CTED

THE UNPROTECTE

How inexcusable abuses and the lack of domestic abuse laws as a child led me towards a path of drugs, alcohol and crime as a teenager and young adult.

INTRODUCTION

SPAWNED INTO HELL
RAISED BY MONSTERS
GREW UP WITH ANIMALS
FOUGHT WITH DEMONS
SURVIVED THROUGH THE PAIN

Obviously the introduction title is mostly metaphors. I don't want you to get the wrong Idea that you're going to read about deadly Demons and Babadook's chasing me through some dark evacuated ghost town or deep in the spooky moonlit woods. The real devil is truly in the details of my life. There were no real clawed, hoofed, horned, hairy creatures coming after me to ruin my life and put me through the hell I have gone through. They were all humans. Flesh and Blood and Bones. The actual title on the other hand. Is all to accurate.

At a very young age I definitely started having the feelings that everyone was pure evil at times. Soulless monsters with an agenda to completely destroy my existence. I have been through a number of travesties in my life that I truly wouldn't wish on my worst enemies. Any of them. And I have had a lot of those throughout my short time on this earth. I would much rather see them die quickly and quietly than to have to see anyone go through some of the disgusting events I have had to endure. There are times in which my hatred for some people has run very deep. But not deep enough to see anyone go through my suffering.

My name is Victor, And I am a human. No matter how much of my humanity has been stripped away from me. At this point in my life I am a forty-seven-year-old unemployed chef trying to make it through just one more shitty day. I did the same thing yesterday. And I will do the same damn thing tomorrow. I have been through some episodes in my past that would make some people just plain give up on life. Put a shotgun in their mouth or shove a handful of pills down their throats and just say good-night and good luck. And I am not saying I haven't thought about it, I have, many times. Especially before my teens. But I was afraid that offing myself would put me in a burning hell for all of eternity.

Suicide is a sin. At least that's what I was forced to believe. So, no matter how horrible, or hopeless, or helpless, living my painfully confusing life ever seemed. I figured with all the disappointments of a broke ass family with no money, the shortage or absence of food in our home, no clean clothes for school, the constant violent abuses, the constant emotional struggling, and the plethora of douchebags that I was dealing with on almost a daily basis. I would still be better off dealing with all of that than roasting in a pit of fire for ever and ever and then some. I always had to weigh my options even as a child. And suicide quickly became the only option that wasn't an option.

When you are at a very young age. And you are receptive to the grownups beliefs that are surrounding you. And because of their beliefs, you believe. 100%. In heaven and hell. God and the devil, Angels and Demons, Santa and the fucking Easter bunny. When you believe in all that. You start to think that maybe being to hungry, or being too cold, or being too hot, or being embarrassed, or taking a severe beating, or dealing with the scum of the earth that force things on you that you know are immoral. Whether it be mentally, emotionally, sexually or physically. You somehow come to realize that with all that pain and suffering, and all the burdens that come with that pain and suffering. Well, At least in my mind. It all just didn't compare to what I was told or believed hell was like.

No matter how extremely horrific my life ever got. Swallowing or ingesting all the horrific evil bullshit the earth and its earthlings had to offer always sounded way easier to me than facing the actual evil that I would have to endure down in the bowels of hell. Who wants to burn in a massive fire pit in hell surrounded by the screams of eternal pain and suffering? Not me. Not one bit. So, in retrospect, what is a broken bone or three here and there from some asshole or assholes here on this earth? It's not too bad. Those bones will eventually heal. In hell, from what I've heard anyway. Hordes of demons break them on you daily. And I'm fairly sure the demons dealing out the damage in hell are going to be much stronger and probably way more brutal than some earthly assholes.

Also, what's an empty stomach here on Earth? A few days without food. Fuck. Maybe even a week. It's probably not going to kill you. Especially when you know for sure if you try hard enough you're going to find something to eat eventually. Even if it's dining out of a garbage can in an alley behind Dunkin doughnuts or grilling up a squirrel under a tarp in the middle of main street or some shit. You will find something to grub on here on earth if you desperately need to somehow, someway.

Now being of a child's mindset, compare that to not knowing if there is even food in hell. Or even if there's water for that matter. And if there is food? You would probably conclude that every bit of sustenance there is probably, wait, not probably, more than fucking likely, horribly burnt. To a crisp. Right? It is hell after all. Eternal fire and flames and what not. And hey? What's a little molestation here and there? You can take it.

You're tough. It's only a human being doing it to you.

Like I said. Flesh and blood. Do you really want to try out getting pounded in your ass by the Devil or his minions with sixteen-inch flame shooting horse cocks eight to ten times a day? Fucking ouch man. I think not. At least for me personally. That is some shit right there that is definitely not on my bucket list. I would hope it wouldn't be on anybody's bucket list. But who knows? Especially these days. Some people are looking for ultimate extremes I suppose. And some others are just simply messed up in their heads. Maybe that's why some people are so damn evil for most of their lives. But to each his own I always say. Just don't push your crazy shit on me please. I've dealt with enough crazy for three lifetimes thank you.

So the promise of a burning tortuous hell kept me from killing myself at my younger age, no matter how bad I was treated. The contemplation of committing suicide as a teenager became something that wasn't an option either. Even though the whole heaven and hell thing was slowly becoming more of a myth to me as the years passed on. I had something to look forward to in the way of a settlement I was getting from, and remember this, it is very important later on in my story. "an accident? That happened to me when I was twelve years old. I was getting the settlement when I turned eighteen. It was in the area of thirty some odd thousand dollars. I wasn't going to off myself before that. That would have just been stupid of me. I figured I'd stick around for a bit. Cash money seems do that to people. Especially when you grow up with nothing.

Not long after I received the settlement I had a daughter. Keisha. Suicide was no longer any kind of option. At all. Fuck the Devil. Fuck the money. I would never let my kids think I gave up in that way. No matter how bad it was or how bad it gets. I know how that feels. And it's not a good feeling. To many friends and to many family members gave up in that way. Again. Not for me. So, I just keep on chugging along and trying to move forward as much as I can. Even though this life, dirty people, and other fucked up elements keep trying to push me backwards off a building, a bridge or a cliff to plunge me into nothingness. It's just not happening. But I will give kudos to all that have tried, and especially to those that have come pretty damn close a few times. I am sincerely sorry for your disappointment.

I currently live in a rundown shit bag apartment, up on the fourth floor. The top floor of a twenty-seven unit building with a leaking ceiling from a ripped-up roof. Also, a leaking kitchen sink. Both of which there is most definitely mold forming from. Five different spots in the ceiling leak when it rains or the snow melts pouring dirty moldy water into our humble $750 a month abode. With nothing included. Unless you count the water from the ceiling. That shits free. We also have a broken toilet, I have to plunge it every single time someone takes a dump. That's a whole lot of fun. There's more, I'm not going to get into it all right now because we're leaving here as soon as possible anyways. And it would take away from the story later. But I will reveal the best part, just for you. The entire building is infested with bed bugs. Not just in our apartment, actually, not just our entire building, the entire block we live on is completely overrun with these little blood sucking bastards, so there's no way to get rid of them for any less than us moving out. We'll get into all that later.

I live here with my wife Patty and our six-year-old autistic adopted grandson in Middletown Connecticut. Just trying to make it year-by-year, month by month, week by week, day by day and sometimes trying to just survive the days hour by hour, just like most everyone else in this mostly failing world. I get it. I'm not alone. But I have to say it seems to be getting tougher and tougher for me as the time goes by. Especially with getting older and my health seeming to fail more and more as the years, even the months now fly by way to fast. With all of what my body and my mind have had to go through the last forty years or so. It does not make anything on me any easier. No matter how hard I try, I just seem to be running into walls. It has happened to me in this way for my entire life. But now it's worse. Every straight away, every turn, every ladder I try to climb or hole I try to dig out of, there always seems to be some kind of wall standing right in my path. WALLED UP, DARK, DEAD FUCKING ENDS.

In writing this right now I am hoping to break down some of those walls, to get past the dead ends and the extreme darkness, and to finally be able to see through to a place where there is some kind of light. And to let everyone else understand where it all went wrong for me. I need to get this all out. There are so many things very deep in my soul that I need to release. There are things I need to get out that a few people know about. And also, a number of things that everybody in my life knows about. An awful lot of crazy, insane, and some just simply straight up disturbing and disgusting things have happened to me, or around me, for almost my entire life. Truman show type shit. The evil version that is. As if Rob Zombie wrote and directed it himself. It was as if someone or something was constantly trying to derail me from having a peaceful and joy filled life.

Because of some of the things that others have seen I have been through. I have always been told that I should write my life story. I have been told, write a book you idiot. You have the stories. You have the events. Get them out there. You've been through just about everything that a person could go through. From dozens of people, hundreds of times, I have been told that I would be super dumb not to write and tell my full recollection of the things I have been witnessed to. Some of these people that have asked me to do this must have missed a few seasons here and there and want to catch up. So here they all come.

This is an introduction of what you will see when you get into my story. It's not all as horrible as it sounds. I mean, it is. But some of it is happy, I didn't go through my entire life with every single second or minute of every single day being purely terrible. There were moments of great happiness. They usually didn't last very long but they were there. Some of what you will see is extremely sad, some of it is haunting, some of it is amazing and awesome. And some, well most, is so terribly awful you will probably have to go back and read a section again here and there to make sure you read it correctly. I have been through some tough periods in my life. Periods that have definitely tested my strength and my will to survive.

I have definitely been through some amazing periods in my life. Periods that have kept me moving forward simply knowing that they may come back around and that they exist. And although it may seem that I am using a good portion these writings and stories to blame a lot of other people for most of the horrible situations I have found myself in, both in the past, and in this place in time I seem to be stuck in now. I lay most of the blame on myself for the bad more than anyone. I truly do.

My birth and my upbringing were obviously not of my choosing. No one gets that choice. No one in the entire world would have subjected their childhood to what I went through if they could have changed it in any way at all. Especially with the horrible, sometimes despicable brutal things I was subjected to, by the people I was supposed to be able to trust as a child and a teenager to look after me and protect my health and safety. But as an adult. I should have known better and picked my sorry ass up and did something different with my life. I should have broken through the walls and jumped over my own hurdles, but I remained stagnant for most of my adult life, always doing stupid things that prevented me from going anywhere in life that could have made me something better. Maybe even someone special. There were times I thought I could. But I definitely dropped the ball on most of them. Way more than once. Just simply settling for what I was and what I had. I had my chances multiple times. I just didn't take them. As an adult it was mostly my own stupidity that has brought me to where I am today.

With that being said, if it does seem I am throwing around some blame. I do realize nobody is perfect. Nobody. But they did this to themselves as well as to me. And this story is going to shine a very nasty light on quite a few people that were tenement in making me who I was and who I am now. Not everyone in my life was a total scumbag. I can't say that. Not everyone sucked. Most did. But not everyone. Everyone has their own beliefs, everyone has their own agenda, everyone has the things in their head and in their hearts that they need to do for themselves, or think they should be doing, and that's exactly what it is going to be for them. You can't change that in people. They are who they are and they do what they do.

Examples. There were a few great people in my life, a very few, but great ones none the less. These people that truly wanted to help me with all their hearts, and protected me when they were able to. It was very obvious that they couldn't protect me most of the time. It wasn't at all their faults. They simply didn't know what was happening to me all of the time. There was a lot that was hidden from them. So, I can't blame them for any of my lost battles.

Some of the people in my life were decent people, with good intentions, I believe that some of them just didn't know what they were doing. People that had some sort of an idea of what I was going through but were confused and scared and had no idea how to get me out of certain situations I was in. I don't blame them either. Even though by sometimes getting only halfway involved in trying to help me instead of sticking with it. They made my life much worse for me. You'll see them as you read on.

Then there were some of the people around me that only had their best interest at heart, these are the people that knew exactly what was happening to me, but had their heads in the sand blind to everything around them and didn't care to help in any way. Some of them, I thought for sure if I made it clear what I was going through, they would definitely step up to the plate for me. I was dead wrong again. They just sat back and watched and did nothing at all to get me help.

And then there were these people, I don't even know if I should call them people, a few more of them than I care to count, "people" with very bad intentions, no sign of any kind of heart at all, evil, dirty, malicious, self-absorbed scumbags. That seemed like they didn't care if I lived or died, they simply wanted me out of their lives and out of their way. And even some that might have actually killed me themselves if given the chance to not get caught, or to get away with it with little or no repercussions. I'm sorry. But there is just no other way to explain it or describe them. It kills me to think back on some of them. But thinking back and writing it all down is now my only therapy. Let's hope it works.

Believe me when I say to you. I am no saint, I would never claim to be. I had a lot of degenerates in my past guiding and directing me through my life. They taught me some very disgusting traits. Which I have to say I have used at times. Some people did try to teach me right from wrong, good from bad and decent from evil. There weren't many of them, but some. For a long time, I really thought the wrong way was just the easier route to go. And sometimes it was. I have done some shady shit in my lifetime that are definitely not the actions of a noble or moral being. I've lied, cheated, assaulted, stolen, misled and just straight up been a douchebag for a good portion of my life. I hope some of the terrible actions in my past are nothing I cannot be forgiven for. I have definitely affected some people's lives in a very negative way. Especially in my teens through my thirties. And I am not one bit proud of any of them.

I am mostly at fault for the position I now find myself trying to dig out from. I could have taken a different path but I didn't. I took the easy path most of the time.

For example, I have worked my entire adult life from the age of fourteen, that is, when I wasn't doing something stupid. I quit school in eighth grade and started my first job. I knew there was no college in my future, and I knew I was going to have to fend for myself and teach myself how to do something. I didn't know what it was yet, but it had to be something. I figured I knew how to read, spell, write and I was really decent at math, and thought that there was nothing else they could teach me in school that would make my life any easier. Looking back, I see I was very wrong. I've beaten my body into the dirt by working over thirty years like an absolute maniac. Working circles around everyone to prove I was better than them. It has definitely taken its toll. I am fairly sure that being an accountant or something like that definitely would have been easier on my body than the route that I took. More than likely, more financially stable too.

I believe what I am trying to explain here, and what you will see as you read on. Is that although I had a terrible life, and was at times a terrible person, and at times I hurt people, some people that didn't deserve to be hurt, and at times I took what wasn't mine to take, sometimes from people that didn't deserve to have their things taken. Although I did these things. I was never just a typical, evil, heartless, sinister criminal type who didn't give a fuck about what other people thought of me. I know at times it seemed that way. And some people think just that to this day, I'm sure of it. But I do have a conscience. I do feel for those I have hurt or disappointed. It just seemed that sometimes in this life, you really do have to do what you need to do to survive. It sucks. But it is a part of this life especially when you grew up the way I did.

I will say that I always felt horrible for just about every bad thing I have ever done. Especially when I was done doing whatever the deed was, and I realized that I did it to someone that may have not deserved it. I am quite the opposite of that deep in my heart. All the bad shit I've done, was mostly because I was programmed at a young age to act a certain way. My heart is filled with love and affection despite everything I have been through and suffered. It always has been. And to the contrary of what some people think. A lot of people do know I am not the bad person that I sometimes portrayed myself to be. In other words. The need to survive often outweighed the need to be compassionate or caring. Most of my friends and family knew I had to do what I had to do.

I have loved many people in my time and my children are my entire life's blood. Even though I can't see them all of the time. Or even talk to them every time I want to. They are in my mind and heart every single second of my awareness. One of the greatest issues in this short life, at least for me, is that there isn't always the time you need to do certain things that you would love to do with all of your heart. Especially with the ones you love and care for.

There is definitely a lot of give and take through the years. Get what you can when you can, and give what you can when you're able. And I've taken my fair share. Taken care of my own needs. No doubt about it. Legally and illegally, with permission and without. I've given plenty, I have showed my compassionate side. I have given all that I have had at times, leaving myself completely broken with nothing left for myself. And I have been taken from exhaustively. From other people's greed. And from other people's wants and needs over all else. It is all coming. No more spoilers here. All of these things will come to light soon enough.

I have always been told from a very young age that I was set up for failure and that I never had a chance, at anything, or to be anything. I was once told at seventeen years old from a boss that I wouldn't make it past twenty years old the way I was living. No possible way. Dude bet me $10,000 to $1 that I most surely wouldn't make it past twenty-one. Once I am able to go into the bars legally, it's all over for me. And if I did luckily happen make it that far. That prison would definitely be where I would be spending most of my life. I was doomed. A lot of people felt the same way as him. And honestly at that point. I couldn't even consider taking that bet just on morals. I agreed with them all.

I should have been dead at least three times in the last thirty years since then. But I'm not. I'm still kicking around for some strange reason. Maybe it's to write this. Something out there wants me to survive. If it's God? Ok. If it's the aliens that are breeding us here? Ok. If it's the doctors that kept me alive more than once when I should have gone bye bye? Ok. Thank you for your concern. Whoever or whatever it is? It definitely wants me to stick around for a little bit longer. No matter how much it hurts. Emotionally. Mentally. Or physically. I'm guessing, that who or whatever it is. It must know by now that I can take the pain and I won't remove myself from the game prematurely.

In my beginning my mother got pregnant with me when she was only fifteen years old and had me when she was sixteen back in 1972, my father was a heroin addict, a painter, and when needed, he robbed banks. From my knowledge he got away with at least two before he got caught and went away for a few years. He and my mother were only together for five years after I was born. And I only lived with him once afterwards, for a single summer, one brutal battle ridden summer it was.

Thankfully, looking back, my father had only a half way decent part in the path my life was to take. Not quite as big as some of the key characters that were around way more. He wasn't around enough to really have a huge impact in molding who I eventually became. I'm sure if he had more time he could have done a much better job fucking me up like most everyone else did. And I'm not saying I didn't love my father. He did what he could when he could. I guess. But he was brought up into fucked up situations and molded into what he was just like me. Just like everyone. He was doing what he was taught to do. Sometimes people just don't ever get the bad or the evil out of their heads or out of their hearts, and they never find a way to change their behavior or the path they were set on. It took me a very long time.

After my father, my mother went on to be with at least four or five different guys in the five years that proceeded him, none that I can recall were very good people, she then went on to marry an extremely violent alcoholic. Then a crackhead. And then. And wait for it. What are the fucking odds? Another crackhead. As you can see, the odds were not that high, at least not as high as THEY WERE all the time. Haha. See that shit. I have some comedy in me too. I think I got that from my little brother Joey. He was definitely the glue that kept me together before my teenage years. Protecting him was my job. Making me laugh was his job. Wait until you hear most of this kids' antics. Some are truly unbelievable.

My life was not at all awesome for a huge portion of it. It was actually quite exhausting. Sometimes excruciating. And always confusing. Especially as a child, I knew the shit going on around me was straight weird, completely wrong on so many levels. Most of what happened when I was younger I can't even explain as an adult. There always seemed to be some sort of life changing event that was going on around me. There was never any calm. It always seemed to be that whatever was going on was going to create an end of the world scenario. These people around me had absolutely no inner peace whatsoever. The fear of where their lives were leaked out of their pores like a broken faucet. Every day was like a nuclear attack on someone around me. It seemed like total chaos at all times. I am quite positive the drugs and alcohol didn't help any of those situations.

I have three brothers all from different fathers, Joey was conceived of my father, Bobby from stepfather one and Donnie from stepfather two. I have three children all from different women. From the time I can remember until now I have lived in over 45 different houses, apartments, trailers, boarding rooms, basements, attics, etc, etc. they were all between Maine, Connecticut and Tennessee. And I have also had over 35 different jobs, most in the restaurant industry, all the way from dishwasher, prep person, pizza cook, executive chef and general manager. Which will more than likely ALL be told in my story here and there.

I have to say, that in writing this and thinking back through my memories, I am definitely opening up some old wounds that have been closed for a very long time. These wounds were never fully healed, but mostly closed. Stitched up to the point that they were ok unless I banged them on something in my mind. Things I haven't thought about or talked about in a long while. Some of them in years, some of them in decades. And I have lived with keeping them hidden away for far too long. And the feeling of helplessness that I have felt through my entire life by keeping it all in, is honestly nothing compared to the feeling of anxiety I am feeling right now letting it all out. But as I said. This has to come to the surface. All of it. I've kept most of it buried away for thirty plus years to long.

I have a lot to tell and will try to get it all in. Even if it means multiple books. I am dedicating my life right now to the truth and consequences of my experiences. And many people will be made to seem straight up evil in this truth. Including myself at times. But the truth is the truth. And I'm on a mission to sell my books and fix my life based on the facts of my history. I believe it's worthy of being told to the masses. If it can help some people to realize that life isn't always easy for others, and by minding your business, burying your head in the sand, and not getting involved in someone else's clear need for your help, especially if you are able to make a difference. You are close to just as much to blame for what that child is going through as the douchebags dishing out the pain.

I've needed help more times than I can count. And I was completely ignored by people in my life that knew my situation and did absolutely nothing to deter what was happening to me.

People that in my mind, and looking back I suppose it was only in my mind, I thought that there was no way they were going to let my abuses continue and get me help. People with standing in the community. Some people in which I Thought had an obligation to get me help. I never understood. But I get it now.

We all have our own problems. But sometimes you should step up, or at least speak up when you see somethings that are completely immoral and hurting someone else. Especially when that someone else is a weak innocent child. It definitely wasn't fair to me, or even my brothers to have to go through the abuses that we did. But thankfully, I fought my way through all the bullshit and got to where I am today. Not that where I am today is anything special or great. I am just saying that I am very grateful to still be alive. Especially with my wife, my family, and my children and grandchildren healthy. And I suppose with my mind and my sanity still somewhat intact. That usually helps.

I am not going to lie to you. If I can sell a ton of these books and make enough money to live the rest of my days with my family more comfortable. You will not hear me complain one iota. I have suffered either in to, or close to poverty, for most of my life. If this is my way out of suffering being broke all the time than so be it. And some of you might not think so, but I think I deserve to have something in my life go right for me. Maybe by the time you're done reading this you will change your view.

I have lived more than likely more than half of my life. I don't think I have twenty years left. I almost definitely don't have thirty more years left to live in this lifetime. My life is running its course close to the end. I've beaten myself up pretty badly over the years. Everyone needs a break someday. Hopefully, this brings myself and my family ours. I want to leave something behind besides disaster to my family after I leave this world. Not just the words of how terrible it was while I was here. And here are some of those disasters.

In my life I have been abused, molested, beaten, hunted down, shot at, ran over by a car that crushed and broke both of my legs, broken my ribs a few different times, broken my nose eleven times, once with a bumper jack, a two by four, nun chucks, etc. Forth degree burns on half of my right leg and foot from three hundred and seventy-five-degree fry oil. Ripped off the top half of my right ear, broken arm my wrist and my ankle, I had three herniated disks in my back, hernia surgery, blew out the meniscus in my right knee, twice, first time torn, second time completely ripped from the bone. I have plantar fasciitis in both of my feet, which I am dealing with right now. I recently had double pneumonia, I almost died from it with eighty two percent blood oxygen levels just six months ago, infected pilonidal cyst last year, my head was split open from a pool stick once and by windshields twice, four major auto accidents in which all the cars were totaled, uncountable staples and stitches. Hundreds of pieces of windshield glass removed from my body, and I suffered my whole life with terrible back acne, even to this day at forty-seven years old it's still quite visible.

You will see as you read on that the skin problems had a huge impact on many of the dreams I would have acted on. But I couldn't. My mother actually wrote a children's book depicting the struggle with my skin problems right before she passed away. And these are just some of the physical things I've been through. Trust me when I say, there is much more of it. The mental damage, and emotional struggles, at least to me, have at times been so much worse than the all physical pain put together. I believe you'll understand soon enough.

With all of that being said I might also have a slight substance dependency problem. Maybe just a little. I have dropped acid and mushrooms a couple dozen times. I have tried things like Ketamine, Xanax, Thorazine, Opium and even Crack a few times. I have been addicted to opioids, alcohol, heroin and cigarettes for most of my life. I have without a doubt smoked a few ounces of hashish, kilos of marijuana and snorted pounds of cocaine in my lifetime. And even though I admit that I have done more of these three drugs than the average human being. It is definitely where most of my money went especially as a teenager. I can't, and I won't say "addicted" to these three drugs. You can argue, and I'm sure you all have your own opinions. But I don't remember ever, never, no matter how much of them I've ever done, hash, weed or coke. And no matter how many days or weeks in a row I used them. I don't remember ever not being able to stop taking any of them, on a day’s notice.

I never got physically sick from stopping any of those three. I most certainly cannot say that about opioids, heroin, alcohol or even tobacco. There is a huge difference. At least to me between wanting a substance and needing a substance. They are two completely different monsters. And I cannot put coke and crack in the same category together. I've seen what crack does to people. First hand. But I've only tried crack twice personally. And It wasn't anything I wanted any part of. You can disagree with my assessment of all of this if you would like. But you're not budging me on my beliefs on this subject.

I started using Percocet and smoking Marijuana at the age of twelve after "the accident". Alcohol and cigarettes started shortly thereafter. Hashish after I moved to Maine at about seventeen. Cocaine and heroin on and off throughout my entire adult life up to 6 years ago. Suboxone for the last 6 years with no apparent way off of it. I have seven DUIs, yes, I said seven, four possession of marijuana charges, felony possession of a handgun in a motor vehicle, smuggling of alcohol and tobacco over the Canadian border but got away, phew, and multiple, countless other motor vehicle and misdemeanor charges.

I have been very lucky, and some might say extremely lucky in the fact that I have never been arrested for any violent crimes like assault or heavy drug possession, even though I have been in multiple violent confrontations and have been in possession of hard drugs more times than I can count.

As of this moment in time my life is in a complete whirlwind. As you could probably guess with just that slight glimpse into my troubling past. And when I say slight, I mean slight. There is quite a lot more to come. Doing what I have done, and going through what I have been subjected to in the past hasn't made anything in my future get any easier. But I do also have to say I have had my shit together here and there, for some years, at some times. The ups and downs that some of us go through, are just an amazing contrast to each other sometimes in this thing that we call life.

I am married to a childhood friend whose daughter gave up custody of her two children about four years ago. The one-year-old daughter Celia was granted to my wife's mother, and her two-year-old son Landon was granted to us. He was definitely, to our knowledge, at the very least, horribly emotionally abused as an infant. Possibly even physically. He couldn't tell us as it took us almost a year to get him to speak. And he was recently diagnosed with autism. And he is a complete handful. Always going going going. I'm telling you the Energizer bunny doesn't have squat on this child. But we love him like he was ours anyway, and I know that he's better off with me than anyone else. Anyone!!! With all of what I have been dragged through in my life, I would never put another human being through anything even close to what I had to endure.

Especially not an innocent child or anyone that I care for. I truly feel I am his only chance at a good life. And I hate to have to say it. You will see more, as you read more exactly why. I don't trust anybody, not anyone. Especially not with a child that is not of their own blood. You might think it is the wrong way to think. But I have been programmed, very coherently, throughout multiple abuses and the actions of many deplorable individuals in my life. I know for a fact, and so do you, whether you admit it out loud or not. that there are some very bad people in this world with very bad intentions. People in this world that even make the disgusting, horrible, people that were in my world, look like Mother Fucking Teresa.

And trusting anybody else with a weak little innocent life like his, I'm sorry, that shit is just not my bag. Not everyone, obviously, but more people than you would care to imagine are just plain dirty. From my experience anyway. And I might not have much to offer, but when it comes to my children or the ones that I love, I would give my life or take any pain in less than a second if I thought it would save them from losing their life or taking any pain. That's what I believe the pain I have taken in the past has made me today. I have nothing but compassion for the weak in this world. And nothing but distain for the bullying, and the harshness, from the people who have absolutely no concern for other people's feelings in this world. Especially the weak ones. No matter what has happened to me in the past. Or even some of the horrible things I have done myself.

No matter how badly someone has hurt me, or ignored me, or whatever evil someone has laid upon me. I feel like it is what has made me who I am today. And although it was a rough and tumble life. And I should probably be dead from a couple of different situations. Brought on by a couple different fucked up evil individuals. I still don't hold much animosity towards most of the ones responsible. I'm not saying they weren't wrong, believe me, I know they were. And I'm not saying I thank them for making me who I am. But without them. I would probably be someone else altogether. Maybe better. Maybe worse. Who knows. But I know I would rather be me than anyone else. I know where my heart lies, I know I am real, and I wouldn't have it any other way.

I have lost my latest job approximately one month ago and I am bringing in no source of income at this moment. My wife is now working two jobs, and I am basically a housewife at the moment, and I suppose a writer, and it's not easy to do. Even with all the drugs and alcohol and through everything else in my past, I have always been the hardest worker in any building, I love to work and love being, and proving, that I am the shit. In any kitchen, at least since the age of twenty-five no one could even come close to keeping up with me. All fucked up on drugs or not. It sucks for me to not be able to do what I love. I LOVE TO WORK. I LOVE TO COOK. Not that the writing isn't work. It is work. But it isn't work at the same time. Not for me anyways. It is very far off from the unchained maniac I am in the kitchen. You can ask anyone that has ever worked with me.

As of now we are residing in an apartment we are currently being evicted from, the reason for this eviction is mostly because I outed the landlord for the building being infested with the bedbugs I spoke of earlier. And, I'm not going to lie, we owe him about three thousand at this point. Between my health, not being able to work, taking care of Landon, plus all the money we spend fighting the bed bug problem. It is all piled up and killing us right now. I am suffering from terrible/debilitating plantar fasciitis on both of my feet, plus disgusting ingrown toenails, and I also have psoriatic arthritis in my right elbow at the moment. Yeah. Not exactly the Hulk as Landon has affectionately named me.

All I would need are the surgeries to be able to get me back to work after a few months to heal correctly, but we have no time or money right now to get them done. Times are definitely what I would call tough right now. But I am working on it. Mostly hoping this book does job that it should be able to do. All of this is just a fraction of a much longer and compelling story of how I became stuck where I am now, and how my family got to where we are today. I am dedicating my all of my time to writing this book. It is either going to pull me down deeper into my hole. Or lift me up out of it and give me the time I need to get back on my feet.

Good luck and enjoy.

Some of what you will read from here on out is not for the faint of heart.
Rated - S.A.D. L.I.F.E

Sexual situations
Animal Murder
Drug abuse

Language
Insane Emotions
Fucking Assholes
Extreme violence

◆ ◆ ◆

PART ONE - BETTER FEAR THE REAPER

The simple fact that I am still around to write this book is absolutely incredible. I am not supposed to be here. I am supposed to be dead right now. I am supposed to be in prison right now. I cannot believe that I am available and able to do this. I never thought, even if I had two hundred years, that I would be able to make the time to do this. I am extremely grateful for the chance to write my life story and I am even more grateful that so many people are interested in hearing it.

I am going to have to probably put the first few chapters together with some broken and slivered memories at best. Some days and events I remember like they happened yesterday and others, meh, not a clue. I don't remember everything and I won't pretend that I can, from birth to three I have no memories at all. So, I think I'm going to have to start when I was around four years old, where my first real memories started on a Christmas morning, before this day? Blank. Like I was born in this moment.

I remember exactly what I got for Christmas that day, as it was the very first event that I can recall. I received a pair of headphones that were bright red, they had a built-in radio with two knobs, volume and tuner. There was also a blue tent where I could crawl through a tube and hide inside. We had it set up in the living room, which also doubled as my bedroom at the time.

Inside of my tent I had a little table and a little light, two pillows and a Scooby Doo and Shaggy sleeping bag. Outside there was a gaudy looking tan and white-ish couch where I slept when I wasn't sleeping inside my tent, a brown rectangular scratched up coffee table, two very un-matching chairs, a small TV, a white bookcase, a stereo with a record player and 8 track tape player with two gigantic speakers, also album covers and 8 track tapes scattered throughout the room.

The records I remember laying around the most were Steely Dan, Led Zeppelin, Aerosmith, Boston and Blue Oyster Cult, and the 8 tracks I remember were Jethro Tull, AC/DC and Fleetwood Mac. There were many more but these are the ones that stood out. I always wondered why the Steely Dan album cover was always moved onto the kitchen table from the living room with rolled up bills and straws around it. Especially when they didn't listen to it that much. I'm pretty sure I know what that was all about now.

I remember laying inside the tent for the first time listening to my headphones by myself, I remember that it was 99 rock WPLR, I remember the first song I heard on them was Black sabbath, snow blind. The second song was Led Zepplin, Stairway to heaven. The third song with the headphones on blew me away. Blue Oyster Cult, Don't fear the Reaper. It's kind of Ironic that I loved this song, and you will see the reasoning for it soon.

This is the point in my life definitely that started my love for music. I've heard the albums and 8 tracks that my parents had playing through the house speakers before. But to be able to lay there alone and take it all in through the headphones with no bother from outside elements felt like the best thing ever to me. It is truly, with the tent, all I remember having for myself at that point in my life.

I'm sure my life had started earlier, obviously, but for me this is where it all began. And although I might have had a loving family. Or people that truly cared for me. I simply don't remember much of that. I've heard of it from different family members when I was older. But I really can't remember. And I am sorry. I honestly think that the bad was so bad that it outweighed any of the good in my life, and totally over shadowed most good memories that I should probably have.

As far as I can recall I lived with my Mother Janice. My Father Victor, and they had guests in and out of the house at all times. My Uncle Joe, My Aunt Laura, My Aunt Cindy. They were all my father's siblings. And then there were whatever people they were hanging out with at the time. It was definitely a party house. I also had a babysitter sometimes by the name of Nancy. At this time from what my mother later told me we lived on Poplar Street in New Haven Connecticut.

As of early memories and from what else my mother had told me, she drastically, emphatically, believed that this apartment was haunted. She would constantly tell me and my father and anyone else who would listen that there was definitely a ghost there that was watching over me. From the story's she would tell me as a kid if I tried to escape the apartment or go outside into the hallway the ghost would flick the cabinet open so I could not escape. It was nice at a young age to think that I had some sort of a protector. Even if it was a ghost. Thinking back upon it now if it really was protecting me it should have let me escape.

I was also told that there was something else there that was not around to protect me. Another being, An evil of some sort. Something that was there to punish me if I got out of line or mis behaved in any way. And that it had its own room down under our home, underground, it had a doorway to its lair from inside the kitchen of our apartment in which I could never enter, unless I was brought down by the being itself that is in charge of my punishments, if I disobeyed the rules of entry and went through that door for any reason I would die a horrible death and never be able to return.

There was always some sort of noises or loud banging that came from under the floor right below where I laid in my tent, and also through that door in the kitchen. I never knew exactly what all the noise was as a kid. All I knew at the time is that it was very loud and intimidating. Like a loud banging music of some sort, but not really at the same time. At the time I had no idea what to make of it in my own mind. My parents always told me it was a ritual going on underground for punishing the bad children that lived in the apartment complex. And if I didn't behave and kept asking questions about it that I would be down there for my own ritual next. The being apparently did not appreciate being questioned.

This other being they spoke of, the being dwelling under our home, the being that was not my protector, the being that was punishing the other children, this being that had a terrible name. What they called it, what it was, what was to be my doom for misbehaving. They called it THE BOOGEYMAN. Whenever I misbehaved, was bad, or didn't listen, they would call it by its name. Hey bogeyman, we need you. Victor needs to see you. It's punishment time. And this is when the shitting my pants would start. It would always take a minute or two before he appeared which made it even worse. And at times they had to call him more than once taking even longer. Maximizing my torture as I was held there by my parents unable to escape.

I would hear him coming up the stairs from the basement, always completely horrified, no matter how much I tried to get away, struggling and crying, kicking and screaming, they would always force me to stand there and wait, telling me this might just be the time he takes you down there to punish you. Once he takes you there is nothing we can do to help you anymore. We will try not to let him take you, but it's his decision on how bad he thinks you were, I remember, always thinking or even asking them sometimes, why would you call him up here if you don't want him to take me? They never had a straight answer for me. At least not one that I recall. The punishments always varied from standing in the corner to losing my headphones to going to bed without dinner. There was always the threat of physical punishment. But I don't remember it ever getting that far, at least by The Boogeyman in this specific apartment.

The Boogeyman would always slam open the door with force. He would make a growling type noise and ask my parents in a deep gargling voice "Why have you summoned me from my torture chamber today? What has Victor done wrong this time to interrupt my slumber? I am at your service to hand out a swift and fair punishment.

Here's the thing. I only remember two times out of the many he came up for me exactly what it was that I did wrong to have him summoned in the first place. The rest I have forgotten. I broke one of their 8 track tapes once, I was put in the corner for an hour and I lost my headphones for a few days. That was one.

This was two. And I remember this day all too well. It has been stuck in my memory like a sumo wrestler stuck in quicksand. I woke up early one morning and was very hungry, no one was awake to make me breakfast so I grabbed a chair to reach some bread from the cabinet and tried to make myself some toast. I still needed another chair to reach the toaster and the dish cabinet that was on the far end of the counter. But instead of bringing the same chair over to the toaster I took another one from the table. I figured I was going to have to put the bread back in that cabinet anyways and there was also cereal in there I was going to grab after I made my toast.

I dragged and scraped the second chair over the floor as quietly as I could trying not to wake my parents up. I pulled that chair over, crawled up on it and I placed the bread in the toaster and pushed the lever down. I reached into the cabinet over the toaster and pulled out a bowl and a plate and placed them both down on the counter. I then got down off of the second chair to go to the fridge to get some butter and milk. I took the milk out and placed it on the kitchen table that was directly in the middle of the room between where the toaster and refrigerator were located. Probably four steps. As I was searching for the butter, for a little more than a minute I think, maybe longer, I couldn't find the butter dish anywhere.

I turned my head to notice the toast was starting to smoke, I ran back, climbed on the chair and tried to stop it from burning any more, for some reason it wouldn't pop the toast up. I tried pulling the toast out with my fingers but I kept burning the tips of them on the metal. I panicked. Knowing what was in store for me if I didn't figure this out quickly. I scrambled, what do I do? I know. I jumped down off of the chair and ran around the kitchen opening up all the drawers searching for something to pull the burning toast out with. I know what you're saying. Unplug it you idiot. I'm sorry. I was four and I guess I just never thought of it.

I opened four different drawers looking for a stupid fork. I don't know why but I didn't know where the right drawer was. I pulled the forth drawer out so far it came off its rails and dropped straight to the floor, and when I say straight I mean straight. Handle down, almost crushing my feet as I jumped away. The drawer made a loud echoing bang and sent silverware scattering throughout the kitchen ringing across the tile floor. This was the drawer I was looking for I guess. Uggh. I snatched a fork up off the floor and jumped back up on the chair and tried to get the toast out before the smoke detector went off or it burned any more. Yeah, I know, not to bright. I was rushing even more now mostly because I was sure my parents and possibly even the Boogeyman heard that drawer and silverware hit the floor and were more than likely all on their way to me right now.

What happened next was just a straight cluster fuck. Not that it wasn't already up to this point. I stuck the fork into the toaster to try to pry the toast out in a rush, panicking, I immediately hit the orange glowing side elements and BZZZZZ. I electrocuted the hell out of myself and actually blew a fuse or a breaker or something. I fell off of the chair sideways away from the toaster stiff as a rail, my right arm stuck straight out in front of me. And I am not exaggerating here, I went at least three feet from where I was standing on the chair somehow. My wrist hit the counter not even loosening the fork from my grip and I slammed the left side of my head above my ear off of the first chair I moved to get the bread in the first place, I hit the floor, and everything got hazy and loud noises started ringing through my ears.

Of course, as soon as I hit the ground I heard these loud noises screaming through my head and I thought it was my brain falling out through my ear or seeping out of the cut on the side of my head. It wasn't that though. It was the damn smoke alarm blaring. BeeDoo BeeDoo BeeDoo. Wha wha wha. Oh God, I can't move my arm or my head. There's no hiding this mess now. I am pretty sure that I am one dead kid.

My parents come running around the corner literally within two seconds of me hitting the floor, they obviously heard the drawer and the silverware hit the tile and were well on their way probably before I even got back to the toaster, they stopped dead in their tracks, peering through the living room doorway into the kitchen. There I am lying on the floor trying to sit up, my neck was all kinds of stiff, my left hand was flat on the floor, my right hand straight out with the fork still in it scorched with a black and blueish purple marking where it touched the toaster elements, there were no lights on, blood was flowing from my head and puddling on the floor, three drawers were sticking out, one drawer was laying upside down, there was random silverware scattered everywhere, there was smoke pouring from the toaster, the fridge was still wide open, and a turned over chair in the middle of the floor, my father starts yelling how the fuck is that smoke alarm still going off with the fuse blown?

Everyone was in a tiff. What a total mess this was. I remember crying hysterically at this point. Not because I was hurt so badly. But I truly thought if I cried hard enough and pretended I was more hurt than I actually was they would possibly have some compassion and give me a pass from The Boogeyman this time. You guessed it. Not a chance in hell.

I looked up at them with tears flowing down my cheeks and I knew I was done, immediately, they looked at each other and then I heard it. In extreme stereo, BOOGYMAN. Louder than they have ever yelled it before this. Both at the same exact time. My dad even looked over at my mother and said jinx, you owe me a Coke Janis. I don't think she was amused. I think we were all in shock.

At the exact moment that my father finished saying jinx, you owe me a coke Janis. Me, as a four-year-old kid, obviously hurt and in a foggy daze, smoke alarm blaring throughout the kitchen and knowing that the Boogeyman is coming right now to propose a horrible punishment on me, also, not really knowing what a fuse box is or where it is located. At the exact same time he finished that quote. Click, BZZZZ? The power in the kitchen comes back on. Both my parents are standing right next to me. I thought to myself how in the entire world that just happen? We're all right here. Why are they not asking each other how the lights just went back on? I was so rattled and frightened. Completely mortified. My answer. The Boogeyman just magically turned the electricity back on and here he comes to get me.

I thought this was it, the absolute end if my existence, if he was going to take me? This was going to be the day for sure. No doubts. My parents picked me up, my father pried the fork from my fingers and walked me over and held me still next to the door, exactly like they always did. Just far enough so the door itself wouldn't hit me when The Boogeyman slammed it open.

As we waited for him to come through the door and approach me. I could feel the warm blood running down behind my ear from the cut on the side of my head and my fingers hurt right up to my elbow from slamming it on the counter and the electricity that just flowed through me. I was wondering why they were calling for him instead of helping me with my pain and my bleeding. What the hell? I don't get it. It even went through my head that if he takes me down there with him at least when he's done the pain will stop. Thinking back on that it was pretty fucked up for a four-year-old kid to think, even for me.

The BOOGYMAN always wore the same thing, a black knitted ripped up sweater with strings hanging off everywhere, a shabby looking black pair of leather or vinyl pants, and black shoes with a large black paper bag type head with large hollowed out eyes. He sometimes carried a large machete type knife or cleaver with him. Not this time though. I don't think he had time to grab either of them. He was in too much of a rush I suppose. I don't know? I could hear him running up the stairs faster than usual as they forced me closer towards the door, at the same time my mother was saying, I'm so sorry Victor but you are really in for it now, we'll do what we can to try to help you, but I think you're in serious trouble this time.

The Boogeyman slammed open the door and stood there peering around the kitchen, looking up and down and side to side. I could hear very heavy muffled echoing breathing coming from him over the still blaring smoke detector. I had never heard the breathing noises from him in this way before. He made me feel even more uneasy than usual thinking he was that angry towards what I had just done. He looked around for about five or so seconds. He made a sudden move towards me faster than usual, way faster than usual. In a flash. This is it, I'm done, I pissed my pajamas. Literally. I'm very surprised I didn't shit in them too.

He flew right past me though, what the hell? It was the first time he ever did anything like this. He didn't say a word. He grabbed one of the remaining chairs from the kitchen table and jumped on it and ripped the smoke detector completely off of the ceiling. He pulled the battery from it and threw it all on the table right next to the milk. And guess what else was there? Yep. You probably guessed it correctly. The fucking butter dish I couldn't find in the fridge was sitting right there on the table the whole time, go figure. And even though the Boogeyman just killed the smoke alarm I could still hear ringing and blaring for a couple of seconds after it was clearly dead. Yeah, concussion type shit.

He stepped down off of the chair, walked calmly over to the toaster and slid a little silver lever on the bottom to the left, POP, the noise I wish I heard five minutes ago. It sprung up revealing the blackened, still smoking pieces of toast. I never even saw that lever. That would have been nice to know. He pulled the toast out and threw it into the kitchen sink and turned both faucets on. I could hear the toast crackle as I watched a mushroomed plume of smoke rise up to the ceiling adding to the rest of the smoke.

He turned around, peering into what seemed like nowhere, glaring right past me almost like he was lost, he walked towards us, both hands on his stomach like he was in some sort of extreme pain, I was thinking that he is so angry his stomach hurt. My senses were turned all the way up at this point. I could hear the water running over the toast, and it sounded like I could here every drop that hit the side of the sink. I could feel where I was in pain. I could feel the blood trickling down under the collar of my pajama top. I could feel my hand, wrist and arm throbbing and I could feel the wetness from my pajamas on my thighs from pissing myself and the smell of the smoke in the air was making me nauseous.

I was very confused and scared, my parents were still holding me by each arm and asking him, hey Boogeyman? What are you going to do about this? This is his mess and he needs to be punished for it. He walked past us and took his usual position next to the opening of the door to his dwelling. All I could picture in my head was being tied down to a wooden torture table and being skinned alive. He placed his hands on his hips, he then looked around once more before looking at me, he was visibly shaking but his breathing was no way more controlled. I heard him take in one deep breath and then he bellowed out. VIC-Toaaahahaha. Breaking out into crazy laughter. He placed his hands back on his stomach.

He looked around once more still cracking up and placed one hand on top of my head, through his laughter he bellowed out in a deep voice again. I think you should clean the blood from his head, you should change his peed in pajamas, clean up this mess and make him some breakfast. Victor is obviously very hungry. He looked over to my mother and said while you're at it you should make some breakfast for the uncle you call Joe too. I sense he will be here very soon. There will be no type of punishment for Victor today. He has punished himself enough. Good luck to you all. Still laughing he then turned around, walked into the doorway, closed the door behind him and that was that for him for today.

My mother walked over to the sink and shut the faucet off. Peered into the sink shaking her head and then scanned around the room. I ain't making no fucking breakfast for anybody. I have to clean this fucking mess up. She then said to my father you take Victor into the bathroom and clean him up. I turned to walk to the bathroom when she yelled wait. Victor, look at me. You got really lucky today pal. Anything like this ever happens again we'll call directly to the Boogeyman's boss and you will be punished to the fullest extent. You better wake us up if you need something to eat from now on. You got it? Don't ever try this again.

I asked boss? What do you mean boss? Who is his boss? There's more of them? She just stared at me and said yes Victor and you never want to find out who any of them are. We obviously have the softee in the bunch. Now get going. Get cleaned up and lay in your stupid fucking tent. I don't want to see your face out here for a long while. I put my head down and said ok mommy as I started to turn towards the bathroom with my father's hand on my shoulder. And Victor. I said what mommy. Not you god dammit. Your fucking father. If your brother does end up showing up here you can tell him to cook his own fucking breakfast.

I walked into the bathroom with my father and he told me to get undressed and stand in the shower. He said pile your clothes behind the door. I asked him if he could turn the water on first please. He said nope. I have to get you somehow for this mess. You are going to have to deal with it. I stepped in. Swoosh. So cold so cold. Be lucky this is all you're getting. He held me under the cold water and cleaned up the blood and rinsed off my legs and that was it. He threw me a towel and said dry off. I wiped my head with the towel and he said oh shit while looking at me. He reached towards my head above my ear. Dammit. JANIS!! WHAT? You know I'm busy you asshole. Do you want to clean this shit up and I'll take care of him? My father yells I think your sons going to need a few stitches. FUCK!!!!! Why is he always my son when there is something wrong? Hang on. I'm coming.

She came into the bathroom. Jesus Victor. That's not that bad. Watch this. She opens the medicine cabinet and tells him to go into the living room and grab the super glue. He asked what are you going to do? Fill it in? She said no you fucking idiot. Just get it. Hurry up. I'll show you what I'm going to do. She pulled out a box of band aids and pulled out the smallest ones. She opened them from their wrappers and set them to the side. What are those mommy? She said butterfly stitches. They'll keep the wound closed.

My father returned a few minutes later and handed her the super glue while she was now shaving around my cut. She then had my father hold the wound closed with his fingers and placed two butterfly stitches over my cut and then superglued over them onto my skin. Don't touch this for a week she said. We don't need a doctor or another bill. Don't touch it at all. You get dressed and go inside of your tent now. If I hear a word from you before I'm finished cleaning up your mess, drinking a cup of coffee and smoking a cigarette I will make him take you down there. I swear to fucking God Victor. Don't push your luck with me. I'm Pretty sure I didn't get breakfast that day. Or lunch for that matter. But I laid there for hours without a word just imagining what the other Boogeymen looked like and how much worse it can possibly be.

I went through this terrifying ordeal for at least a year on and off from what I can recall. I'm sure I don't have to tell you that I behaved as much as I could, and mostly hid in my tent and listened to my headphones, and I never went into that door in the kitchen, not even anywhere close to that door if I could help it. No one at the age of four can be constantly behaved though, four-year old's get into shit, it's what they do. I'm sure I did some things to warrant them calling for him, at least in their minds. I just simply can't remember what most of them were. And I don't think it ever got physical like I said earlier, but I do remember that the threat was that he was going to drag me down the stairs to skin me, cook me and eat me if I ever did anything worse than the things I was doing now.

So, one day, very soon after the kitchen toaster debacle, which is what my mom always called it, my parents had called me into the kitchen. Where the door to the bogeyman's room was located as you already know. They told me they wanted to get back at the Boogeyman for all the times that he had terrified me, and that they thought it was time for him to leave his lair and move on to other children besides me because I was getting to old for him, and all I had to do was show that I could defend myself from him, and that I am not afraid of him anymore and he would have to leave.

My father told me that no matter what happened they would protect me, but I had to throw the first blow so he knew I was serious. I tried with everything I had to convince them that I couldn't do it. He would just take me from you and kill me. What happens when his boss finds out? You said there were more of them. Oh no my father said, you have nothing to worry about. We're moving out in a few weeks and they would never in a million years be able to find you. Only the one that is attached to your soul can follow you if you don't do something to stop him. But the rest can only live here in this building. They kept pressing and pressing and pressuring. For some reason this was extremely important to them. To important. I remember thinking that they were going to lie to him about something I didn't even do when he got up there and they were trying to get rid of me forever. They didn't want me anymore and this was their way out.

They pressed on over and over and convinced me that they would keep me safe. Swearing to god multiple times. Even grabbing a bible and putting their hands on it. And as a child a parent swearing to God on the bible is a big thing. At least it was for me. Would they really chance burning in hell just to get rid of me? I reluctantly agreed to do it on their promise of safety.

They had told me when he comes up and opens the door and he comes near me they're going to let me go instead of always holding me for him and that I should punch him squarely in the balls. They handed me what I believe was a roll of nickels wrapped in masking tape. They showed me how to hold it to hit him with the most force, and exactly what angle to hit him, fist clenched around the object in an uppercut motion. I actually knew this would work because he always stood the same way, with his hands to his hips with the knife in his palm pointing behind him and away from his back if he had it, and his feet spread out a bit more than a normal human. They said as soon as we release your arms you hit him as hard as you can. If you hit him hard enough he will disappear into thin air and he will have to find a new child elsewhere never to be seen by you again.

They explained to me that this would be the only way to rid him from my life, and to show him that I'm not scared of him anymore, and they said that this will drain him of his power over me. What happened next was an epic day in my life. Perhaps the first one beside getting my headphones and my tent. My parents held me each by an arm like they always did. And they called his name, hey bogeyman, Victor is here for you. Take your time, he's in big trouble and not going anywhere. A few minutes later I heard him coming up the stairs and I was fairly horrified. But trusted in the safety of my parents.

He opened the door, he started walking slowly towards me, he had the machete with him this time, as he got within about a foot away my father said you won't be needing that today, can I hold that for a second? The Boggymans head turned to the side like a confused dog would. He handed my father the machete and he placed it next to us on the counter. The Boogyman took his normal stance, and right as he was about to ask why he was summoned here today, my parents let my arms go. And I let my little fist go. Boom.

It was a perfect shot straight up the middle that dropped him dead to his knees. I hit him so hard I expected him to vanish, but instead he put his hands between his legs, dropped to his knees and started falling sideways to the floor, he was shrieking and crying in pain, with the sounds of my parents now screaming behind me, and seeing him falling like that I knew he didn't vanish like he was supposed to, but as he was falling sideways I was starting to close my eyes in fear of a swift retaliation and noticed something weird as they were closing.

Ok, he didn't disappear, that was obvious, but I hit him so hard I knocked his head off. I saw it, I saw it falling off as I closed my eyes. I know I did. I kept them closed for only about two seconds processing what had just happened and hoping that his head really came off and he was dead. I opened them quickly waiting for some sort of retaliatory impact. My mom and Dad were still screaming behind me so I thought he might be getting back up. As my eyes opened all the way it hit me.

There, lying on the floor, still clutching his testicles, with a paper bag head laying behind his real head, there lied, not a Boogeyman, but my Uncle Joe, still wrenching in pain with tears actually flowing from his tightly closed eyes. The screaming from my parents behind me in which I thought were screams of fear turned out to be uncontrollable laughter. My father was actually on the floor in a ball muttering how he was going to piss his pants this time. Haha. Very funny motherfuckers.

I do remember for a second feeling so proud of what I just did, happy for a moment that doing what I just did made my parents that happy. Even if just for a moment. I was proud that I had the nerve to stick up for myself against something that has terrified me for as long as I could remember, but also feeling a sense of anger that I was lied to all this time, feeling bad because I just clobbered my uncle in the balls like that and he was clearly in pain, and also feeling a sense of relief that there wasn't really a Boogeyman. All this time it was just a jerk in a paper bag. And I was a little confused as to why my Uncle was now calling me a little asshole instead of being mad at my parents? I believe it was my very first sense of total mixed emotions.

I would later come to understand that the reason my parents had me do this to my uncle was to get back at him for laughing about the toaster debacle and not helping them clean up the mess and asking my mother to make him breakfast that morning. And the whole Boogyman story was to make sure I never entered the basement. Looking back this is really a sick and twisted way just to keep a kid behaved and to stop him from entering a certain door.

After the nut punch my parents brought me into the living room and my uncle disappeared for a few days. I thought he was mad at me and was never going to come back to visit ever again. I asked my parents how he was getting down there so fast to come up to get me and they told me that he lived only a few houses down and there was a separate door from the outside in from his house. Whatever the fuck that meant? They then told me I was still not allowed down there because that was the adult space with very dangerous stuff and no kids should ever be allowed down there.

So within that next few days I do believe, when I was there alone with my babysitter, Nancy, everyone else was gone and I noticed she was on the telephone and not paying attention to what I was up to. I remember sneaking over and opening the door to the basement, staring down the stairs I was still quite scared shitless to say the least. But as I was slowly walking down I started to realize that it was really just a regular person's bedroom. No ovens, stoves or butcher blocks, no other door from the outside in, no axes, swords and cutting tools hanging from the walls that they had all mentioned to me were down there. You know, so he could skin me, cook me and eat me.

The black clothes that the so-called boogie man was always wearing and the paper bag were all sitting on a dresser. There was a bed, a couch, a few chairs, a larger dresser and a big round coffee table in the middle of the room that was filled to the brim with beer cans, alcohol bottles and drug stuff that at the time I had no idea what it was. And oh yeah, I noticed something else, there on the coffee table in the middle of all the garbage was the machete. Of course, I grabbed it. Plastic. Fake, Bendy. I was never in any danger at all from this thing. It was all still pretty messed up and confusing though. I can still remember the scene for some unknown reason like it was last week. I started noticing, not that I hadn't already kind of figured it out. All of this stuff was my uncles, he carried around a green "tobacco bong" sometimes when he was over and two of his jackets were hanging from a pipe.

I realized quickly that was my Uncle Joes bedroom. What the hell? I never ever ever saw him go down there or come up. The only one that ever came up or went down there was the Boogeyman. I always thought that when my uncle Joe left the house through the back door he was going somewhere else. I never knew he actually lived there with us.

Apparently, every time immediately after he would tell me goodbye and leave the house to go home, that's when my parents would make me go into the bathroom to wash my face and brush my teeth. That gave him the opportunity to sneak back in through the back-kitchen door and make his way down there without me noticing. He could make as much noise as he wanted down there because they all had me convinced it was the fucking Boogeyman. And people wonder why some kids turn out to be dishonest douchebags or insane axe murderers?

There was one more thing down there. And the reason I got caught trespassing in my uncles' room for the first and only time by myself. A very shiny silver machine with big and small golden discs in which I've never seen in real life before. And this was the realization of what the loud noise that was always coming up from under the floor was. There was a big, bad ass drum set. This was the most awesome thing I've ever seen in my life to this point. Two sticks sitting on the snare drum just screaming my name and I just couldn't help myself. I slammed the hell out of those things, maybe four or five minutes, eventually my babysitter Nancy came running down to put a stop to the racket.

I'm pretty sure I wasn't any good at it. But I have to say I fell in love with drums immediately. It's one of the main things I wanted to do and become for most of my life after that moment. Sure, I had a few other dreams since then. But most of them were squashed pretty quickly. You'll all hear more on that stuff later, in book time, as their being crushed, I don't want to give away too many spoilers. Anyway, I remember her promising me that she wouldn't tell anyone that I was down there because she didn't want me to get into any more trouble with my uncle after I smashed his nuts. Awww, that is so nice of her.

Well, as with anyone who's ever owned a set of drums, you can always tell when someone has messed with your stuff. And I was questioned, for hours, I said no, it wasn't me. Maybe it was Mom? Maybe it was Dad? Maybe it was the real Boogeyman? I tried the guilt trip thing. I Thought that I could get away with it after everything they put me through, I thought maybe they would just let it go. Hell no! They called Nancy back to the house and only had to ask her one time before she broke like a cracked egg. Yeah, he was down there, he was slamming on the drum set when I found him. I made him stop and come back upstairs. I was going to tell you but he asked me not to. So much for not wanting to see me get into trouble bitch. It's ok, I get her back soon enough. Way back. And front. You'll see.

As I recall it was my very first belt spanking. Pants down, bare ass, ten to twelve hits by my father. It was fairly brutal with every smack of the belt coming with a word. Don't-you-ever-lie-to-us-ever-again-you-little-bastard. This really started me down a path of hating and mistrusting most people terribly. How could you, after what you've already done to my mind. Scaring the hell out of me almost daily. Thinking I was going to be skinned, cooked and eaten by a monster that lived under the house. Lying to me constantly, Hitting me like that? Really? I believe my uncle felt bad for me after all of this went down and I remember a couple times before we moved out he actually let me go down and play with the drums and hang out in his room with him when my parents weren't around. These are the last of the memory's I had in this apartment. But not even close to the memories of violence that came after.

◆ ◆ ◆

PART TWO - THE FATHER COMPLEX

We had moved into a different apartment complex still in New Haven, I don't recall the name of the street. What I do remember is as we were moving in my mother was just starting to be visibly pregnant. With what would soon be my little brother Joey. I remember the moving truck, I remember moving stuff into the apartment, I am pretty sure that once again my bedroom was in the living room because that's the only place I ever remember putting my stuff. Besides in the hallway next to the bathroom upstairs when they had guests. I didn't have much for a room anyway. I still had my tent and my headphones and that was enough for me.

I remember a girl from across the street who was approximately my age coming over and introducing herself as we were unloading the truck. She said hello, my name is Alice, do you have a bike? I said no, she said that's OK, you can share mine with me. I live right across the street and my mom lets me ride my bike in this parking lot whenever I want. And this was my first real friend in the world. But like most else in the world for me. It was pretty much short lived.

I truly do not remember an awful lot about life in this apartment, as it was also short lived? I remember I had a big parking lot to play in and a church at one end that had a bell tower and it would ring every morning at 9 o'clock. Myself and my friend Alice would play out in the parking lot quite a bit alone. She had a basket on her bike and would bring toys over with her. Matchboxes, action figures, Barbie dolls, yeah yeah, fuck you, I was four years old and she was my only friend. We took turns picking our sorts of playtime. Yes. I was a gentleman. Thank you. Sometimes anyway. There was a good-sized wooded area right behind our apartment, about fifty feet from our back door. This is where we played most of the time.

We would take sticks and rocks and sand and whatever else we could get our hands on from inside or right on the outside of the woods to make little houses for the dolls, or forts for the action figures, or ramps for the matchboxes or just for whatever we wanted to do. It was usually peaceful and as far as I can recall no one ever really bothered us. We would be able to stay out there all day as long as we were both home before the sun started going down. Do you remember when kids actually did that?

On one of the days I do remember the most with her, it was very early in the morning as while we were playing outside I remember the church bells going off after we were already outside together for quite a while. Not long after the church bells rang we noticed a light blue Cadillac Eldorado pulling in a few spots next to us. It was my grandfather Frank that came to visit. "Gramps" My mother's father. We were in our normal spot playing matchboxes. I know it must have been a Saturday because he wasn't working and my father was home.

It was a complete surprise to see him. He always went roller skating on Saturdays. But not today. He got out of his Caddie. He always had a Caddie. And he told me to climb into the car and push the yellow button in the glove compartment. He took me by my hand and told me to close my eyes. He led me to the now opened trunk and told me, go ahead, open your eyes. I opened them and I saw that he had brought me a pair of black roller skates with bright white laces. I think Alice was more excited than me because now she can ride her bike and I could skate next to her. This was my first time ever roller skating. I was so excited to have something else that allowed me to play outside more.

He stayed with us outside for like four hours and taught me how to skate on them while Alice pretty much circled us on her bike. He told me that I was actually picking it up very quickly especially being on rocky pavement. I learned how to go forward and turn and how to use one foot for a break to stop. I was having no problems going from one end of the lot to the other by myself within just a few of those first four hours. I was getting so good so quickly I was even trying to skate backwards on my first day.

After the first four hours I was clearly doing well and Gramp's asked us if we wanted to go out for lunch. We said yes, I asked Pizza please. He said of course. My mother called Alice's mother and she said it was no problem. We went to Modern Pizza on state street. Me and Alice ordered a medium pepperoni and each had a birch beer. This was the first soda anyone ever let me drink. Gramps ordered a small sausage and pepper pizza for himself.

The pepperoni was not cut into slices but rather there were little chunks spread all over the entire top. It was anything but round and it looked very greasy and I was skeptical to say the least. It didn't look good at all. I took a slice and gramps sprinkled some grated Parmesan cheese over it for me and said go ahead. Take a bite. It tastes way better than it looks. I took a bite of this pizza and my mouth exploded. Sweet Mary mother of baby Jesus. The favors were absolutely the best thing I had ever put in my mouth. I remember my grandfather had to make me swallow it because I just kept chewing. I never wanted it to leave my taste buds.

I finished the first slice and had to get up and give him a hug.

I told him I never want to eat anything else for the rest of my life. Gramps and Alice were both laughing so hard. Alice looked at me and said I'm sorry. Your parents definitely need to get you out more. Have you ever eaten Chinese food before? I said no. She said wait until you do. It's pretty darn good too. I sat back down and we finished the entire medium pizza and I even had a slice of Gramp's pizza and had a soda refill.

It was the most I had ever eaten and drank in one sitting. And probably the most for years to come. Between the pizza and the birch beer I was absolutely in love. I didn't know how I would survive without it. Between that and the birch beer. Best thing ever. Modern pizza forever. I actually work here twelve years later and it was just as good as it was when I was younger. Gramps actually bought me a second medium pizza on this day to take home with me, and bought my mother and father a large for them. He was such a great guy.

We left Modern and he drove us home. He pulled back in to the same spot and I ran inside to put my pizza on the table. My grandfather walked in behind me with their pizza and told my parents that he got them a large sausage and peppers and the pepperoni was for me for dinner tonight and for lunch tomorrow. We went back outside and I put my skates back on and tried to roll around like before. No go. At least not right away. I was way to full. It took a while to digest all that I had eaten. I skated and Alice rode her bike for about two hours while Gramps was inside talking to my mom and dad while he was watching us from the doorway.

Before he left he told me that I should take them off and put them inside so I don't get hurt without him around. He said its only two or three hours before dinner time so I should relax and play with the toys on the ground. And hey, Victor. Come here. He whispered in my ear as he put a twenty-dollar bill in my hand. Use that for something you want and don't tell anyone about this or the soda. I didn't let your mother drink soda until she was thirteen years old.

He smiled and gave me a kiss on my cheek and looked at Alice and said it was nice to meet you, you take good care of my grandson, ok. She said yes sir Gramps. I always do. He said thank you dear, goodbye. He jumped in his El Dorado and off he went. Me and Alice were now outside playing in the same spot as earlier shortly after he had left. She had gotten bored playing with the toys and started riding her bike around the lot. I had snuck back into the apartment and took my roller skates back outside without my parents seeing me. We still had a little more than an hour before it was to start getting dark. Let's roll.

I never said I was smart. After almost an hour, when we knew we had to go inside very soon. I don't know why but Alice and I thought it would be a good idea to race each other from the church to the curb near the woods. In one day, I thought I was the fastest skater in the world for some reason. We went a little farther towards the church than we usually did. And from the church towards my family's apartment and the curb near the woods was a slight downward incline. We got to our mark. I held her handlebar with my right hand so our bodies were perfectly even and told her she could count down. I probably should have lined up with the front tire.

1-2-3 go. As I pushed off to get out in front of her, and it wasn't on purpose, just the way it happened when I tried to leave the starting line. I had pulled her handlebar so her tire pointed towards me. My knee actually hit the tire. She laughed at me and said I'm going to catch you anyways slow poke. I got out on her about ten to twelve feet pretty quickly. In about four seconds I turned my head to see how far out front of her I was. She was directly behind me already. Like four feet away. I looked behind me to the right, there she was. I looked behind me to the left, there she was.

Ah hell. She's going to hit me. She was coming up fast. Too fast.

I knew her tire was about to hit my skates. I put my arm out to the left hoping that's the way she would go and tried to dart right. No chance, as soon as I moved to the right my right skate hit a rock in the parking lot and down I started. I didn't even make it all the way to the ground when I felt her front tire dig into my ribs, and when I looked up over my left shoulder she was flying over me without her bike. Crash. Let the bodies hit the floor.

I can remember scraping up my right knee, hand and elbow really bad. Little pebbles and sand all through the cuts. She was bleeding from her nose and her fore head. Her hands were all scraped up and her bike was a total mess. Chain fell off, handlebars were crooked, front spokes were all bent up and her seat was even sideways. I believe it was my father who was the first to notice all the commotion as he was the first there. He yelled for my mother and picked Alice up off of the ground and she immediately threw up pizza all over his face and in his hair. He looked over at me and yelled get inside now and he ran across the street to bring her to her parents' home. I felt so bad and was hoping that she wasn't really that hurt.

My mom freaked out yelling at me that my grandfather told me no more skating today. I know I didn't listen, but hurting her was obviously a mistake. I explained to my mother that I would never hurt Alice on purpose as she was trying to remove my skates. She said she didn't care. You didn't listen and when your father gets back you are in big time trouble. You are definitely getting the belt. He came back into the house and went straight into the bathroom yelling that he had to clean the little chunks of pepperoni puke out of his hair before he deals with me. As soon as he was finished this was the second belt spanking I ever remember.

I can't remember the actual spanking in too much detail, pants down, belt on butt, my hand, knee and elbow were already hurting and still bleeding so I think that numbed the pain of the leather against my skin. I remember that it was upstairs in my parents' room and that after the spanking I was crying and I was pulling my pants back up as my mother grabbed me by the back of my neck, dragged me down the stairs and put me in the kitchen corner and said this is where you stay for an hour. No less. Any noises or complaining. It will be two.

There was Mom, Dad, Nancy, Uncle Joe and someone else there in the kitchen that I don't remember. They were all drinking and playing cards at the kitchen table about fifteen feet away from my corner and the sun had just went down. It was about twenty minutes into my sentence when my nose that was full of snot from all the crying started drying up. Every time I would breathe a little out of my nose it would start to whistle slightly. Like the sill of a window when the wind is blowing under it. It started getting slightly louder as the time passed and I had heard someone ask if the wind was really blowing that hard outside.

I waited a minute or two and did it again, shhhhwwww out of my nose. My father got up and looked out of the window and said what the fuck is going on out there. Not one leaf on any of these trees are moving at all, how is there wind just outside of the window. My mother said that she should call Alice's mother to see if she died because of me and her ghost was trying to get through the window to get back at me. I knew that was bullshit because I was the one doing it. Nice try though mommy.

My mother then actually tried to call over there and there was no answer. I waited a few more minutes after they both sat back down. Shhhhwwwww. Shhhwwww. They all got up and ran towards the door this time and opened it and went outside. Someone is fucking with us. Victor, are you making noises over there. Answer me. I didn't want another hour so I lied. No. I'm not doing anything. I heard it too. What is it? Is it the wind? Never mind, you just stand there quietly or you're not getting your pizza tomorrow. OK Mom. I thought to myself I guess that means I'm not getting my pizza tonight.

They all sat back down. At least that's what I thought. All I can see is flowered wallpaper in a corner. Now they're actually talking about the weather. Snow, cold, hurricanes, blah blah blah. In my mind I'm telling myself don't you do it, you're going to be stuck here for another hour if they catch you, you're almost done and can go clean yourself up and listen to your headphones. You still have your pizza for tomorrow. Don't do it idiot, you're going to get caught, don't do it, don't, and... Ahhh, you won't get caught. I just couldn't stop myself, it was to funny. I turned my head a little to the left and shhhwwwwwww. CRAAACK, Back right side of my head Immediately. My face smacked against the wall to the left, straight nose shot. That's not very surprising. I have a pretty large sized nose, and in pulling away after smacking my nose my head hit the other side of the wall, my nose started bleeding through the dried-up snot and I heard my mom scream, I knew it was you. I fucking knew it you little bastard. What the fuck is wrong with you?

She turned me around with everyone else laughing, that was great someone said. We really thought the wind was messing with us. My Mother had told me I had bought myself another hour. But everyone else was kind of still laughing and asked for me to get a break. Let him go clean himself up and play in his tent. That was to funny to punish him for. So, I was allowed to go upstairs in the bathroom. No one even came with me or helped me clean up my face though. Or my cuts from the accident that were now dried and starting to scab over. I went into the bathroom and had to clean it up all by myself. My nose bled for at least five more minutes. I rinsed the other cuts with Bactine in the tub and sink. I made sure to clean up all the blood in the sink, tub and on the floor so I wouldn't get yelled at or punished any more.

After all that I go into the hallway next to the bathroom where my father threw my tent. As I said earlier I can't have it in the living room here on this night or any like it because there is no wall between the living room and the kitchen and that's where they partied all night. I am now laying in my tent not long after I got myself cleaned up, listening to my headphones, Steve Miller band, go on take the money and run was playing, I was thinking about how far I could get away from them on the money my grandfather gave me when I felt a kick to the side of my head right through the tent. My headphones flew off and I could hear my mother calling me a filthy scumbag. You had to use the yellow towel to clean up your blood, didn't you? You couldn't find a darker colored one to use? We have brown or black or dark towels everywhere. You just had to use the yellow one. I can't believe you have to ruin everything I have in my life. Go to fucking sleep. Now. Don't even let me here you move in there again until the morning.

All I can remember thinking that night as I laid in my tent, listening to the grownups in my house hooting, hollering, smoking, drinking and doing whatever drugs they were doing to make them so irrational all the god damn time, I remember thinking, at four fucking years old, how in the world is it ok for these people to even think of having another child. How in the world is my mother still in that kitchen drinking and smoking cigarettes at about seven months pregnant with my little brother or sister.

And how in the world am I going to protect a child from this obvious evil when I am nothing but a child myself? How am I going to protect a baby from the madness that obviously controls these people's lives? A four-year-old child should not have to have these worries in their lives while all their trying to do is listen to some music and fall asleep. This is around the time where my insomnia started. And it would have a huge impact on me for many years to come. When you see how my childhood was robbed from me in later chapters especially. You will realize why my teens twenties and thirties turned out to be what they were.

And on a side note, the next day and the week to follow the bike accident and the corner windstorm joke, my eyes both turned black and blue, my nose was clearly broken and crooked with a nice lump on it, and no one ever said a word about it. No one had ever even looked at it. The only thing that was ever said when someone asked anyone what happened? The answer was It happened on his roller skates when he collided with the little girl on her bike. And as you probably figured when I went into the kitchen the next morning in the middle of the table with all their empty cans and bottles were also two empty pizza boxes. I cried like a baby. And people always wondered why I was such a bitter troublemaking prick once I started school and all the way through.

Besides the memory of this specific event. As far as living in this apartment goes, most everything from here on out is an on and off blur. Except for one more ridiculous night. Our last night there. As best as I can recall it, and as myself and my mother had talked about it afterwards when I got older more than a few times. And in some of those conversations I also was informed that in between me and my brother Joey she was pregnant twice. And aborted them both. I don't know to this day how to react to that information. I am 1000% against abortion any time after there is any possibility that the baby can feel the pain of it. But on the other hand, I couldn't imagine how much worse my life could have been or what kind of hell those children might have had to go through if she had them. It is a lifetime of intercranial conflict I have always had to live with.

Anyway, back to this day. My mother was about none months pregnant now and ready to have the baby literally any week, and she had been working still. She was a lifetime waitress. But did dog grooming on the side. I believe she was supposed to be waiting tables on this specific day because I vaguely remember a black apron with pens sticking out when she left the apartment.

My father was supposed to be working a late night as far as he told my mother earlier in this day. He exclaimed he had an extra painting job for that night, and that he would more than likely not be home until way after she got there. They both left for work at pretty much the same time. Even as a kid I felt a tension in the air like I've never felt before. Something was off and terribly wrong. I asked Nancy if everything was alright and why they were acting like this towards each other. They always gave each other a kiss and a hug goodbye even if they were arguing, but not today. She told me not to worry about it and that everything should be fine. You are way too young to be worrying about adults' situations. You wouldn't understand. You can go outside and play if you want, I'll call you in for dinner when it's getting dark.

So I went outside to play, by myself, did I mention I never saw Alice again after the bike and skate mishap. She ended up breaking her wrist and getting stitches in her head. It truly sucked, but this is something I would have to get used to through the years. It is what it is I suppose. Losing friends and loved ones is just a part of life. Even if they are still alive. I learned this at a very young age and learned how to deal with it in my own way. So, I was outside for a few hours playing by myself, mostly skating around.

I was up by the church sitting on a curb re-tying one of my skates when I noticed my father's car pulling in to the entrance of the parking lot. It was right before it got dark and as he was pulling in to his parking spot, Nancy yelled for me to come in for dinner. My father walked in before I skated to the door and he went straight upstairs. I called out for him to ask if he would help me take my skates off as he was about half way up the stairs but he ignored me. Nancy helped me take my skates off and set a plate up for me on the floor right in front of the TV. I asked if my father was alright and she said not to worry. I'll go take care of him, he'll be just fine.

I still remember exactly what I was watching when Nancy walked up the stairs. And right to the skit a few minutes later, and I also knew what was going on in the apartment upstairs was something weird, something that was not supposed to be happening. Nancy had gone upstairs right after giving me my dinner, I could hear them talking and giggling and I heard the shower start, I didn't really think about it too much at that time and just ate and watched TV. I was watching the three stooges. Moe, Larry and Curly were all laying down in the same bed sleeping. Larry was snoring really loud and wakes up Moe. Moe slaps him in the top of the head and says "Wake up and go to sleep" I blew a piece of ham out of my nose that actually stuck to the TV. It was the funniest thing I have ever seen or heard in my life up to then. I reached over to pull the ham off of the TV screen laughing hysterically when the front door flew open.

My laughing stopped immediately. No pause from my mother, where is your fucking father Victor? I looked back at the TV hoping to escape into it. I wanted no part of this whatsoever. VICTOR, WHERE IS YOUR GOD DAMN FATHER???? I can't be sure but looking back on it I believe she never went to work on that day and hid somewhere to see if my father came home early or not. It's something I think I never asked her. So, I am fairly sure I will never have the answer for that. Everything else about this night is crystal clear though.

I will always remember my answer to the where's your father question. I paused for a couple seconds after I was asked. Victor, please. I had to think about it. Do I tell her? I think where he is is wrong? I don't think he is supposed to be there, I can't do this to my mother. She asked me again. Where is he? I looked up at her and realized that she already had an idea. It was the saddest I ever saw her up to that moment. From the funniest thing I ever saw in my life on the TV to the saddest I've ever seen my mother in less than a minute. That is honestly the underlining story of my life. Where is that fucking whore Nancy? Victor, Is she still here? You tell me right this instant. I thought about it for only one more second. And then I had thought about all they had done to me up to this point in my life. The Boogeyman, The Spankings, The Broken Nose, The Ratting On Me Over The Drum Set. All of it. I'm sick of it. FUCK THEM ALL. THEY ALL DESERVE THIS. Nancy's upstairs washing daddy in the shower!!!

I remember her face turning bright red and her running towards the stairs, going quickly but I think trying to be quiet at the same time to catch them in the act. Everything bouncing around and my feeling that that baby is going to fall out of her belly if she keeps trying to go up the stairs like that. She made it to the top of the stairs as I walked over to the bottom to try to see what the hell was going on up there. For some reason I knew they shouldn't be in the shower together but I had no idea what they were really doing in there. In my mind they were probably just washing each other. Right, I'm four years old, it's 1976, nobody has taught me anything about sex yet. I don't know what that is. But I'm about to find out in the worst way. Well? Maybe the best way. You'll see.

So I look up at my mother at the top of the stairs, she was facing the bathroom door, I could see the top half of the door clearly from the bottom of the stairs to just maybe a foot above the doorknob. My mother took like a half a second, took a deep breath and reared back and kicked the door open, one shot, pretty damn impressive for a girl about to drop a baby any week now. Actually, a pretty scary chick if you think about it. As the door flew open the first thing I noticed was the steam billowing from the top of the door jam and the first thing I heard was Nancy scream.

My mother took two steps in and B lined it straight for the shower, I could hear the rings from the shower curtain scrape across the shower rod and then it happened. YOU FUCKING CUNT WHORE GET THE FUCK OUT OF HERE. NOOOOOW. And then a few choice swears and Italian words I'm pretty sure I never heard before this came out of her mouth. So many feelings and thoughts and questions were flowing through my mind at this point, I had no idea what was about to transpire. All I know is she's pregnant, and I also know there is definitely about to be a terrible battle that she shouldn't be a part of in her condition at the top of these stairs right now. There isn't anything stopping this. And all I could do was watch. It was a terrible feeling of helplessness. Again.

Peering up the stairs I could see the light fixture hanging from the bathroom ceiling, the medicine cabinet to the right and my mother's head facing the shower to the left, in which I couldn't see the shower through the wall from the bottom of the stairs. I could see my mother lunge towards the shower still screaming as she disappeared behind the wall. Nancy came flying out of the shower as I could see my mothers' hands trying to reach for her, she started to fall down but gained her footing and reached down to scoop up her clothing and started towards the stairs. My mother turned her absolute attention to my father. Nancy took three or so steps to the stairs from the bathroom, as she started to come down she was definitely slipping and sliding here and there. It was in such slow motion to me. It seemed like the whole way down a single flight of stairs took her a solid minute although it was probably twelve to fifteen seconds.

All I could hear was screaming going on upstairs from inside the bathroom, the plastic shower curtain making a crumbling noise and then the rod breaking and also squeaking from my mothers' shoes on the bottom of the porcelain bathtub. It sounded like they were wrestling in there. Probably because they were. It was quite loud. I heard the shower turn off. And all I could see now, was Nancy, coming right at me down the stairs, butt ass naked, fumbling to keep her clothes in her hands and up against her body while also trying to reach for the stair rail to keep from falling.

I don't think she knew as she was coming down the stairs with me standing right there staring up towards her which part of her body to cover up. She kept moving her clothes from up to down, from front to back, dropping pieces on the way and stopping and bending down to try to pick them up. Everything just hanging out. Boobies bouncing, butt bouncing, water spraying everywhere from her still soaking wet flailing hair. I could feel the spray on my face and I'm sorry, it was all just so fucking awesome. From start to finish.

As she was bumbling and stumbling I think she was trying to find her underwear because she was paying more attention to her clothes than the stairs she was trying to navigate as she got closer to the bottom, she made it to three stairs from the bottom when her feet came out completely from under her, I couldn't keep my eyes off of her, and I didn't move an inch. I was inspecting every possible crevasse of her body, I was in awe.

I was following her every step from top to middle all the way to me. Literally. As her feet slipped out, she landed on her butt as her clothes flew up into the air, she had hit my feet with hers as she hit the bottom and I landed directly on top of her. She pushed me off to where I was sitting upright against the wall facing the steps. She looked at me and said I can't believe you didn't tell us she was here you little bastard.

As she then tried to get up she put both hands on the floor to boost herself to her feet, I truly don't know what came over me, I really don't, because this is messed up for any four-year-old, even if I was to be five in a few weeks? As her hands were down flat on the floor and her boobs are pointing towards the floor, something in my mind said, you have to know what those feels like, I cupped my little hand, reached forward, pushed upwards, grabbed and squeezed. It was very water balloon like. I couldn't stop looking and I didn't want to let go, but, smack, open hand right across my face. The look on her face was all kinds of things at the same time. I still can't explain it. But I'm pretty sure it was mostly surprised and disgusted, I don't know why she'd be surprised? Her and her people made me like this.

You little fuck she yelled, then she pushed me back up against the wall in a sitting position again, she got up to her feet and turned back towards the stairs. As I stared at her back side, still riled up about all that was going on around me, and all that has happened and is still happening, especially the booby, she put her right foot on the second step and bent over to gather up all of her clothing. Holy shit. A feeling came over me that I had never felt. An epiphany of sorts, as she was bent over, retrieving her belongings, two feet in front of my face, it hit me, I am right now seeing my first live vagina, up close and personal, that's what they were doing in the shower, that is what a penis is for. Talk about an awakening. No one ever had to tell me about sex. I figured that shit out right then and there. Daddy was having sex with Nancy in the shower and that's why mommy is losing her mind right now.

She stood up, clothes in hand, I couldn't even say anything, the noise from upstairs is now just muffled random sounds, I think I'm in shock. Again. She walked to the middle of the living room and struggled to put on her shirt as her hair and skin were still wet, she walked over to the kitchen table and grabbed her pocket book, I still couldn't stop glaring at her, the image of the vagina I just experienced flashing in and out of my mind. She turned towards me one last time before she would leave and said, stop staring at me you little asshole. I wouldn't. Fuck you you little pervert prick, you're messed up in your little fucking head, and your mother is a filthy cunt. She screamed as loud as she could towards the stairs. FUCK YOU JANIS. And then she just walked out of the door, leaving it wide open, only wearing a shirt, no underwear, no pants, no shoes, just out. And I'm the one who's messed up? I then heard her car start and pull away as I was now focusing on what was going on upstairs. The noise became clearer and I knew this battle inside the house, even with her now gone, was just getting started.

Obviously my mother and father kept bickering and fighting and yelling and screaming upstairs in the bathroom, I could see my father trying to get his pants on as my mother kept yelling and swinging on him. My father grabbed her by her hair and pushed her head against the medicine cabinet cracking the mirror and growled like an animal in her face. He let go and started walking down the stairs with his pants in his hand, with her just a step or so behind him holding up her belly still screaming in his ear, this lady had no type of give up in her at all. I remember saying out loud, be careful please, I think the stairs are still wet from Nancy. Please don't slip and fall. Not even a glance from either of them.

They made their way into the kitchen through the living room, walking past me like I wasn't even there. The argument ensued back and forth for about twenty seconds. My father came back into the living room and sat in the chair still trying to put his pants on, head down shaking it back and forth like he couldn't believe this was happening to him. All was quiet for about ten seconds besides the sounds of my mother crying and sniffling in the kitchen, and then it wasn't. I heard the wooden kitchen drawer open and the silverware rack slide from the back to where it hit the front. For some strange reason I knew this wasn't going to be good in any way.

She came screaming around the corner like a monster on a kill mission, and my father jumped up out of the chair and just stared at her. She screamed in a scratchy broken voice, I'M GOING TO KILL YOU, YOU CHEATING MOTHERFUCKER. She drew her arm back and that's when I saw it, Michael Myers size butcher knife. Everything went into slow motion again, but this time it seemed even slower to me. She had the knife by the handle and I thought she was going to rush him while he was standing there. She looked at me for a split second and as soon as she turned her head towards him she let out a blood curdling scream and threw that thing at him as hard as she could. This lady meant some business. Insanely pissed off would probably be an understatement.

I could see the knife leave her hand and as it went through the air a million thoughts were flowing through me. I thought he was going to die, she was going to jail, I was never going to see the baby, I have no place to live and life as I know it is over. The knife hit him directly in the chest as closed my eyes and I could vision it perfectly sticking out of his chest, I could vision the blood, I could vision the look of horror on his face. I heard the knife hit his chest with a hollow thud with my eyes closed as tightly as I could get them and turning my head away so I didn't have to see. But a second after the thud, TING. The knife dropped to the floor, she had hit him with it perfectly, just the wrong end, it was the handle that had made the impact. All I thought was Phew.

I looked at him and he absolutely snapped. I guess the Phew I thought was dead wrong. What followed next is one of the most devastating moments in my young life. For some reason, even at my young age, I knew this was the end of my mother and father being together. Life was definitely about to change. For better? For worse? Who knows? But nothing from here on out is going to be the same.

My father kicked the knife to the side near where I was standing and then ran full speed and grabbed my mother by her hair again and dragged her over to the coat rack by the door, he grabbed a belt off the coat rack, he then pulled her over to where the knife was by my feet. He tossed the belt over his shoulder and picked up the knife, he looked at me and said I can't take any chances leaving this near you, you're just as fucked up as she is.

He tossed the knife into the kitchen and said now don't you move, you stay right there and watch this. It's far past time this bitch learned some respect. He dragged her still grasping her by her hair over to the chair he was just sitting in, he sat down and he pulled her towards the chair and he threw her over his knee, he ripped down her maternity pants, pulled the belt off of his shoulder and began to beat her with it while she was literally nine months pregnant. She was flailing around crying and screaming trying to get away.

He wasn't just hitting her on her behind either, he was reeling back hitting her everywhere. Butt, back, legs, head, like I said, everywhere. He beat her for at least two minutes straight in the sitting position with her over his knees, he just wouldn't stop. I never have seen anyone that angry before and to tell you the gods honest truth, it scared me more than the Boogeyman ever came close.

All I can remember thinking was that he was going to kill her and the baby inside her. And I was also terrified that Nancy was going to return and tell him what I did grabbing her boob, and he was going to kill me too. Even to this day the memories themselves make me feel strange and awkward. And the realization that this was my life that young, and the fact that it even gets increasingly worse later, is just absolutely mind blowing to me. But what the fuck are you going to do? Right?

He eventually threw her off of his knees into a ball on the floor in front of him and kept whipping her with the belt for another solid minute, yelling a single word with every smack, he finally stopped and stood over her and told her to look at him, she turned her head towards him and he spit directly in her face, he then bent down and screamed in her face that she minds her own fucking business. He said that they were done, why would I want a fat pregnant cunt like you when I can have her. He said I know that baby isn't even mine whore. I saw my mother visibly shaking trying to reach up towards him with one hand while trying to pull up her pants with the other.

He walked over to the coat rack as she was still trying to pull her pants up and gain her composure while still crying hysterically and he placed the belt back where he got it from and grabbed a shirt. He looked at me and said that's exactly what that fucking cunt deserves and don't let her tell you any different. She's nothing but a fucking bitch and she'll ruin your life just like everything else she touches. Trust me he said, you just wait and see. My emotions were flying, this was all my fault, why did I tell her? I can't believe this is happening.

He turned back towards her and he spit on her one more time and said that's right you fucking bitch, you can go cry to your father and brother now, we all know that's exactly what you're going to do. They should leave you on the street where you fucking belong. Good for nothing fat cunt. He then walked back towards me, he patted me on my head, I couldn't even look at him, he said good luck with your life and your little bastard brother kid. I love you but I can't stand her. It's not worth it. Goodbye. And he calmly walked out of the front door.

I could hear him yelling from the parking lot. I don't want to see you here when I get back tomorrow. I'm warning you. You'd better be fucking gone. I will send whatever's left to your father's house next week. That's when my mother looked at me and told me to pack whatever I wanted to bring with me. She said grab your skates your tent some clothes and your headphones. We will never be back here ever again and you will never see your father ever again either. I am completely done with this. He's nothing but a drug addict cheating piece of shit. And that was the last time I saw or heard from my father for quite a while.

◆ ◆ ◆

PART THREE – WALLYWORLD

We moved in with my grandfather in Wallingford, his house was in the middle of a decent neighborhood. Mostly families with teenaged kids. There weren't a lot of kids around that were close to my age, there were a few so it was a little more than just the one friend I was used to, it was definitely a family neighborhood. Soon after my little brother Joey was born. I have to say, and this absolutely sucks, that a lot of my memories from here on out, at least for a few years, are broken into pieces to say the least. But the ones I do have I believe are the most important. At least I hope so. If there are any memories worse than the ones I remember. I don't think I want to know. I always wished my grandfather was around more to see what was going on. But he worked all the time.

My gramps, Frank. Italian as can be. Nicest guy I can ever recall meeting in my life. He was a freezer stock worker for Stop & Shop warehouse in North Haven when we moved in with him. He would get up at four o'clock every morning and go off to work before five and not be home until six or seven at night. He was formally a milkman and was in the Navy for some years during and after WW2. When he wasn't working, he would dress to the hilt, straight up 1930s mafia boss Chicago gangster looking guy. He was definitely a snazzy dresser. He was commented on how sharp he looked wherever we went and was always singing a snappy tune or whistling a melody, at least he was when he didn't have a cigarette hanging out of his mouth. It didn't matter where we went, grocery store, bank, roller skating. Smoking a cigarette. The guy was just who he was and he didn't give a rat's ass about what anyone thought. Which is probably why everyone loved him to death. Everyone.

From what I heard he was married at around twenty-five to my Grandmother, Violet, I never had the chance to meet her. I believe they met when he was in the navy. She was pure French. They had two children Bob and my mother Janice. They bought the house on Sorrento road in Wallingford and settled down there. From my mother's stories my grandmother was very ill right when she was pregnant with me. She had psoriasis of the liver from what I remember her saying. From what my mother told me my grandmother would never stop drinking. She drank every single day and drank herself to death. She died in front of me and my mother in the living room at my grandfather's house about a year after I was born from what I remember my mother telling me. I never knew much about her besides that. And I obviously don't recall her death. No one ever really talked about her. Gramps would marry again, but that's a later, even sadder story.

Well now we were living in this neighborhood in Wallingford at my grandfather's where I had a much nicer place to play than a slab of parking lot. There was an actual front and back yard, the deal with my mother and my grandfather was, if you leave the yard you can't go past two houses on either side, you have to stay on our side of the street and you need to be in the house before the streetlights go on.

To the left of my grandfather's house was the Peddifrins, that's a made up name, you'll see why very soon. To the right of my grandfather's house was the Fairchild's, and directly in the backyard was a family called the Consiglio's. The Consiglio's had a few grandkids which I would play with in the backyard every now and then. Cheryl May and a few others that would come over to their house to visit their grandparents. We would play running through their sprinkler in the back yard when they were there. The Fairchild's children were a lot older, Doug was a police officer and his brother was a hippie, his name was Steve. Fairchilds and Consiglio's were great people all in all.

The Peddifrins on the other hand. Actually, in my other fucking hand, were a couple of pedophile faggot pricks. As you can guess by the last name I gave them. I don't want to get sued using real names calling out scumbags. And you can call me a homophobe all you want. When you see yourself at six or seven years old realizing that a couple of cocksuckers are using you to get off, fuck what anyone thinks about what I think or how I feel. And fuck them. Here's what sucks the most about this entire situation. I didn't remember all of what they did to me until I was in my mid-twenties. I had blocked it all out somewhere along the way. Fragmented it in my mind. Some of it is still blocked out. And since then a lot more had happened with both of them that should have made the memories flow back to me but they just simply never did until it was too late.

Harry and Greg were friends with my Mother and Uncle Bob, Greg was the older one by maybe two or three years. If I was to guess I would put them at eighteen and twenty years old or so at this point. I really don't remember much of what exactly they did in earlier events. I wish I could but at the same time I'm glad I don't remember more. Because for some reason deep inside of myself I truly think it was worse than I can recall. Not that what I recall wasn't bad enough.

Let me explain who these guys were in my opinion and in my recollection. I know that they had watched me in both my grandfather's house and in their own house if my mother needed a babysitter. Greg was a fat dude, talking like two hundred and seventy-five to three hundred pounds. He had a pigeon coup in their back yard. He would always bring me back there to watch him let the pigeons go and to show me that they would always come back home. He also had a chicken hawk in a cage up against his house that he would always come to get me when it was feeding time. He fed it live sparrows. It definitely grossed me out but I think I was still intrigued with the brutality of it all. That's all that I really remember of him personally.

His brother was the younger one. A typical teenager in the late seventies from what I would believe. He had a room in his house that was pretty much a basement room with its own separate entrance. He had a beer can collection on shelves all over his walls that even at my young age I still remember being impressed with and jealous of. He had your usual rock and roll posters on the wall. There was a black lighted Black Sabbath poster I remember for sure. I wanted that thing so bad. He had a few masks also on the walls and normal teenage paraphernalia lying about the room. I remember a little red bong, three Polaroid cameras and packs of Kools and EZ Widers that were always on his table. I distinctly remember him always playing with his cameras. This is really all I can remember about him personally. Now here is what I remember of them otherwise.

These are the two distinct memories I have of what each one of them did to me. Each is just one occasion but they are the most important because they are when I made each one of them stop fucking with me. All by myself. I recall watching TV in my grandfather's house. Greg was babysitting me and Joey and no one else was there. Joey was napping in my mother's bedroom. I know it was during the day with the sun out because I remember a glare from the picture window on the TV screen from where I was sitting.

I was sitting on the couch on the far end of the room away from the TV and he was in my grandfather's recliner which was much closer. I don't remember what we were watching exactly.

I remember asking him if he would please get up and close the curtains for me because of the glare. He said that the curtains wouldn't help and he got up and moved the recliner so it was more in front of the TV and it was actually blocking my view now. I asked how is that going to help? Now I can't see it at all.

He then said, I moved it here so you can sit with me and be closer to the TV. Come over here and sit down next to me on the recliner. There's plenty of room. Come on. You're going to miss the best part. I couldn't see the TV anymore from where I was sitting so I did. I went to squeeze in next to him and he said you'll never fit in there, you can sit on my knee. It's fine. You're not that heavy, I can take it. I don't remember feeling anything before I sat down with him as far as fear or remembering anything weird in the past. I don't think. I can't honestly say either way. I just don't remember. But, how easily and quickly he did what he did most definitely leads me to believe that he's one hundred percent done this to me beforehand. I just can't remember it in any detail that would matter.

What I do remember is watching the television, him laughing, my butt being uncomfortable on his thigh and then hearing him unbutton and unzip his pants slowly. I had no idea what he was doing and didn't think about it at all. I was concentrating on what I was watching and out of nowhere about five minutes later I realized that my hand was wrapped around his penis with his hand over mine controlling it up and down. I could feel it going up over the head and back down. That is what got my attention. For some reason I just knew this was dead wrong and not supposed to be happening at all. I just said enough and snapped.

I completely remember looking at him and saying I know this is not supposed to be happening like this and if you don't stop I will tell my grandfather and Uncle Bobby. I recall him letting go of my hand and gently pushing me off of his lap. I turned and looked at him as he put his penis away, I pointed at it and said if you ever put that thing near me ever again I'm telling everybody. I know that it is wrong and I don't like it one bit. Don't you dare do that to me ever again. He zipped his pants back up and promised me he would never do it again and to please not tell anyone. I even remember him crying as he pleaded with me not to tell. I don't think he ever did it again. I think I would remember if it happened after that. And I think because he never did is the reason why I never told a soul until I was much older when these memories came back. And what happened next with his brother was soon after and much clearer.

It was Halloween. 1979. And you are probably asking yourself how in the world would he remember the exact date? Well I'll tell you how in the world. Because miraculously, I have a Polaroid picture of the exact day this all transpired. My mother who had recently passed in 2017 had it with the rest of her pictures in a box I found in her bedroom in New Orleans. As soon as I saw it I remembered all the details like it was yesterday. I always knew that Harry, besides his brother had also done something to me because I remembered how I confronted him to stop. I remembered the exact words that came out of my mouth and exactly where we were at the time, but until I saw the picture I couldn't remember the entire situation that brought us to the moment when I made him stop.

I was seven and my little brother was two. Almost eight and three because our birthdays were only two months away. We were getting ready to go out trick or treating. My little brother was dressed up to be a clown and they put on his makeup at my grandfather’s house. I wanted to be Ace Frehley but they all wanted me to be Paul Stanley. Sorry, for the younger people, that's Kiss. Detroit Rock City. I Wanna Rock and Roll all Night and Party Every day. You know it. Don't lie.

As they were applying my makeup there was some sort of snag with the star that was supposed to cover and surround my eye. I didn't remember why, but Harry had told my mother he had something in his room that would help fix it. He would bring me over there and that he could make it look perfect and we'll be back in a little while. I remember the feeling of uneasiness flowing through me, at this point I think I knew he had done things to me in the past also. Because I know for sure his older brother did at this point. But I went anyways. I think I figured if he did, his brother told him to stop. Nope. Sure enough, as soon as we stepped into his room he pulled down his pants and pulled his penis out and sat down on the bed and grabbed my hand to place it on it. We have to hurry up he said.

Once again with the ease of which he did this just like his brother did, I know he did this to me before. It was just a feeling before. But now I know for sure. I guess my mind has blocked out much of what's happened to me during this period in my life and I am extremely grateful for not knowing it all. I can't think of any other reason I don't know every single thing for sure, the memories just aren't clear. The human mind is an amazing piece of equipment.

I can remember every detail of entire days and entire experiences from a few years earlier but these two years are mostly a blur. I've thought about going to a hypnotist to try to pull the memories out after the few came back. But this was in my mid-twenties. If I had found out any more, if I had found out it was any worse than just my hand. I would have killed any piece of shit who was involved without taking a single breath over it. Just saying. Zero tolerance for anything that might have happened besides my hand.

So on this day I do remember for some reason I was more afraid to stand up to him than to his brother, but I did it anyways. I thought back to the Boogeyman and I told myself I can definitely do this. I knew it was wrong and knew I wanted absolutely no part of what these fucking douchebags were doing to me. Because I do have to say, even back then, with absolute certainty. I knew I was a vagina guy. This shit that they were doing was dead wrong to me. Nauseatingly disgusting in my eyes.

And I have nothing against gay people. I really don't. I know a few. I respect them, they respect me. Do what you do. As long as you are not doing it to someone that doesn't want it to be done to them. I don't care. Hey, You like dick, cool. I like vagina. Go to town on that dick all day long. Your own town though. Not mine please. I wouldn't try to drag an unwanted vagina across your streets, so don't try to drag an unwanted cock across mine. I hope you caught all of that exactly how I was throwing it. If not and you just happen to be a douche. Don't go trying to spin it into your own words to follow your agenda. You know what the fuck I'm saying.

Sorry about all that. I got a little carried away. Back to Harry. My exact words were. You are going to stop doing this to me or I am telling everyone. I pulled my hand away from his penis. He grabbed it back with both hands and said come on, just one more time then I won't do it anymore. He tried to place it back on his penis and I kicked him in his shin and pulled away as hard as I could. Seriously he asked? You won't do it for me just one more time?

I can't believe that this is what this fucking puke said to me. Like I was his fucking girlfriend or some shit. I said no way, let go of my hand right now, I'm serious, if you ever touch me again or even go near my little brother I'm telling everyone what you're doing. I'll make sure I tell Doug next door first and you will go to jail for this. I know you're not supposed to be doing this to me. He immediately let go of my hand and put his penis away and said all pissed off. Ok, fine, I thought you were my friend, fuck you. I'll stop but if you tell anyone about this I will kill you, your mother, and your little brother. I will kill everyone. I left and walked home. I guess I believed him because I don't have any recollection of ever telling anyone or even seeing him anytime soon thereafter.

Until. Four years later, when he actually did almost kill me, which looked like a complete accident at the time. Now? And with what happened a few months later. There are more than a few people out there that think that he might have been trying to take me out all along so I could never tell anyone what he did back when I was younger. But that's still four years down the road. I'll tell that when we get there. It is truly an incredible awakening for me and there are going to be some people that read it that are going to say, hmmm, it all makes sense now. I still have some other memories in between which I don't want to forget or leave out. It never really got any easier from here especially with the hell that came next, and next, and next. Take some deep breaths Vic, Deep breaths. OK, Ready? let's do this.

Over the next year or so living with gramps and my mom things seemed to be like they were going to be ok. I believe our dad only visited us once or twice, I think that was it, my uncle Bob and aunt Debbie were there a lot. My uncle Bob had a dog kennel in my grandfather's back yard where he bred beagles. He had Boy and Girl as his two main doggies and then Bull and a bunch of puppies. He also used them for hunting. Gramps had a collie named King Louis. I played with the dogs a lot. I only had a very few friends living here.

My mother, to say the least was quite promiscuous while we were living here as I explained in my introduction, there were at least four or five different guys after my father she would have in and out of gramps house while he was at work. And I know for a fact that they weren't playing cards when she brought them into her room. I saw her and to many fucking guys naked running around the house in and out of her room to use the bathroom or go to the kitchen or some shit without even covering up with a towel. She was, at least in the eyes I see through now, completely out of control. Maybe it was to get back at my dad for cheating. There was one guy named Victor "she must have dug that name" that I guess you would call her main man for a little while after my father. He was really the only one that gave me or my little brother anytime at all. The rest were obviously there for something else.

There was one crazy black dude too. I don't remember his name though, I don't know where she met him, how she met him, or what connection they had to each other whatsoever. All I know is this guy would pull up to my grandfather's house, in a different brand-new looking sports car every single time and just laid on his horn screaming my mother's name, until, for some reason, within less than a minute or two, two or three police cars would come flying around the corner and chase him down the street. And then nothing for a few days, and then, it would happen again. Exactly the same.

The last time I remember it happening I was with a friend named John outside his house about four or five houses down playing matchboxes in the middle of the actual street when we heard the sirens. John looked at me and said don't tell me that's the cops chasing your mom's boyfriend again. I laughed and said no. He was here yesterday. And he's not her boyfriend. Just some crazy black dude that she doesn't even like. And what the hell do you know. A bright yellow corvette comes screeching around the corner. You could hear the sirens getting closer and closer.

John said I told you so as the sports car dude pulled up in front of Gramp's house. He stopped only for a few seconds, he got out of the car wearing a long brown fur coat with a black furry collar and pointed a hand gun at my mom who was on the lawn raking leaves, which I think I was more weirded out about the coat than the gun at the time because it was very warm out as I recall. He yelled something at her, only about five or so words I couldn't hear and got back in the car and sped off down the road straight towards me and John.

As soon as he hit the gas I looked at my mother who was

screaming at me and waving me to get off of the street. At that same time there were three Wallingford police cars coming around the corner. Billowing smoke from the tires of all four cars involved. It was absolute craziness and ultra-loud mayhem, something that you would definitely see in a car chase movie. It was just insane smoke and loudness all happening in about a hundred-yard space. John ran off to the side walk to get to safety, and I just stood there, like a complete ignoramus waving my arms back and forth trying to get him to stop, in my mind I thought to at least slow him down enough for the cops to catch him.

It happened so fast, I didn't even see Johns father. All I know is this crazy fucker didn't look like he was going to stop at all looking straight at me and I don't think he would have stopped. Luckily, Johns dad pulled me out of the road just in time. I felt the wind from the car brush up against me and felt my cloths flapping in the breeze as he passed. None of the cops even stopped or came back to see if everyone was alright or what the fuck. They just chased him down the road out of sight and even the sirens seemed to stop way before they should have. I never saw any of them ever again. No questions no nothing. I asked my mother about it and she would never tell me anything at all. Just that he was insane.

To this day I can't figure out what in the actual fuck that was all about. Was this guy some dirty pimp that had a thing for my mom and wanted her in his stable? Where was he getting all these brand-new cars from? Why did he have a gun? Why did he point a gun at my mother and not shoot? What did he say to her? What the fuck was with that coat? Why were the cops always right behind him? Was he a terrible car thief who always caught the polices attention before he came to our house? Was he a cop? Was he getting all these cars out of an impound yard or something and using his cop friends to either intimidate my mother or to impress her? How in the fuck were there cops always immediately behind him but never caught him so he couldn't do it again? Why did the sounds of the sirens stop immediately after they left our neighborhood? This is one of the biggest mysteries I've ever had in my entire life. It has always baffled me to this day. And just another set of episodes I will never get a straight answer to.

During all of this I don't really remember seeing that much of my father, I have a picture of where I was around eight and Joey was around three where we are with him, Uncle Joe, Aunt Laura and her son Travis. But before that picture was taken, nothing. I don't really have any memories of seeing him or even talking to him until definitely just a bit after the cop car dude. I remember because it was the winter I was turning nine years old soon.

One day we were all watching TV and my mother received a phone call and seemed to be getting very upset, she said she can't talk over the phone right now and my grandfather new immediately it was something to do with my father. My grandfather and my mother got into an argument over him not wanting her to see my father anymore. I heard my grandfather telling her how he was no good and asking her why she would always go to him after what he did to her. He's no good Janis.

My mother told him it was none of his business and stormed out of the house with her keys in her hand. As she was walking towards her car he was yelling at her that it is his business when he has to support her and her kids because he's a no-good junky bum. She jumped in her car and drove away. All he said to me when he walked back in is I don't know what's wrong with your mother Victor. She never listens to me. She just keeps on ruining her life. He made me and Joey some lunch and we watched TV.

She came back a little later in that evening and I can remember my grandfather was still clearly upset. I stayed up and waited myself, and as soon as she walked into the door they made me go into my room, but they let my little brother stay out with them for a little while, I think probably because he was too young to understand what was going on. Mine and my little brothers' room was right off of the kitchen and the living room hallway, there was a door on each side of the room, the gateway to the whole house you might say, and twelve years later was named by dozens of friends as “The Game Room". Some crazy days there. Those will be fun to tell.

Anyway, the room had a set of bunk beds for me and Joey, he had the bottom and I had the top. The reason I'm telling you how we slept will become clear in the next half a dozen paragraphs. It's not really part of the story of what happened with my mother and father but it is to fucking funny to pass up the chance to tell it, even though the story itself is sad in a way, I just could not leave this part of this specific night out of it.

The house was filling up, people were coming and going left and right, I didn't know what to think, I kept thinking because of my grandfather’s words and my mother’s actions and reactions that maybe my father or at least someone close to us was dead. It soon became clear to me that that wasn't the case though. I can remember that I had asked for a cup of water before I went into my room. Once I entered the room I chugged it as fast as I could. I had asked for the water so I could bring the glass in the room just for the purpose of putting it up against the door and my ear after I drank it, like in the movies and TV so I can hear clearer what they were saying.

And what I was hearing through the cup and the doors were the words that were being used the most. Money, bank, guns, robbery, money, money, money, fifty thousand dollars, bail, police, jail, New Haven, Court, why, why, why, what a fucking idiot, where is he now? He deserves whatever he gets. I told you he was a piece of shit. It kept on for a while and I pretty much had the gist of what was going on.

My no-good idiot piece of shit father robbed a bank with a

gun, got caught, and either needs or made bail, from my grandfathers' tone, my mother either paid it, or wanted to pay it, probably with Gramp's money, and now he has court and is more than likely going to jail for a very long time. Well even though I pretty much had it all figured out, I kept listening anyway. I got so distracted from concentrating on the words that I didn't hear my mother bringing Joey into the room through the opposite door for bed. I got caught listening in. There was no real punishment, I think that they thought of it as funny because of the use of the glass. Anyway, my mom takes the glass away and makes me go to bed and tucks Joey in telling him if I move off the top bunk for any reason to call her. Trying to turn a three-year-old into a rat. Bad parenting. Ahhh crap. I'm stuck in bed now. I know I can't hear anything from up on the top bunk so I turned on my radio.

I have to tell you, there is a song from my childhood that freaked me out from the first five seconds of the song until the end. It made my skin crawl and made me feel like it was the apocalypse every time it came on, I thought that when this song was playing, something really bad was going to happen to me, or I was even going to die. This fucking song bothered me so much. I can handle it now obviously, I'm a grown man, but back then, holy shit, end of the world type shit for me, The Eurythmics, here comes the rain again. And this night it was actually raining.

So, as I'm lying there processing everything I just heard from the living room, knowing everyone in the house is now in the kitchen, and this song that's trying to kill me is playing on the radio. FLASH. A bright light shoots through the bedroom. WTF? MOM, MOM, HELP HELP HELP ME. SOMEONES TAKING PICTURES OF ME. She comes blasting through the door, what are you talking about Victor? MOM., someone's taking pictures of me in here. I swear. I saw the flash. She says, well, no ones in the room besides your brother and he's sleeping now. Are you sure it wasn't lightning? No mom. It came from inside the room. I know it did. Ok, turn the radio off and go to sleep. I'll see you in the morning. OK.

I can still hear people in the kitchen awake and talking, my mother, my grandfather and I believe my Aunt Debbie and Uncle Bobby. Not 100% sure on them. But someone else was there. Now I'm lying there and I close my eyes, laying on my back so I stay awake, falling asleep on my back is something I have never been able to do and I still can't do to this day. I close my eyes for just a second, and as soon as they're open, FLASH. MOM, MOM ,MOM, GRAMPS, SOMEONE IS TAKING PICTURES IN HERE I SWEAR. So, in comes my mother and grandfather. She says to my grandfather, there was definitely no lightning this time because I was looking out the window when he screamed, he asks if maybe the TV keeps flashing, is it off? They check the TV, and then unplug it to make sure. They check and open the closet, look under the bed and even walk around the outside of the house to make sure no one is taking pictures through the window. Greg or Harry maybe? Right? They are not exactly not scumbags.

This honestly happens to me two more times, but quicker in recession. Finally, after this had happened for the fourth time, Joey is somehow sleeping through the whole ordeal. And they are getting more and more angry with me. They are now saying I am looking for attention and there is absolutely no way that anything is flashing in my room. I feel like I am completely losing my entire mind. I am fighting my case telling them I'm not lying or making this up and there is someone taking my pictures. So, my mother and my grandfather decide, after four damn times, to leave the door open just a crack, and not to my knowledge at the time, my grandfather grabbed a ladder and stood outside in the rain looking into the window to see if something is really going on.

A minute later. FLASH, FLASH. Before I could even get the word mom out of my mouth she rushes into the room, my grandfather starts pounding on the window yelling incoherently, Janis Blah Blah something something. To tell you the gods honest truth these three seconds were scarier and crazier than anything that happened the entire night. I seriously thought that somebody had taken my pictures and was starting to attack me and my mother and grandfather were trying to get them away from me. Everything happened so fast and as my mother starts frantically looking under the bed where she thought the light had come from, my grandfather bursts through the door and runs right towards the bottom bunk.

Joey open your eyes. Joey, I said open your eyes right now you little shit. Joey opens his eyes and looks up at Gramp's. Give it to me, right now. Right now I said. He hands something to my grandfather as I'm looking down from the top bunk still shaking. My mother asks my grandfather what the fuck is that? What did he just hand you? A camera? Nope. This little bastard, while all the commotion was going on over my fathers' antics stole someone's lighter and brought it to the bed with him. He was down in the bottom bunk pretending to be sleeping this entire time, and flicking a god damned Bic whenever nobody was around scaring the ever-living hell out of me.

I thought somebody this entire time was taking my picture and just waiting to kill or hurt me. It was the funniest, cutest thing ever, to everyone else besides myself and Gramps, I was scared shitless and he was pissed. I think mostly because some stupid clown let a three-year-old walk off with their lighter. This fucking traumatized the hell out of me and no one gave a fuck whatsoever. I always seem to be the brunt of everyone's fucking joke. Whatever, life goes on. And thinking back. If it happened now where I was the adult, it would probably be quite amusing.

After this had all transpired I got to hang out with my dad only once, the day before he had to go to prison, on the front lawn of my grandfather's house with my grandfather right there. We threw a baseball back and forth. How American lifetime movie of him. My grandfather wouldn't let him take me anywhere. Or let me out of his site for that matter. I don't blame him, not for a second, I never could. He truly is the only one who at all times tried to protect me from everything and everyone he possibly could, including my mother and all the bad choices she made. He was my one and only protector. When he could be. Obviously, he didn't know some things. Well. Most things.

From here on the next two or so months seemed to be pretty quiet, mine and Joeys birthdays had passed, my grandfather was working, my mother was working, my father was away, did I mention he was with Nancy now, sorry, slipped my mind. No more Greg or Harry coming around, their choice I supposed, I guess they didn't want to be around something they could no longer have, dirty scumbags. I had a new babysitter. Stephanie Lazzaro. She was really good to me, she let me watch whatever I wanted, let me play outside and even played card and board games with me and Joey. She had a brother Michael who was about my age that came over once in a while too. Life was actually going really well.

At this point everything was going so well that we were able to go on vacation for a long weekend in the beginning of spring, Thursday thru Monday, there was a huge plan for all of us to go camping up in Massachusetts and go to riverside and the water park on its opening day. Uncle Bob had a camper and we had a bunch of tents. It was a great start to what was supposed to be a super fun weekend. Me, my Mother, Uncle Bob, Aunt Debbie, Joey, Gramp's and a bunch of their friends. We got there on Thursday and set up our campsite.

I remember cooking outside, playing volleyball, frisbee, horseshoes just a bunch of different outside activities. On Friday night we all sat around a campfire cooking hotdogs and roasting marshmallows. It was the best time I ever remember having before this. There was absolutely no stress whatsoever and wished it would never end. I remember my mother telling me to take Joey and go inside the camper and go to sleep. She said to try and get a good night's sleep. Tomorrow we go to riverside and get to play in the water park so you will need your rest.

Me and Joey were so excited sleep wasn't really too much of an option. We kind of just kept saying and thinking why are these people still outside with the fire and not going to bed themselves? We finally fell asleep and I was the first one to wake up jumping out of my skin waiting to go to play in the water park. I started trying to wake everybody up immediately. While some people that I woke up were waking other people up, and others packing stuff and getting ready to head out for a day of fun, I was getting very antsy. Are we ready? Are we going? Are we ready?

My mother asked Steve Farchild to try to keep me occupied while she made me and Joey breakfast and everyone else was getting ready to go. He grabbed a frisbee and asked me if I wanted to play. I said hell yeah. My mother looked over at us as we were playing and told me to put some shoes on so I don't step on a piece of glass or something. I said ok mom, give me one more second, I want you to watch this, go ahead Steve, throw me the frisbee. Mom, watch.

He rears back and let's it go, it went off to the left a little, my right, I Started running towards where I thought it was going to land, the frisbee did a bobble going upwards so I took two steps back and jumped backwards with my hand up to grab it, it slid over my fingers and I landed. My right foot landed first, and then my left. As my left foot hit the ground I noticed that something didn't feel right with my right foot, for a split second I thought I cut my foot on a piece of glass and thought to myself why didn't I listen to my mother.

I started to fall backwards and looked down at my foot to see how badly I had cut it, and as I went down and my foot came up I then realized what I had landed on. Or should I say in. As my right foot came up, so did the red-hot burning coals from last night's campfire. A puff of smoke rose up and I let out a scream that got everyone's attention. My mother was the first one there and trying to wipe the coals off my foot, you could see the skin peeling off with every wipe.

I was there crying in pain while everyone was trying to figure out what just happened. I still remember the look on my uncle Bobs face and I felt like I just ruined everyone's weekend. Someone came over within about a minute with a five-gallon bucket of water and stuck my foot in it. Don't ask me how they called, I never asked, but like ten minutes later the ambulance showed up, all I can remember was telling everybody over and over that I was so sorry. I'm so sorry I ruined everything. Again. I can't do anything right. Everyone was telling me not to worry I didn't ruin anything, I felt so bad for my brother, he has never really gotten to do anything that would even be close to this fun. The last thing I remember is looking at Joey and saying that I was sorry and the ambulance driver sticking a needle in my arm and that was it. Outies.

I was out of commission for a few months with forth degree burns on my entire foot. I remember the pain and that I was mostly stuck in my room. I remember eating in my bed and watching TV a lot. I'm pretty sure they gave me Tylenol 3s, you know, the ones with codeine. I fell in love with them immediately. I could actually lay on my back if I wanted without my legs twitching. They made me feel so comfortable. I don't remember very much at all in those following months besides that. I wonder why?

After I healed up on the weekends when Gramps wasn't working he would take me every single Saturday to go roller skating. He was a pro, gliding around the rink like he had wings on the skates. He was most definitely a smooth motherfucker, he had all the girls eating out of his hands. He was a good guy to learn from. I loved these days, Billy Squire, the stroke and dirty laundry were my favorites to skate to. I learned to skate better than in the parking lot with the help of Gramps pretty quickly and couldn't wait to go every single weekend. It was so much easier without having to roll over the pebbles, rocks and sticks in the parking lot. I loved it.

That was just on Saturday's, on Sunday's we would go to Nonnie's house, Gramp's mother. She always made an awesome Italian dinner and always made an ice cream cone for me before I went home. This was my solace, this was my getaway. This was my freedom from the reality of my life. But it didn't last long. Only a few months. My mother met a new guy, Brian. And she was pregnant. Again. And everything was about to change. And not for anything better I can assure you. God didn't help me. This was my new rendition of hell for a long time. Buckle up. This is going to be one scary fucked up ride.

◆ ◆ ◆

PART FOUR - WELCOME TO MERIDEN

This is rough, I'm just going to start with the first thing I can remember from this period. My mother had a new man we were moving in with soon. His name was Brian. How to explain this guy is not very hard. I just go to 1980s WWF. And I am not talking about the World Wildlife Foundation. He was 6'2" 215 lbs. He was a good-sized dude. No noticeable fat. Jacked. His favorite saying, and it spewed out of his face like uncontrollable reoccurring diarrhea of the mouth. THOUGH I WALK THROUGH THE VALLY OF THE SHADOW OF DEATH, I SHALL FEAR NO EVIL. FOR I AM THE BADDEST MOTHERFUCKER IN THE VALLEY. He said that shit so much I would hear it in my dreams.

He loved watching wrestling and took on their personas, He thought of himself as a mix of Hulk Hogan, Randy Savage, Sargent Slaughter and Jake the Snake Roberts. Here's the problem with all of this. Take these personas. The testosterone, the attitudes, the egos, and the muscles. You take all of that. Add it all together. And then blend all of that with a case of beer and a pint of Jack Daniels a day. You now have the uncontrollable concoction that is Brian. Every once in a while, you can throw down a shot or two of Rambo with it just to top it off.

I only started to recall him when my mother was already a few months pregnant with what would be my little brother Bobby. I don't think my mother brought Brian around my grandfather's house at all. But when I first met him he was just like any other guy with a new girl. A little sweet, trying to impress, going to work, nice to her kids, you know. Completely full of shit.

The first time I had my doubts about him started pretty soon after we first met him, a few months before we moved in with him. We went to a beach somewhere in Rhode Island. There were about ten people in their group all together not including us kids. I don't remember how many exactly. I don't remember much about the entirety of the day. What I do remember is there was a small grill they were cooking hot dogs on, some lawn chairs and a few coolers full of sodas and beer.

I remember that Brian was turning hot dogs on the grill, Joey was making a sand castle with a few more kids, I was throwing a tennis ball with Brian's German Shepherd Zane, and all the other adults were playing volleyball. I walked over to Brian and told him I liked his dog. He's so cool. He said he's your dog now too. He then said to me you should go swimming for a little while before you eat something, your mom won't let you go in the water after you eat for about a half hour because you'll get cramps, so go get it over with now. Let's see how far you can swim out. I'll watch you.

I ran over to the water and started swimming out from the beach. I wanted to impress him. I didn't go out that far when I turned around to look and see if he was watching me. He waved to me to keep going so I did. I doggie paddled pretty far out when I realized I was getting really tired and had to turn around. When I turned I noticed the people that were playing volleyball and the kids were walking towards the grill now and Brian was now sitting on one of the coolers with his back towards me. I could see Zane barking towards me running back and forth on the edge of the beach as I was screaming for help.

I started to try to swim back but I was clearly not going anywhere. I was kicking and screaming and could see that no one was looking at me at all. There was a currant trying to take me. I could feel it pulling on my legs like there was a wet blanket wrapped around them. I was almost completely out of strength when I noticed Brian get up and start walking towards Zane. Then I went completely under for the first time. I fought with everything I had to swim back up to the surface and I tried to lay up straight on my back and float but I couldn't lift my legs all the way up. I got sucked under again.

As I fought my way to the surface one more time, I had looked to the beach to try to see my mother or see if anyone noticed me one last time before I went back under, but there was a wave in my way and I couldn't see anything besides water! I knew this was probably the end of me and I half way accepted it. I knew it was going to be a painful way to die not being able to breath, it was always my worst fear next to burning alive, but in my head, I also thought it would be quicker. I took a deep breath and screamed for help once more straight up into the air.

I looked back towards where I thought they all were, and I had noticed my mother and others on the beach were now all screaming and pointing towards me from that area. I looked across the water and I noticed an arm splashing down much closer to me than where the beach was, I took one last half breath and I got sucked under one last time. I could taste the salt in the water and I could feel that I was going to have to try to take a breath any second. I was kicking and using my arms as hard as I could with what little strength I had left to try to get to the surface. I could feel that even my hand was completely under the water now and I knew there was no way I was getting back up for air. Everything had gotten blurry and I thought I was going to die right then and there when I felt a hand grab my arm, then everything went black.

I dreamed of a Boogeyman wearing an all-white tuxedo with a regular brown paper bag on his head and white magic marker type eyes and a mouth drawn. He said with his magic marker mouth moving. "This is going to be the greatest day of your life" when I felt two hands grasp my face and all of a sudden there was a strange guy and my mother looking down at me. I asked where did the White Boogeyman go and my mother just started balling her eyes out.

I remember them standing me up and then making me lay down on one of the lawn chairs. I looked up at Brian and asked what happened. He said he saw me swimming back towards the beach and thought that I would be fine and that he was sorry he stopped watching me. My mother said that he was the one that pointed out that I was stuck out there. And that the other man swam out and saved my life. My chest hurt very bad and I had a booming headache. Brian carried me to the car and laid me in the back seat and I fell asleep almost immediately. I don't even remember the car starting. I do remember that when we got home to Gramp's house he wasn't home and I went straight to bed and fell asleep again completely drained of energy and exhausted. This was the first time I believe that I probably should have died. And it is very possible that I did.

I don't remember what my grandfather had to say about the whole thing I just remembered that he wasn't happy with my mother or Brian. It was only a few months later that we moved to Meriden in a new apartment with what would now be my new father. Or should I say Daddy.

We had moved in to the downstairs of a duplex in Meriden with a fenced in yard. It was my mother, my brother Joey, myself, Brian and his German Shepard Zane. First thing when we moved in I could remember that it was very quickly when the first demands started. He made me immediately start calling him Daddy Brian. This is something I really wasn't all that happy with. But I did it. Because I learned very quickly that you do exactly what Brian says or you are most definitely in for a world of pain. So, for now, Daddy Brian it is.

There was no physical abuse right off the bat, just some verbal discipline. You all know how I was disciplined in the past, but something about all of this seemed different. He hadn't physically touched any of us yet, but with his posture and in the intense way he made his demands of us, especially me, it was pretty clear that disobedience was not going to end well. There was an aura around him that let you know, listen to what I say and obey everything I command or you're fucked. You're smaller than me and I will fuck you up because I can. Yeah, He was 100% one of those guys. In simple wording. He was a bully.

You could see it in the way he treated Zane also. Whenever other people were around especially, he would make that dog stand right next to him at all times unless I was playing with him. If he didn't obey what Brian said. He got either hit or kicked. He would do this kind of thing without hesitation no matter who was around. No one ever said shit. And of course, he had everyone convinced that this dog was the most intensely trained attack dog in the country. Just with a command of attack or sick and a point of his finger he could get this dog to attack and rip out the throat of anyone who threatened him. He even had me convinced that if I ever needed the dog's protection he would attack for me too.

He would also always tell everyone that he was a Vietnam vet who was deep in the shit for three tours and he had six confirmed kills, most of them with a knife or with his bare hands. I believed his stories for years, I thought he was a straight killer. It would not come to light that he was full of shit until a few years later when myself and some friends did the math and realized the math was just all wrong. We confronted him on it once. Only once. It went about like you'd think. There will be more on that later.

Well let's get to it, there was just a slight preview of the man I had to deal with for the next 5 years of my life. And the easiest way to break those years down is like this. 5 years is approximately 1800 days, out of the 1800 days he was drunk or high for 1500 of them, out of the 1500 he was an angry drunk for 1200, out of the 1200 he was verbally abusive for 1000, out of the 1000 he was out of control breaking shit for 700, out of the 700 he was physically abusive or threatened physical abuse about 400, out of that 400, 100 or so of them Myself or my mother or Joey or Bobby or a pet or all of us took a pretty nice beating, out of that 100 there are 20 or so that stick out like a broken hand. And some of those are the ones you are about to hear. Most of them have a story or a situation behind them, or I simply remember where we lived or where we were at the time of the abuse.

Like I said before, we were now in Meriden. We only lived here for maybe four months during the summer as I remember, but just like everywhere else in my life there are plenty of events and stories. Even in that short time. Here are a few. While living here I would try to stay outside as much as I could, I really didn't want to deal with him, he made me feel very uncomfortable, so like at my grandfathers, I would play in the yard mostly, playing with Zane like I would with the beagles or King Louie. He was a very energetic dog and fetched pretty much anything you would throw. He had a tan and black coat and a brown leather collar with his name burned into it. And for a 70+ pound dog he was very gentle and playful with me and Joey.

We would wrestle all the time and he would fake bite me. I always had fun and felt very safe in the fenced in yard with him always by my side. I guess you could say that it didn't take long before he was my dog more than he was Brian's. I don't think Brian appreciated that in any way, shape or form. He started with some very strict rules around a month in. Walking the dog was now my job in which I really didn't mind, don't leave the yard, taking out the garbage, folding my own clothes and making my bed were my sole chores, but not just making my bed like a kid would make his bed, or folding my clothes like a normal kid. But making my bed and folding my clothes military style, he even had a ruler he would keep on my end table to make sure I got the creases right.

If I got it wrong in any way he would tear my bed apart or empty out my dresser drawers onto the floor and make me do it all over again until I got it all perfect. I have never had to do this stuff before. And I didn't want to now. I was only nine years old, I didn't want to take an extra hour making sure I got everything perfect, who would want to? He hadn't started hitting me yet over it. But it was coming.

There was a girl that lived next door by the name of Laura that was about my age, she was just on the other side of the fence and was always watching me and Zane playing together. There was another kid across the street and a few houses down by the name of Freddy who usually just sat on his porch reading. I knew his name because his mother or her boyfriend were constantly yelling at him and it wasn't hard to hear. He was about two years older than me and always peered over at me playing with the dog with a disgusted look on his face. He was much larger than me too, no worries though, I have the fence and Zane. Be as angry as you want kid. I'm safe

Across the street to the right was one more kid about a year or two older also, but in this case, he was a little smaller than me. He was also a porch dweller, I never saw him leave it for the first month or so that I lived there. I actually thought he lived out on the porch. Just like someone I actually know. From what I heard his name was Miguel from other kids walking by that would always talk shit about him. He was Puerto Rican and most of the other kids around our neighborhood were white.

Behind our house up on the hill was a street where I would always hear kids outside playing, but I wasn't allowed out of the yard at this point so I didn't know who was up there. It was constant, there must have been twenty kids playing up there. It took a lot to control myself and not take a shot at it. But like I said, I knew if I did something Brian told me not to I'm pretty sure it wasn't just going to be a spanking like my mother or father gave me. It was going to be something else.

One day while out in the yard the girl that lived next door came over to the fence and just said hey, hi, what's your doggies name, I said Zane, she said that's a cool name and he's beautiful, I'm Laura, who are you? Hi I'm Victor. She asked if I could leave the yard. I said no, I'm supposed to stay in the fence with the dog. She asked if she could come inside the fence and play with me and of course I said yes. We hung out and played with the dog together in the yard for a couple days straight. As we were playing one day we saw Freddy walking up the street towards my yard. He was walking to the corner store for his mother.

Laura looked at me and said I really don't like that kid, he's always giving me dirty looks. I said I know he's always looking at me too. He's just a jerk. So out of nowhere I look at him as he's passing the yard, and I don't know what I was thinking, at all, because looking back at me at nine years old I wasn't even breaking 60lbs, and this kid was definitely tipping at least mid-90s. Well, maybe I was thinking, impress the girl, you got me at almost 60lbs and Zane has 70+lbs. Fuck it. DEAD FRED HAS A BIG UGLY HEAD.

This kid didn't even blink, walked right to the fence and asked what did you say? I said DEAD FRED HAS A BIG UGLY HEAD. And if you even think about coming over this fence I will have my dog kill you. He looks at me and says, that dogs a pussy, and just started climbing over. I truly wasn't scared at all, I knew he was fucked as soon as he hit the ground. He gets over and as soon as he landed he turned towards me and I said Zane, SICK HIM. ZANE ATTACK. I looked over at the dog and he went from the sitting position to laying down. Oh shit, I looked back towards where Freddy was coming towards me and all I saw was a flash. Welcome to Meriden bitch.

I hit the ground. God damn it. Not my nose again. I got up immediately and I don't think he was expecting it but I rushed him like a maniac. Wrapped my arms around his waste and just dug my feet forward, luckily for me Zane was still laying in the same spot and he tripped backwards over him. I expected Zane to attack or at least bite him for tripping over him but nothing, he just got up and walked away. I landed on top with my blood pouring all over him from my nose and threw one punch, but I missed, I hit a damn rock right next to his head, sweet, sprained hand and broken nose and I never got a shot in. Ahhh, first real fight, whatever.

After I hurt my hand he bucked me off pretty easily and mounted me just as easy. He lifted his hand up to hit me again and Laura yelled at him to stop. He looked up at her, he asked why should I listen to you? You never even look in my direction, none of you even like me. She looked down at me and I was waiting for her to say something like you're right and I was about to get clobbered again, but she looked back at him and said, you're always sitting on your porch just giving us dirty looks, we always talk about asking you to come over and hang out with us but we thought you didn't like us.

He looked confused, I didn't know what he was going to do. He kind of just smiled and got up off of me, he put his hand out to help me up, I grabbed his hand and yelled because mine was hurting excruciatingly, and WTF would you know, within a second from the noise coming out of my mouth, Zane attacked ME, viciously, went right for my throat, just like Brian trained him to do. Lmao, got ya, No, I'm just kidding. Freddy was obviously right, dog was a god damned pussy. Brian didn't train shit. Sit, lay down, fetch and heel, that's about all he had.

So Freddy helped me up, blood pouring from my nose, he said you're a pretty tough kid and definitely got some balls for as skinny as you are. I looked over at him and he pulled off his top shirt, he wiped my blood off his face and handed his shirt to me. Go ahead man. Stop that from bleeding before your father see's you. I know how it is, my parents are completely awful too. He seems like the kind of parent that would hurt you for getting hurt. I said He's not my father, but your right. I have to hide that this happened. He reached down, gave Zane a few pats and said I'm sorry about calling your dog a pussy, he's actually really cool.

We all went into the back yard so I could clean myself up and not be seen. I still don't think I completely trusted him, for some reason I thought he was going to hit me again. I'm sorry but it's just the way he looked, very angry looking all the time. I was wrong. We sat down at an old broken-down picnic table in the back and talked. Laura ran to her house and returned with a bowl full of ice, a towel and an ace bandage for my hand. As we were talking I learned that his father had died just a year earlier, and the guy who lived with his mother was always yelling, screaming and hitting her, and that's why he was always on the porch.

He said he never wants to go inside his house, he'd rather sleep outside in a tent or something. He exclaimed that his mother always came outside to yell at him because her boyfriend is always inside beating on her and yelling at her and he doesn't really blame her because she has no other way to get her frustration and anger out. As we were talking, Laura was sitting on the edge of the broken picnic table bench wrapping up my hand. I was explaining some of the crazy stuff that happened to me while living in New Haven.

There were all kinds of noises coming from the hill above where we were sitting and talking. I was in the middle of telling the

Boogeyman story when I stopped and asked, where is all that noise coming from? Are there a lot of kids up there? Is there a park or something? Laura told me that there was another street up there, it was a dead end that ended right above our houses and all the kids gathered to play there because it was the safest area in the neighborhood. She pointed up towards the hill and said that she had friends that lived up there too, but because the hill was too steep to go up that way, and to get there from our street you would have to walk by a biker gang clubhouse, she wasn't allowed to go up there very often.

Like on cue we could hear her mother calling out for her to come home, we all laughed as I said, she must have thought we were planning on going up there and put a stop to that quick. She slid over to me, and kissed me on the cheek, she told me she was sorry for all the stuff I've dealt with from my parents. And she knows that life will get better. She walked around the table and kissed Freddy on the cheek and said the same. She started walking away as we followed her to the gate to get out. She stopped right before she opened it and said, I'm very happy we all became friends today. See it's already getting better. And she went home.

Me and Freddy hung out for a little while with Zane, and I showed him a few of the tricks I was trying to teach him. We talked a little more about our unbearable parents and really started to become friends. Our problems were most definitely close to the same. We talked about how we would be better off just running away and living in the woods past the dead end. It would have probably been better. We looked across the street and he asked me about Miguel and if I ever talked to him before. I said no. He never leaves his porch.

Freddy said that we should definitely go over there tomorrow and see if he wants to hang out with us. He's always by himself and probably has the same problems as us. He said he hears yelling coming from over there too. There's three of us now, and though we really don't think Laura has a life anything like ours, it's nice to have someone that's not always angry because their family sucks. An anchor of sorts to keep us grounded.

He said I have to go home now, actually I have to go to the store first, my mom's going to kill me, I left to go get her cigarette's three and a half hours ago. He called Zane over and got down to one knee and hugged him. He said he really is a cool dog and I'm glad I've met you, I always thought you were an asshole but you're not, I'm sorry I hit you and sorry you hurt your hand, it looked like a good punch, I'm glad it didn't hit me. I'll talk to you tomorrow. I hope you don't get into too much trouble. And never, ever, call me DEAD FRED again. We both laughed and he left.

I went back into the back yard instead of going inside right away, I didn't know what I was going to say, I wasn't worried about my nose. It's been broken before and after Laura cleaned it up her and Freddy said that it still looked pretty much the same. I was worried about how I was going to hide my hand. It was throbbing like crazy, the pointer and middle finger knuckles were scraped up nicely. I was pretty sure that if we all sat at the table for dinner one of them would surely notice. I gathered my courage and Zane and we went inside.

I walked inside the front door, I sat on my bed, took off the ace bandage, hid it under my pillow and kicked off my shoes, Zane walked immediately over to his doggie bed which was directly at the foot of my bed, he looked like he was going to lay down and stopped, looked at me like he was confused. He looked back at his bed and swear he sighed like a human being. He turned to the left in the far corner of the room where his food bowl was and started eating, very slow. I think he wanted to lay down and sleep from exhaustion with all the commotion and playing all day but realized he was hungry. I started laughing with myself and could actually feel my hand throb with every breath of the laughter. I got of the bed and went to put my sneakers on the shoe pile.

OH SHIT. sorry again, I'm not a perfect writer, I never said I was, and this proves it. I do my best and I go by memory, thinking back on the events in my life like I was trying to re-live them on the specific days they happened. So, some things slip, and instead of going back and writing them in, I'm just going to add them where my memory puts them in. When stuff like this happens, please bear with me. Writing from memories sometimes is way harder than making shit up. And harder or not. Every line I write is just as important as the last. I'm getting what my life was like out. Writing it perfect or correct isn't my first obligation. My story is and the facts are.

So, me walking in and kicking off my shoes, and the doggie bed at the foot of my bed, and the food bowl in the corner, and the shoe pile all in the same room directly through the front door wasn't any kind of writing or memory mistake. The front door opened up into a screened in mud room. Which, is pretty messed up looking back, like it usually is in my life, the screened in mud room, well, it was also my bed room. Yep, I Basically lived outside on the porch. Of course, Brian called me the porch monkey every chance he could.

I put my shoes down and walked through the front, front door, yeah, the one to the actual house. Through this door was the kitchen where I expected to see my mother and Brian, they were usually sitting at the kitchen table, but there was just my mother. Cooking dinner. American Chop Suey, I'll always remember that. It was one of my all-time favorites. My mother said I saw you in the back yard with Laura and a new friend, is that the kid from across the street whose parents are always yelling at him. I said yeah, that's him. We're friends now. His parents are really mean and he has no friends so we're going to be friends with him now. I think Zane likes him too. The way she was asking I thought maybe she saw everything that happened out there but she didn't.

She says that's nice of you and turns around from the stove and looks at me. She knows something happened now. What happened to your face. Nothing, don't lie to me. Ok, I got into a fight. Where? In the yard. With Who? My new friend Freddy. What? Why? Why are you friends now then? I explained that it was my fault and I was calling him names and being mean and it was a fair fight that I started. I just lost. She said that it was ok and that she wouldn't tell Brian.

I told her I hurt my hand too. She looked at it and said she didn't think it was broken, it was swelled up pretty good though and definitely sprained. I asked her where Brian was and she said he was at his sisters and wouldn't be home for an hour or so. I asked if I could eat dinner before he got home and just go to bed. She said yes and that she would just tell him I was sick and sleeping. I ate dinner and went and laid in my bed, it was only around seven o'clock. I heard a car door close and him say goodbye to someone through the screens. I heard the metal door open to the porch and him walk in. I had my body facing the wall and my head buried in the pillow under the blanket.

As he was walking bye I could hear him start talking to himself and getting angry that my bed wasn't made, my mother opened the front door and just as he was trying to say something about it I heard her say, ssshhhhh. Victor is really sick and he's sleeping. I was wide awake though. Eyes wide open but facing away. He didn't check. He asked if I ate dinner and she said just a little bit, but I was complaining I wasn't feeling well so she let me go to bed. He said whatever. More for me, and walked in the house. I laid there for a while, the heat, the light, my hand throbbing, and the noise outside sucked. But I fell asleep before it even got dark.

Seemed I only slept for about two minutes when I heard, GET UP. GET THE FUCK UP. I jumped out of my skin and knew immediately. Jesus Christ. Can anyone in this fucking world keep a secret for me? My own damn mother is even throwing me under the bus now. What happened yesterday? I asked yesterday? Nothing happened yesterday. Let me see your fucking hand. I showed him my hand and he grabbed it. I let out a scream in pain. It was cabbage patched. Something happened yesterday, what happened? I again asked yesterday? He yelled yes Idiot. It's morning. Yesterday? I thought it was still the same day. I was extremely confused.

The whole hand above my knuckles looked like it was filled with air. He looked up at me and said stop being such a pussy, it can't hurt that bad. He pinged me in the nose then laughed as he said, your face looks worse. I saw my brother Joey peering through the doorway, I have to say, he was smart. He turned around immediately and went back into his bedroom. He hid and stayed away as much as he could. He's in a few of these encounters. But not many.

So Brian says to me, at least you weren't a complete pussy, his face must look just as bad as yours if your hand looks like this. I wanted to lie, so bad, I could have lied, so easily. But, my mother. She already knew what happened, and even though she looked at me with what seemed to be approval to lie, I didn't. And do you know why? I didn't trust her. She just ratted me out five minutes ago and that shit was still fresh in my mind. I never hit him I said. But I swear I tried. I got him down for a second but he moved his head when I was trying to punch him and I hit a rock instead of him. That's why my hand is like this.

He still had my hand in his hand and he gave it another squeeze, I didn't make another noise this time, I knew better, but between the pain of him squeezing it, and the fear he was going to do something to me, a tear rolled down my cheek. You didn't hit him at all. I said no, he was way bigger than me and he got the best of me. I'm sorry, that was the first fight I have ever been in. Are you serious? Really? He asked. By your age I was in dozens of fights and won every single one of them. He was probably full of shit. He usually was.

He looked over at my mother and asked what kind of boy are you raising here, no son of mine is going to lose a fight and then cry over a swollen hand. "I guess I'm his son now? Lucky me" He looked back at me with another tear rolling down my face, and I could see the anger starting to build up in his, he pulled my hand towards him, reached to the table behind my bed and grabbed the ruler he used to measure the bed creases. You want to cry little baby? I'll give you something to fucking cry about. He grabbed my wrist and placed my hand flat down on the bed, puffy side up, my mother said don't you dare, if you hit my kid like that we're done. I don't think he gave a fuck. Whack, Whack, Whack. He looked at her and said you're not going anywhere bitch. Go make me coffee before you get the same.

The fucking pain, holy shit, I still remember how bad that hurt. He didn't use the flat part of the ruler either, he used the side of the thing. But I have to say, he didn't rear back with all his force, it was pretty much just from his wrist. But it still really sucked. And It wasn't just my hand, that shit ran up my whole arm and straight into my brain. It gave me an immediate headache. My whole arm felt broken. There, he said. Now you have something to cry about. And no outside unless it's to walk the dog, and no talking to anybody you're fucking grounded. For a week. He started walking away and looked down at Zane. And speaking of the fucking dog. Where was he? Was he in the yard when you were fighting?

Again I didn't want to answer. But again, I didn't want to get caught lying. He asked again. Where the fuck was Zane? I said he was right next to me. He asked why he didn't do anything to stop this kid from beating on me? I said I don't think he knew what to do. And I never asked him to help. I never told him to sick. I didn't want him to bite the kid and get in trouble.

He said that's what he's trained to fucking do either way. What the fuck good is he if he won't protect you. Without hesitation he reached down and grabbed Zane by the collar and the middle of his back. By the skin, like you would pick a cat up by the back of its neck. I could see his skin stretch over his rib cage as he lifted him up and spun and threw him through the door into the kitchen.

His hip hit the door jam and started to spin the opposite way. He landed on the floor backwards, landing on his paws. But as he landed on the tile floor, facing the opposite way from the direction he was moving, he looked like he was trying to run forward and his legs came out from under him very quickly. Like a dog when they're dream running. His body slammed on the floor and he slid into the kitchen table knocking everything off of it. Brian ran up to him and kicked him once in the side. He slammed up against the side wall now out of my view. He yelped with the impact of the kick, but it wasn't loud, it was weird, it was like a breathless gasping yelp, like he had no air in his lungs. It was a very frightening sound. I thought he had killed him.

I could see Brian from my bed through the door into the kitchen. But couldn't see Zane anymore after the kick. He was too far to the side now. My mother looked at him and asked, what the fuck is wrong with you? He walked over and grabbed Zane by the collar and dragged him into my room. The poor thing was still trying to catch his breath, I thought he was going to die right there. Brian said he'll be fine. I'm done with both of you for now. Make your fucking bed. And it better be right.

My mother asked again, what the fuck is wrong with you? Why would you do all that? He said mind your fucking business woman, you want him to have a father and learn how to be a man? This is how it's done. It's how I had to learn and now it's his turn. I'll teach him, if it fucking kills him. I'll teach him. Now clean up this fucking mess and make me some breakfast, I'm taking a shower. I could hear my mother start to clean, talking to herself, I heard her say I can't believe I have to deal with this shit again, my father's right, I'll never learn. I was making my bed and Zane had caught his breath but was still just lying there. Glaring upwards towards me with the saddest eyes. I gave him a pat and said, I'm sorry buddy. I wish we were strong enough to kill him. He's a jerk.

My mother had cleaned and was now making breakfast. I was done making my bed, it took me like twenty minutes to try to get it perfect with my still throbbing hand. I heard Brian getting out of the bathroom complaining that my mother still hadn't finished his breakfast. Hurry up, I gotta go. But first I have to check Victors bed. It better be done right or his hand will be the least of his problems. I remember being nervous I did something wrong, the corner angles weren't right, it wasn't tucked in tight enough, I measured the seam wrong, it wasn't far enough from the head. Even though I knew it was perfect. I was still in complete fear. As soon as the door flew open Zane scrambled, claws scratching on the wooden floor trying to stay low and crawl under my bed.

He was so scared of him, I had never really noticed it this bad before, but now it made much more sense the way he acted around him. Whenever Brian became loud or angry he would literally tuck his tail between his legs, put his eyes down and his posture would completely change. I never knew what that was or meant until this day happened. I remember as he was scurrying under the bed I was extremely nervous he was going to mess up my folds, but he didn't. He just crawled under and never looked back. All you could see was the tip of his tail hanging out.

Brian walked over and pushed the rest of his tail under the bed with his foot. You could tell he had no remorse for what he just did to him in any way. Pussy dog. He said, the bed looks good, but let's make sure. He grabbed the ruler and moved my pillow. Blanket is 18" from the head of the bed, 4" seam and your 45^ angles are perfect. See, a little bit of discipline and you just might learn something. My mother yelled in, your god damned breakfast is ready master. He said, do you see that now? Everybody's learning around here. He reached his arms across my bed from top to bottom. Ripped the blanket and sheet off of the bed and threw them on the floor. Do it again. Practice makes perfect. He went inside to eat.

It took me about another twenty minutes to do it again. All I could think about is how much I hate this guy and I can't believe my mother hasn't packed up our shit and got us out of there already. He finished up his breakfast and I could hear him gathering up his fishing poles. My mother asked where are you going? Are you going fishing right now? He said yeah, I need some time alone away from you and your fucking kids. You said you left their scumbag father for drugs and cheating. But I know that's bullshit. The more I'm around all of you, except for Joey, He's quiet, he hasn't had a chance to be poisoned by your shit fucking family yet. But the more I'm around you and that little prick on the porch, the more I believe he ran to get away from you. He probably got himself thrown into prison on purpose just to get away. I wouldn't doubt it for a second. Fuck you. Don't expect me back anytime early tonight.

He walked out of the door, fishing poles in hand. My mother sitting at the kitchen table crying now. Victor, come in here. I walked in the door. I sat down, How's your hand? I'll make you and Joey some breakfast. She got up and walked over to the fridge. I never answered her about my hand, I don't think she really cared and she never asked me again anyways. I think she was looking for sympathy. I'm sorry. That was my feeling then. And that is still my feeling today. She did this a lot after confrontations even if I was the one who took the beating. Oh, sorry me. Always.

I did feel bad for her a lot of the time though. But the more and more and more she let these things happen without her sticking up for herself or for her sons. The less and less and less I cared. I loved my mother. I really did. A lot. She was my mother. And I know she loved us. Sometimes. I think. But I have to be honest. Whatever man she was with was always a step or two more important than we ever were. Just the facts. Everyone in our lives saw it just as much as we did. And it really had a strain on our relationship for most of our lives. Even as I entered into my late twenties. It took me until at least my mid-thirties before I ever forgave her.

So I'm sitting in the chair at the kitchen table. I see Joeys head pop around the corner, he pops back in, and right back out, he looks at me, then my mom, then he looks around the room. He whispers. Is it safe to come out now? Is he gone yet? Yeah, he's gone. Come on out. He says Ok, runs out, phew, finally. I gotta poop so bad it's about to come out of my nose. I thought I was going to have to poop in a shoe and wipe my butt with a sock. Daddy Brian's a mean guy. And he ran to the bathroom. He actually had me and my mother laughing for a minute. Some of the stuff that came out of this kids' mouth was just ridiculous.

I truly expected my mother to ask us to start packing our stuff after Brian left and we ate breakfast. I even asked her, can we go back to grandpas. Please. He's going to get drunk today and come back and hurt me or Zane. I don't trust him. I don't like him. She said No, Absolutely not, No way in hell. I'm not going back to my father's house with my fucking tail tucked between my legs like that stupid dog hiding under your bed. It's not going to happen. And we have no money to go anywhere anyway so we're stuck. You're just going to have to learn to behave and deal with it. Be happy you have food and clothes and a place to sleep. Most kids don't even have that. Yeah, great. Thanks, Pretty soon hereafter. As things got worse. The clothes and the food were pretty sparse. At least I had a bed now. Lucky me. Even if I had to walk on mud as soon as I woke up.

Here's the thing with my mother not wanting to go back home. Gramps did not approve of Brian, not in any way, I think even more than he disapproved of my father. He didn't like my father, but he despised Brian. And my uncle Bab did as well. I heard them before we moved out of Gramp's house, more than once, tell her she was making a huge mistake, constantly arguing about the matter. They would try to convince her, go get another abortion, don't you dare have a kid with this guy. They exclaimed that this wasn't the right guy for her and especially not for me and Joey. He was a mean drunk and was in trouble with the law more times than he wasn't. And those are just facts, the guy was a total misfit. She obviously didn't heed their warnings.

My uncle Bob and Brian actually had a past before my mother even knew him. He wasn't just talking out of his ass. From my knowledge, they always hung out at the same place, and even had a lot of friends and acquaintances in common with each other. They all hung out in the same circles. Wallingford was a small town back then. Some years earlier, there was a fight at Sporty's bar, where they mostly hung out, and Brian ended up breaking my uncle Bobs nose during a scuffle. The details of this fight are not to my knowledge. But it has been confirmed by my mother, Brian and uncle Bob that it actually happened. Why my mother would date, have a kid, and later get married to someone who hit her brother was always beyond me.

She didn't want to prove them right, so she wouldn't go back to my grandfathers. I've even heard her say it out loud way more than once. She just couldn't swallow her pride. She put us in danger, and even herself in danger for years with this guy just because she didn't want to admit what kind of scumbag she had chosen over listening to them. I was nine at the time so that put her age at twenty-five. I guess her teenage rebellion years stayed with her for a little bit longer in life.

So Joey comes out of the bathroom and my mother feeds us breakfast. She goes in her bedroom without a word. Like she was mad at us for something. Like it was our fault that he was getting more and more angry. And because of that, I always thought that it was my fault. It took a long time to realize that it wasn't. He was just an asshole.

We finished our breakfast and I went to check on Zane. It took a few minutes to lure him out from under the bed. He wouldn't budge with food or a milk bone. It took both me and Joey grabbing his leash and his tennis ball to finally get him out. We took him outside into the yard and let him relieve himself. It was almost noon by now and he hadn't gone outside all day. We tried to play with him, but he was definitely off. Didn't want anything to do with the tennis ball. He was looking around the yard like he was afraid Brian was going to come around the corner any second now. I asked Joey to stay with him for a minute. Zane was just lying on the grass. Joey pretty much just stood there bouncing the tennis ball off of Zane's nose, then fetching it for himself. I think Zane might have still been hurt. And I think Joey might have been part clown.

I waved Laura over from her yard, now looking around the same way as Zane, not knowing if I can even talk to someone through the fence when I take him outside. Scared shitless and nervous as hell that he might come home and see me. She said nice nose and asked me how my hand was? She then asked me what all the commotion was outside on the porch. I explained to her my hand was hurt worse and why. I let her know what happened. I told her I was sorry but I probably wouldn't be able to see her for a while and to please do me a favor, and not come over to talk to me when she sees me outside because it would just be easier than dealing with him, just in case he's in a bad mood.

She agreed and said she would let our new friend Freddy know as well, if she sees him. If that was ok with me? I said of course. I never told Brian who it was I fought so I wasn't worried about it. She said she had talked to her friends who lived up on the hill and told them about me, she said they said they couldn't wait to meet me. Obviously, that's on hold for now though. I told her I had to go. I yelled for Joey who was now standing next to the dog trying to bounce the ball off of his own nose. I asked him what he was doing and he said he was pretending to be a dog seal. We laughed as we took Zane inside.

We went inside and asked if we could watch TV. She said ok but we have to stop as soon as Brian comes home if he comes home at all. We had a new VCR with only 1 movie. Indiana Jones and the Temple of Doom. We watched that thing at least 250 times in the coming months and years. I think we watched it three times on this day. Quiet, on the couch, just waiting for the maniac to come home and ruin the night. Me and Joey didn't talk much back then. We just chilled and watched TV together.

My mother just sat in the kitchen on the phone talking. She would talk to one person and soon as you heard her say goodbye, you would hear the rotary dial. Hey, what are you doing? Then blah, blah, blah. Talk, talk, talk. My mother was always on the phone, and she had this certain problem, she just couldn't help herself. No matter how many times she got caught, no matter how many fights it caused, no matter how many people told her it was going to get her in trouble if she didn't stop, from as far back as I could remember, until the last time I ever saw her on the phone. Always and forever. It was the worst habit I ever saw.

Notes. She took fucking notes. Of every single conversation she had on the phone. Not full sentences mind you. Just notes. They would always start with the name of who she was calling, before they picked up, or even if they didn't pick up the phone at all, she would write their name. Then whatever they were talking about, there would be snippets. Just a word or two here or there. Victor, Fight, Broken Nose, Brian, Threw Dog, Kicked, Ruler, Fishing Poles, Fucking Animal, Alphonse, Carol. Have to leave, so dumb, and so on and so forth. Envelope, napkin, random pieces of mail. It didn't matter. If it could take the ink from a pen or the lead from a pencil, and she was talking, she would write on it. Always scattered all over the kitchen table. Lady couldn't even keep a secret from herself. If that makes sense.

Dinner came and went. No Brian, Joey went to bed and I went into my porch and nervously waited for him to come home. It was a few hours, way past dinner so I would put it at around 9:00-9:30. I didn't hear a car pull up but heard him mumbling to himself walking up the steps to the porch door. He opened it quietly, and as usual, I pretended to sleep. You could smell the alcohol leaking from his pores and this scared the shit out of me. I knew there was going to be some shit. I could still hear my mother talking on the phone, but to me it was just a muffled voice through the door.

He snuck over to the house door like he was trying to hear what she was saying. He stood there for about three or four minutes but I don't think he could hear clear words either. He finally opened the door and throws his fishing poles next to Zane on the floor. She scrambles, he's home, I have to let you go. He kept the door open, I wish he didn't. Who were you talking to? She says Cindy, Victor and Joeys aunt. She called to see how they are doing. Your ex-husband's sister? Yes. I told you. She was checking on the boys. He snorts, just make me my fucking dinner. Ok. She said. Calm down. Just let me go to the bathroom, I've been on the phone with her for a while, I'll go pee then I'll heat it up.

She disappears into the bathroom. He sits at the table and takes his muddy boots off. I could see the dry mud falling on the floor, and after he took them off he actually beat them together right there under the kitchen table. I remember thinking it was better than in my room, but I was still going to have to sweep that up in the morning. While my mother is finishing up in the bathroom I can see him start to move the papers around on the table. Standing up to reach the other end to grab them all. She comes out and asks what are you doing? He sees some of what she wrote and you can see the change in his posture.

He again says. Hurry up. Make my dinner, I'm starving. Get me my fucking food wench. And I'm not kidding. He loved that word. She walks over to the fridge, and as she's putting together his meal at the stove he's telling her, I don't want you on the phone talking about me when I'm not hear bitch. You will be fucking respecting me, and not tell anyone what goes on in my fucking house, or in our fucking lives. If I ever hear you talking about me again I will fuck you up. She said I'm talking to my ex sister in law, what are you worried about. Her brother treated me like a piece of shit so what do you care what she thinks.

He says I see who you're talking to right here. She says, no, that's who we were talking about. He says I don't care, you've been warned. He grabs all the papers and crumples them up and makes his way over to the garbage can. But instead of throwing them in, he grabs a napkin out of it. He opens the napkin and turns around. He takes two steps and throws the other papers back on the table. I saw it coming. He walks behind her and without saying a word, grabs my mother by the back of her hair, yanks her head back and stuffs the napkin in her mouth. You filthy cunt, your sister in law huh? How many fucking times have I told you I don't want you talking to that fucking black faggot. The name written on the napkin was Alphonse.

Quickly, I will describe Alphonse. Not a big part of my life, so there's not much for me to tell. He was someone my mother went out dancing with, and I only met him a handful of times at my grandfathers if he picked her up there. I usually saw him only outside. Gramp's, well, he wasn't really digging on him either I don't think. This was before Brian was a thing. He needed to hate on someone my mother chose to hang out with. She didn't really make smart choices to say the least. And I'm not judging her or him. I'm just saying, that especially back in the early eighties. This guy's style wasn't the norm. Not at all. At the very least not in Wallingford CT.

Here's Alphonse in a nut shell, he was a very flamboyant black gay dude. Feathered headdress, platform shoes, makeup, the whole nine. Cross dresser, drag queen. Whatever the politically correct term is today as opposed to yesterday. Basically, Ru Paul before there was a Ru Paul. He later died of AIDS. But for me that's neither here nor there. My mother loved him, and for a while I believe besides the on and off guys she was with, he was most definitely her best friend.

Brian screamed. What the fuck did I tell you, spitting the words directly into her face. You have no reason to talk to this motherfucker. Especially about me. Brian never let go of her hair during all the yelling and screaming. He smashed her face on the table sideways where the other papers were, and started trying to push them into her mouth also. You fucking bitch. None of them. You talk about me to none of them. He lifted her head off of the table, her hair still grasped tightly in his hand. With his other hand he grabbed the phone and ripped it out of the wall and he threw it across the room. He then flipped the table over on its side. At this point Zane is on the bed with me trembling and I can hear Joey crying from his room on the other side of the kitchen.

He dragged her from her hair across the kitchen heading towards their bedroom. He said I'll teach you not to fucking talk about me when I'm not around, you think your husband spanking you was something, I'll show you how you get a bitch to obey. I remember my little brother opening his door as he dragged her past. Don't you hurt my mommy he said. Brian grabbed him by the face with his free hand and pushed him back in his bedroom and said mind your own business or you'll get a beating too. These little fucking bastards of yours have no fucking respect and all that shit changes right now. He slammed my brother's door and dragged her into their room.

He slammed their door and all I could hear was slamming and crashing from inside. She was screaming bloody murder and although I could no longer see what was going on, I knew what it was. Joey opened his door again and looked through the kitchen to where I was laying with Zane. He whispered, can I come lay with you and I waved him over. He ran so fast through my door he tripped and landed perfectly on the bed. Dug himself under my blanket and wrapped his little arms around me and Zane at the same time somehow. He asked why is Daddy Brian such a mean guy? I want my gramps house.

After about five minutes of yelling and beating on my mother he emerged from the bedroom saying, you're going to fucking listen to me now bitch, I guarantee it. And if you don't teach your kids some fucking discipline I will. He went over to where the table used to be, grabbed a chair and started to put his boots back on. My mother comes out of the bedroom clearly beaten badly. I could see her eyes were puffy and she had scratches all over her face and body. She started screaming, where do you think you are going? You just got home. You're going to come home and start a fight with me and then leave. This must have been your plan from the start. Where are you going? What girl are you going to see? Please stay here. Don't leave me here alone.

I'll never forget, Joey looks at me and pulls my head close to his mouth. Is mommy ok? I think he knocked her brains loose. Why won't she let him leave? I want him to leave. I said I don't know. I hope he leaves too and never comes back. Brian turns towards us. You two shut the fuck up in there before you get the same thing she just got. My father would have me in the back yard buried up to my neck if I was like you two. No respect for your elders at all. I'll teach you. Don't you worry about that. If not, you can both get ready for military school. If I can't fix you they sure the fuck can.

My mother was still standing there crying and bleeding, begging him not to leave. He finishes tying his boots and stands up. Walks past her into the bedroom and grabs himself a new shirt. He starts walking out of the bed room and she tries to snatch the shirt out of his hand and she says you're not going anywhere. He yanks the shirt back from her forcing her closer to him and grabs her by her throat and slams her against the wall. If you ever try to grab anything from me like that again I will fucking kill you, don't you fucking doubt it. He lets go of her throat and she dropped to the ground with her legs folded up under her butt, now crying even more hysterically. He takes the keys to her car and heads towards us.

She yells at him. You're a scumbag, I know where you are going, fuck you, fuck you, fuck you. He steps into the mud room and looks at us and says, your mothers fucking crazy, I'll think about coming back tonight. He then kicks the bed and says get that dog off of your bed and get the fuck up and help your mother clean up that mess. It better not still be like that when I get back. As a matter of fact, take that retard dog outside and chain it to the fence before it shits somewhere in the house. If he does I'll rub your nose in it instead of his. He walked out the door, my mom still screaming. Shut up bitch, I'll be back when I get back. And off he went.

I took the dog out and chained him to the fence. I went back inside and my mother was still in the same exact spot with her face buried in her hands. It took a couple of minutes to get her up off of the floor. Mom you have to go clean yourself up. Your bleeding. Come on, we'll help you. Fuck you, this is all your fault. I'm going to always be alone because I had you two. And now I'm pregnant with what's probably going to be another retard. Your father is a no-good drug addict and ruined my life with you little bastards. Joey says, you don't mean that mom. I'm fricken perfect. And you can't blame Victor. Look at how many times he's been hit in his head. She kind of laughed for a split second with gross snots blowing out of her nose and wet tears all over my arm. She looks over at me, I thought she was about to give me a hug. She wipes the snot tears off of my arm and just says, help me with the table.

We picked up the table, my mother and Joey went into the bathroom for her to clean herself up. I was once again confused. I went to check on Zane. Is this real? What the hell did I do to deserve everyone hating on me? I was outside actually talking to the dog. Crying. Telling the dog, I was better off killing myself. I really didn't understand. I didn't do anything wrong. I hated my life. This was honestly my first contemplation of suicide. The whole world sucked to me.

I went back inside and my mother and brother were now cleaning all the papers off of the floor. She told my brother to go ahead and go to bed. He asked if he could sleep with her and she said ok and to go ahead and go lay down in her bed and she'll be in there soon. He gave me a hug and asked me if I wanted to sleep in his room instead of in the mud room. Maybe he won't know where you are and leave you alone. I agreed. If Joey was in Moms bedroom it was a good place for me to hide.

Me and my mother eventually finished up cleaning the kitchen and she said she was going to bed and I should do the same. I set up Zane with fresh food and water in my room and went into Joey's room to go to sleep. I laid down, I actually fell asleep pretty quickly. It was a long day. But once again, after falling asleep, it didn't seem like I was out for more than a few minutes. Wake up. I looked up, and there was Brian holding Joey who was still sleeping in his arms. Or faking. Who knows with that kid.

Get up and go to your own bed right now, this is not your room and you don't belong in here. This is Joeys room and I don't want you in here at all. Let me catch you again and you get the belt. Go. Now. So, I go into my room not even looking back. The only thing I notice, is that where I swept up the mud under the table before I went to sleep, was all muddy again. Typical douchebag narcissistic asshole. I close my door and lay down. Zane is in his bed and I try to go back to sleep. All seemed quiet. Maybe they both fell asleep. I laid there for about forty-five minutes and I became very thirsty. I remember almost drinking out of the dog bowl just so I didn't have to leave my room, just in case they were still awake.

I had an idea. Instead of opening up a cabinet and getting a glass, and taking the chance of him hearing the water in the kitchen. I'll just pretend I have to use the bathroom and drink from the faucet. On the way I can hear noises coming from my Mothers and Brian's room. Uggg, they're not sleeping. I thought they were arguing and fighting again with the door closed so I just rushed in to get some water. I walk back out into the kitchen. I stop for a minute and listen.

Against my better judgement I wanted to make sure that he wasn't hurting my mom again. As I got closer I started to realize that they weren't fighting at all. It was much worse. I couldn't believe it. After all the stuff that happened earlier this morning to me from this guy. After throwing and kicking Zane the way he did. And all the shit that went down with my mother when he got home earlier. And him leaving for hours when she begged him not to. After all that. Are they really having sex right now?

I was absolutely completely deflated. I was completely disgusted. I had a glimmer of hope that with the beating. Just like after my father spanked her. I thought for sure she would hate him and maybe tomorrow, if he didn't come home tonight, she would come to her senses and possibly leave him. I thought for sure it was just a matter of time before we packed up and left. This moment was the most disappointing moment of my young life. I knew that THIS was now my life. And there was no way out. There was nothing I could do. Nothing she would do. We weren't going anywhere. Life can't get any worse. At least that's what I thought. Once again, I was dead fucking wrong. This really felt to me like it was becoming a pattern.

◆ ◆ ◆

PART FIVE - THE GROUNDED

The next two weeks I was obviously still grounded. I basically just hid in my room, as much as you can hide in a room that is the entrance to the rest of the house. I only left the room to either take out the dog, eat, or use the bathroom. They would have people over and they would always ask why I just sat in the porch. Brian would say I don't know, he's a fucking retarded porch monkey. He's grounded from going outside so he just stares outside all day at the other kids playing.

One of these days that I was grounded, a few days before the end of my sentence we had guests over. I am not going to throw names out on this event. I am just going to say that many years later I had found out that the younger daughter in this family was badly molested, for a very long time, at a very young age, by a very scummy guy. There was a mother, a father and two daughters that came over.

And I am only telling this in my story because it is in a huge way connected to another major event in my life that happened about one year later. Plus, it is an event in itself that messed with my head for a very long time. It was weird, and wrong, and gross and embarrassing. But in the greater scheme of things, it is important to tell. And at nine years old. Sometimes you just don't know right from wrong. And you simply do what's in front of you at the time. And you take the consequences later.

We had a cookout and one of the daughters was around my age and the other a little bit older. They actually let me outside to join in with the party. And they even let Laura come over to play with us. I don't remember if it was for anything special, or just a cookout. I had met the daughters only one time before but we all got along great. It was a beautiful sunny day and we stayed outside until dark. We played frisbee and horseshoes and had a little kiddie pool and a slip and slide for the day.

We played tag and fetch with Zane, and ate and played, and all in all it was the best day I had in a very long time. As we were playing I remember the younger of the two daughters was getting very close to me, she kept asking if Laura was my girlfriend. I said no we are only friends, we're to young to be boyfriend and girlfriend. She lives next door and we play in the yard with Zane sometimes. She seemed very excited by this and stayed right by my side the entire rest of the day. I remember Joey saying, at only 4 years old mind you. About Laura, you are fricken crazy dude, if you don't want her, I'll take her, she's a beauty man. What's wrong with you kid? Everyone died laughing. I believe it's the first time I ever heard the word dude come out of his mouth. And then twenty million times after.

As it all winded down, Laura went home and the rest of us went inside the house. They put all the kids in the living room and my mother pulled a box out from behind the couch. She then said, I was going to wait until your punishment was over to give you this, but you were all so good today the hell with it. Your grandfather stopped over earlier and dropped off something for you. I looked up. YES YES YES. ATARI. I couldn't believe it. I was so happy. Why didn't gramps say hi? She said he was in a rush. I'm sorry honey. He told me to tell you and Joey he loves you and will see you very soon. I know why he didn't stick around, she did too. She just wouldn't say it. You know why too.

We played for about three hours. It really was a perfect day by all accounts. I needed it. Desperately. Not being trapped inside all day was such a relief. Brian was even decent for the entire day. I think he stopped drinking for a bit after the blowout the week before. And as the day turned into night and the other family was getting ready to leave, me and the younger girl were taking turns playing a game of frogger. I was just starting a new game when someone said come on, get up, it's time to leave, say goodbye. The girl asked if she could please just play one more game. I handed her my controller and said here, you can finish my game.

The parents all looked at each other and one of them said, why doesn't she just sleep over tonight. She said please, please, please. The father said yes immediately. The mother said no you slept at a friend's house for the last two nights, it's time to come home. You have to clean your room tomorrow anyway. Please mom, I'll clean my room when I get home and I'll even do the dishes for a whole week. I'll be so good and even go to sleep when I'm supposed to. I promise. Please!

Finally the mother broke down and she said Ok. She asked my mother where she was going to sleep and her father said without hesitation. Victors room is fine. It seemed weird to me right off the bat. He said that beds big enough for the both of you. It's the nicest room for a breeze, there's a fan in there and I know you don't like the heat when you sleep. She went out to the car with them and she came back with all her stuff. PJs, toothbrush and a sleeping bag with She-Ra riding a white winged horse.

We played for a little while longer after her parents and sister left. We were now playing pit Fall. One of my all-time favorites. When Brian came in and said, ok, it's late, you promised your parents you would go to bed early. She said ok, He said go into the bathroom brush your teeth and get changed into your pajamas. I grabbed my pajamas and waited outside the bathroom door. Changing in my room freaked me out as the walls were pretty much just a line of giant screen Windows. She finished changing and Brian had her bring her dirty clothes into the living room and I went into the bathroom to change.

Now this isn't any kind of kiddie porn, so no details, just quick facts, and the download of this situation in my mind, and how I had to process what had happened for the rest of my life. As with a lot of things. Downloading and processing. We laid down in bed. At some point while we were talking she took my hand and had me touch her where I shouldn't have and she touched me where she shouldn't have and we kissed way too much for kids our age to kiss. That's as far as I am going with that. It happened that night and we never spoke of it again. This event I believe pushed me into another event about a year later. And that's one of the main reasons I told it. The confusion of why or how it happened and how and why I didn't have the common sense to stop it is the other reason I told it.

She left, it's over. It won't be talked about again. Not about her or her family or what happened to them later. I realize she did what she did for a reason, and It's not my place to say that to anyone else. Nothing that happened within their family had anything else to do with anything else in my life. So that part of this story is over for me.

So that day is over and I am still grounded. For a few more days. I felt like the Rapunzel chick up in the tower trapped in my room. Being able to watch and hear everyone outside playing killed me. This shit wasn't even close to being invented yet, but I had a serious case of FOMO. The last few days went by without any events besides taking forever. I finally got to go outside.

Not to long after I got out, Laura and Freddy were both over. There wasn't any playing though right away. They wanted to know why I was grounded for so long and what it was like dealing with my parents. I told them all, well almost all. With my confessions of what I was going through inside my home, they both opened up and told me their stories as well. It's almost like we all got a little older in the last few weeks.

We sat at the back-picnic table and just talked and talked and talked. We spoke about our lives and talked about our parents. It was an eye-opening conversation. This is where I first learned I was not really alone. Freddy was going through the same things that I was. His Mother's boyfriend was a heavy drinker just like Brian and very abusive to him and his mother, and that he has been going through it with this guy since his father died. He explained in detail, as I did, some of the actual abuses that he has gone through "it's not my place to tell about his so I won't" And with all the crap I have seen and have been through, I still felt bad and cried for him.

Then he hit us with something that made me so jealous. Maybe my first real feeling of jealousy. Except for maybe my uncle Joes drum set. He said that he's fine now though, not worried at all anymore. While I was serving my punishment inside, his mother and her boyfriend got into a huge argument and he slapped his mother around pretty good. Freddy hid in his mother's room and called the police while it was happening. When the police showed up the mother denied that anything had happened. He said she was scared he would kill her if she opened her mouth about anything.

The police were there for a good half hour. He said he was extremely frustrated trying to convince his mother to tell them everything when another squad car pulled up in the middle of the other officers questioning. He said the newest officer on the scene got out of the car and told his mother's boyfriend to put his hands behind his back. We have a warrant for your arrest. Well I guess he didn't want to go. He hit one of the officers and tried to run back inside the house when they tackled him to the ground, after a slight struggle they got him cuffed up. They stood him up and put him in the quad car.

They went back into the house with the officers while his mother's boyfriend was kicking at the door and window of the police car. They told Freddy and his mother that bail would be super high for assault on a police officer and damaging police properly, and that he was more than likely going to be in jail until court, maybe even longer if a judge decided. The officers asked her again if she would like to press charges, they said it would probably give them more time to figure things out and get them out of the situation they were in. She was reluctant but Freddy begged her. So, she finally did it.

Freddy said that his mother even got a restraining order against him a few days ago while he was still in jail, and his brother came over and picked up all his stuff that morning before we all went outside. From what he told us, no one would pay the bail for him and all together he was looking at fifteen years in prison. Freddy seemed like a totally different kid at this point. Way more relaxed and just plain happy. He said his mother was worried about paying the bills for them without any help, but she was ok with all of it rather than dealing with the abuse. Me and Laura were both happy for him. And I was less likely to have to deal with another broken nose due to Freddy having a really bad day.

From Laura's story her parents were saints. Completely opposite of what we were dealing with. They were church going twice a week kind of people. She told of how they would do anything for her, never yelled at her and never fought with each other. Her being only nine years old she told us they have only ever had one complaint or criticism towards her.

And not really a complaint in her words, more of a suggestion. The suggestion was that she be extra careful and mindful when being around Victor or Freddy. She told us that it wasn't because her parents didn't trust us, they said we seemed like nice boys, but they realized that we both seem to have extremely tough lives. And if Brian or Freddy's mother's boyfriend was around outside that she should stay on her side of the fence or even go back inside.

She said that her parents always told her that she was a very intelligent young girl and very mature for her age, and that if something looked off to use her judgment and remove herself from the situation immediately. They knew what was going on around there. And I agree, she definitely acted like she was at least three years older than she actually was. She was very mature and wanted to keep me and Freddy from getting into any trouble. Well, any extra trouble anyways.

I always thought that it was just me, I thought that there was something wrong with me. I thought that I was a worthless piece of shit. I thought that this is what I deserved for ruining my mother's life. I thought that I was a bad kid and couldn't do anything right. This conversation with Freddy and Laura taught me that I wasn't alone, and it had nothing to do with me, or who I was. I realized that there were some decent people out there. I just didn't know many of them in my life.

I realized that the whole world wasn't out to get just me. Other people had these problems too. It is just certain people throughout other people's lives that fuck everything up. I realized that there are scumbags everywhere. And it is them, they are at fault. I haven't done anything wrong to deserve the way I am being treated at nine years old. They are the ones that have the problems. And I had a huge revelation with Freddy and Laura's help, it was that these other people have no remorse about projecting their hate and insecurities on the closest one's around them. Usually the weakest one's. The one's who can't fight back.

I can't say this conversation changed my actions. I was still angry at the way I was treated. It only changed my outlook on certain things and certain people. I was still the same kid. And it certainly didn't change the way I was treated at home at all either, obviously. It did change the way I thought of my situation and the way I dealt with it internally. It made me think that someday I will be an adult and all I have to do is get through these rough years and all will be ok in the future. Knowing there was someone in almost the same exact situation as me, and seemed to have gotten out, gave me hope.

And knowing someone else in the complete opposite situation also gave me a little hope. Maybe Brian will mess up and go to jail too? Maybe my mother will leave him eventually? Maybe she will find a nice guy someday? I can get through this. And if I take her parents advise. And I stay on my side of an imaginary fence away from Brian, I might just get through this portion in my life with everything intact. I have to say. They both gave me hope. It turned out to be false hope. But it was hope none the less.

A few days later I woke up to what sounded like way more kids than usual running around right outside my room. I looked out towards Laura's yard and noticed her, Freddy and three other kids playing kick the can. I yelled hi to them and they said hurry up and get out here. These guys want to meet you. I hurried outside with Zane and they introduced me to two girls and the Puerto Rican kid Miguel from across the street. The girls were identical twins named Tabitha and June. They were two of the girls that Laura mentioned lived up un the hill behind our houses.

We played outside for the full day. Kick the can, tag, hide and seek, and even had a beauty contest. In which I have to brag about. I won. Hands down. All three girls. It must have been my beautiful hair. It was a great day until it came to a screeching halt when Brian pulled up. The girls all went home, pretty damn quickly. So, it was me, Miguel and Freddy still standing in the yard. Brian being Brian started talking shit. Which one of you broke this little faggots' nose? I know it was one of you, No one else even talks to this dirtbag kid. I didn't want to have to deal with him for long, so I just told him the truth. I said I already told Mom it was my fault and I deserved to get hit. He looked at Miguel and said, it was you huh. Figures he'd get his ass whooped by someone smaller than him. Freddy stepped right up and said it was him. And that I actually put up a good fight.

Brian, like usual, took offense to anybody talking back to him, puffed his chest out and said, well you're lucky I don't smack the shit out of you kid. Freddy took a step back. Miguel looked over at Freddy and said come on let's get out of here, we'll go to my house. Brian than says no. These two fought, how about you fight Victor. You're closer in size. Miguel said we're all friends and we're not going to fight. Of course, Brian eggs it on. Fucking kids these days. No heart, no balls. Come on. I know one thing, Victor can take a beating, so your little punk ass won't have a shot. Wow, a compliment. Miguel said I'm two years older than him, I'm not going to fight him. My mother would kill me.

Brian kept pushing it, mostly on me now. I told Brian I can't fight. My hand is still swollen from the last time and it still hurts. We never even went to a doctor to look at it. He said ok, just wrestling then. No punches. Come on you pussy. Fight him. Come on. Show me that you're not a pussy. Come on. Prove to me that you deserve to be called my son. Come on, Come on, Come on.

I finally got so frustrated and so angry at Brian that something snapped and I pushed Miguel. I said fine let's go. To this day I wish I didn't. Brian said ok. Now where talking. Let's go to the side of the house where there's more room. He didn't do it for more room, he did it so no one would see two kids fighting with an adult cheering them on. We went to the side of the house behind a line of bushes. Once we got there he went over to Miguel and was actually giving him pointers against me. He told him that punching me is fine, don't worry about it. He's a wimp and can't even hit you back. Have a little fun. I'm not going to lie. That shit hurt worse than the fight itself. This is who my mother chose to be my dad. Aren't I just the lucky one. We squared up and started fighting. I had no intention of a real fight with him. I just wanted Brian to be appeased and leave us alone.

Me and Miguel fought for this fucking douchebag, and I pretty much got my ass handed to me. The whole time. I had no desire to do this in any way. We rolled around in the grass mostly wrestling. My mother came out of the house yelling for us to stop but Brian just yelled over her and said, he has to learn how to be a man someday. Miguel got on top of me, pinned my shoulders to the grass and said, there, are you happy, I win, I'm done. Brian said you're not even close to done. Punch him in the face or I'm going to punch you in the back of your Spick fucking head. Well, I guess that got Miguel's attention. He hit me like three times in the face and my mother finally broke it up.

Typical cunt wench, Brian said, when he grows up to be a little girl faggot we'll know why. Miguel looked at me and said he was sorry, and Freddy just turned around and left. Brian yells, get the fuck inside. You couldn't beat a kid you have almost fifteen pounds on. Disgraceful. He said to my mother, you need to put this little prick in military school. They'll whip him up into a man. He told me go to bed, no dinner tonight. I don't want to see your face at all. I laid in my bed still dirty from the grass with blood from my nose again just wishing I could kill this fucking guy. Stab him in his sleep or poison his ignorant ass or something. FUCK. Fucking guy even opened the door to my room so I could watch them all eat dinner without me. It wasn't the first time, and it sure wouldn't be the last.

Grounded for a week. Again. For nothing. Because I didn't win the fight. Watching my friends from the window again. Dying inside, wanting nothing more than to talk to my friends. This to me alienated me from most of them. Nothing was ever the same. I could see sometimes that it seemed like they were laughing at me while I was stuck watching them through the screen Windows. I believe it might have all been in my head. But they absolutely treated me different when I was allowed to go back outside.

Three days in to the new sentence I got the news. My mother came into my room with Joey and they both sat down on the bed. She looked at me and said we're moving out of here in two weeks back to Wallingford. I jumped up and gave her the biggest hug and kissed her on the cheek. I gave Joey a huge hug and started crying. I said thank you mommy, I love you. She asked me why I was so happy to move away? You made some very close friends here and I thought you loved Laura. I said I do, but going back to Gramp's house and getting away from Brian will be worth anything. I just wish we could keep Zane.

She looked at me like she didn't know what to say. She then said we are keeping Zane. I said I hope he gets along with King Louis. She said Victor. Listen to me. Joey looked at her and asked, Brian's coming with us? Isn't he? She said yes. I said but Gramps hates him, how is that going to work? I don't want him hurting Gramps. She stood up and said stop talking and just listen. We found a new place in Wallingford. Not with your grandfather. A new place and a new beginning.

Brian promised to stop drinking and we are going to make this work. And you two are going to help. You both are going to have a new brother soon. This is just the way it is. You have two weeks. Make the most of the time you have left with your friends outside. She just walked away and shut my door. Joey just stared at me and said I'm sorry big brother. I hope the new kid isn't anything like daddy Brian. Two of them would just be way too much. I would probably run away if I was you. Living in the woods with the bears or a Bigfoot would be better than him. He gave me a hug and walked away to his room.

I remember my last week in Meriden. I was able to return outside, while they worked on packing, I tried to fit myself in by asking them if I could help them but Brian said I would just fuck it up and be in their way. Go outside and play with your ghetto friends. You're always complaining you can't go out and now that you're allowed you want to stay in. Your son is a fucking retard Janice. You know that? She snickers and just says, why don't you just leave him alone, you promised you would stop. Victor, just go outside. Take your little brother with you.

So me Joey and Zane go outside, somethings different now though. There's no one around. As we made it to the back yard I can hear kids up over the hill playing. I can hear Freddy yelling June's name and knew they were all up there playing now. I asked Joey to stay in the yard with Zane, don't leave this yard Joey. I won't be long. He asked where are you going. I told him up the hill to tell my friends we are moving in a few days, I said I don't know if I will have a chance to say goodbye to them. He asked if he could come with me. I thought about it for a second but I told him he needed to stay and watch Zane. He bought it. I climbed up the steep hill using the tree branches and roots sticking out of the ground to get up there.

I got to the top and they were all playing tag at the end of the street. I yelled I'm free. They all came over to me, I got a few hugs and I got a few dirty looks. There were a few older kids I didn't know. I explained that my parents were making me move with them to Wallingford and I will be gone in about a week. They asked if I could stay and play for a little while right now. I told them no I had to hurry back, I'm not supposed to be up here right now as it is, and my little brother is in my back yard with the dog. If Brian ever finds out he will kill me.

Miguel takes me and Freddy to the side and says, well if your leaving, I want a recount on the beauty contest thing we did. You're not going to be around anymore so we want to see which one of us the girls like more. I said ok, I don't care, but just for a minute, I really have to go. We call the girls over and tell them what's going on. They do it. Right away the twins both say, it's still Victor. Laura looks at us and hesitates before she says,

Miguel and Freddy are tied for me.

Everyone knew what that was. She was so nice and pure and sweet that she felt bad they weren't picked and didn't want to leave them out. She even hinted to that as being the reason. I could tell they weren't happy. But all they said was let's get back to tag. I gave the girls a hug and shook the boy's hands. As I let go of Freddy's hand and said goodbye he tapped me on the shoulder and said TAG, your it. They all scattered. Like a dummy, I chased them.

Up on the street, on top of the hill, behind my yard, there were cars parked on both sides of the street where we were playing. This is where all the kids ran to keep away from being tagged. I remember I was chasing Freddy first but he was way faster than me. I came up with a strategy. I was chasing him around a car on the right side of the road. I saw either Tabitha or June standing across the street behind a car on the left side of the street laughing and giggling. As I was chasing him I lagged behind on purpose and waited for the girl to look towards him.

As soon as I noticed her look away from me and towards him I darted towards her. She started laughing and running around the car. I had a huge head start in the running and as we were turning the corner at the back of the car I reached towards her and Tag. I couldn't even get you're it out of my mouth before disaster. As I touched her back our feet got tangled up with each other's. She started tripping forward and. And, to this day, in all my memories, I don't know how this happened at all. I swear. Another fucking mystery that has haunted my mind forever. I didn't even know which one of the twins it was at the time.

As she was tripping forward. Somehow? Someway? Yeah, question marks. She went head first into the wheel well of the car we were running around and got stuck in there. Wedged in between the tire and the wheel well. Against all physics. It was insanity. It was an accident. It was a mistake. Well. Not to everybody I guess. As parents ran across the street and towards the car to get her out, I was just standing there, in shock apologizing. I am so sorry, I kept yelling, I'm so sorry. It was an accident. I didn't mean to hurt her. I'm so sorry.

As the parents are getting her out I'm just staring at them. As they finally get her loose she is the only thing I am concerned about or concentrating on. Her head has a huge gash and she's bleeding everywhere. I'm still saying I'm sorry when I feel a push from behind. I turn around and there is Freddy and Miguel with another two older boys I've never met. I think one of them was the twins' older brother. I apologized again. I'm so sorry. Is she alright?

The brother says, does she look alright you little asshole? He asks Freddy, where does this kid live. Where the fuck did he come from. Freddy points towards the hill. Right down there. He looks at Freddy and Miguel and grabs me by my arms. Miguel and Freddy and the other kid join him and start hitting me as they're all pushing me towards the hill. Laura is yelling for help and telling them to stop that it was an accident and not my fault. Someone please help him. You guys stop this instant. I remember as this was all happening, time had slowed down for me once again. Just like Nancy coming down the stairs and my mother throwing the knife at my father.

I knew I was going to get hurt, I knew I was in trouble. I didn't care all that much. As they were pushing me closer to the ledge, Laura screaming to stop. I looked over to where the twin was to see if she was ok. I didn't care about myself. One of the parents looked me straight in the eyes and shook their head and turned their attention right back towards the girl. Don't come back up here ever were the last words I heard before I felt a push and my feet slide out from under me and behind me.

No more ground under my feet. My face hit the grass and down I went. Sliding backwards down the hill on my belly and face.

Trying to claw at the hill in front of me to stop my descent. I can feel the rocks from the hill cutting my stomach so I tried to turn to my back. As I was almost to my back my shirt ripped off over my head from a root or a branch or something sticking out of the ground. I tried then to sit up on my butt and slowed down and grabbed a tree about four feet from the bottom.

I was a disaster. I was bleeding everywhere. I was all kinds of dirty, I had no shirt on anymore. No more friends. And in all honesty, all I kept thinking about is was she going to be ok? That thought was pretty short lived though I must say. I was looking down at my stomach still holding the tree when I heard in a thunderous voice. WHERE THE FUCK WERE YOU. I looked straight ahead. There was Brian walking towards me all puffed out again. My mother was sitting on the picnic table bench with my brother sitting on the top of the picnic table itself towards her. She had a bottle of peroxide and was pouring it on a towel.

Brian took a few steps up the hill and he grabbed me by my hair and ripped me from holding the tree. I asked what about my shirt? He said, fuck your shirt, you'll be lucky if you get to wear one again. As he's dragging me across the lawn I see my mother putting the towel on Joeys knee. He lets go of my hair right next to the picnic table and reaches down to grab me by the back of my neck. He tells my mother to move the towel away from my brothers' knee. He then puts my face right against it and says again. Where the fuck have you been? Why were you not watching your brother like you were told to? Where the fuck did you go?

My brothers knees both had a bunch of scrapes and small cuts on them. My mother then says, your little brother tried to climb up the hill to follow you. Why would you go that way and leave him down here by himself? What's wrong with you? We heard him yelling your name and when we looked out of the window he was at the bottom of the hill holding his leg crying for you to come back. Did you not hear him? I said no, I'm sorry, there was a lot of noise up there and I couldn't hear anything. She said don't you never, ever leave him alone again like that. You're in more trouble than ever mister. And what happened to you dummy? Why are you bleeding all over like that?

I was just about to answer when Brian pulled me up to my feet, what the fuck does it matter? It's not getting him out if this no matter what happened. He started dragging me towards the house, pretty much just slapping me in the back of my head over and over. My mother yelled to him not to hit me anymore and that I was hurting enough. He yelled I'm not beating him this time, don't worry, it obviously doesn't get through his thick scull anyways. I have something much better in store for him this time.

We go into the house and Brian pushes me to stand in the corner. Don't you dare move you fuck. I can hear him moving things around in the cabinet. My mother and Joey come back inside and Joey tells me he's sorry. Brian says don't apologize to him it's his fault you got hurt. Janice. Where the fuck is the rice? We had a full box of rice. Where the fuck is it? I threw it away she said. We're starting to move all of our shit in like three days. It was expired. I figured we didn't need it. Brian said Well I fucking do. Right now. Where is it? She said in a bag on the curb. Go get it. Are you kidding me Brian? I'm not going out through the garbage for a box of rice.

Yes, the fuck you most surely you are he said. Unless you want to watch me beat your fucking kid to a bloody fucking pulp. You said you didn't want me to hit him right, now go move your fucking ass and do what you're told. She huffed a little but did what she was ordered to do. And out the door she went. In the meantime he was screaming in my face what a worthless piece of shit I was and how my little brother could have died trying to climb that hill, or how he could have tried to go around and get hit by a car. And now I am going to feel what his father used to do to him when he didn't listen or fucked up. Oh yeah, I'm gonna learn you now he said. It was one of his sayings. He had plenty. Every one of them proving he was an idiot more than the last.

My mother came back in about two minutes later with the box of minute rice in her hand and threw it on the table. She sat down and said, come on, please get out of his face like that. He knows what he did was wrong. And he is obviously already hurt. Look at his stomach. Look at him shaking. Why did you need the rice so god damn badly? You'll see right now. He grabs me by the back of my neck again pulling me away from the corner. Stand right there, don't you fucking move. He grabs the box of rice off of the table and rips the top off.

He walks towards the corner and pours half the box out onto the floor. As he's spreading it around I'm thinking he's going to make me stand on it. I can take that. No sweat. He puts the box on the counter and grabs me by the back of the neck again. Apparently, that's also one of his moves. Two steps towards the corner he demands me to kneel. My mother asked what do you mean kneel? I said fucking kneel. My mom said no, if you're going to do that to him, just make him stand on it. He said fuck you, my father did this to me and it most certainly worked. This kid needs to learn some fucking discipline. Now shut your mouth and tell him to kneel or I pull the bullwhip out and make his back look worse than his stomach.

He kicked the back of my knees and pushed me forward and I slammed down on the rice. It was extremely painful especially landing on it at first. Unexplainable. Just pain running through my legs. He said, now don't fidget around too much, if you try to escape the pain, it will only make it worse, take it from me. I heard my mother say you're a sick man and I heard her take Joey and go into the living room, telling him he better make sure he listens and behaves so this stuff doesn't happen to him. Brian then puts one hand on my shoulder and pushed down slightly. It really was very painful. I was shaking and crying. He said, just like your mother just told Joey, if you learn how to listen and behave this wouldn't happen to you. Now tell me why you left the yard and why did you try to run down the hill and fall like that? Did you hear your brother after all?

I was obviously still crying and trying to explain that I wanted to go and say goodbye to my friends and only thought I would be gone for a minute. I then was about to explain what happened with the coming back down the hill, I was thinking of lies to tell and whether I should go with the lies or tell the truth when. Knock Knock Knock Knock Knock. He yells who the fuck is that? Don't you move. If you fucking move I will come back here and make you lick up every piece of rice off of that floor. He walks towards the front door. I was praying to everything possible that it would be the police. Someone finally called them. Finally. Please take him away, please even take me away. Please. Do something.

As soon as he was out of site I started trying to pick the rice from my knees, my mother's voice as she was walking towards the door said I wouldn't do that if I was you! if he catches you it will get worse. I promise. As she was walking bye I heard him open up the door. Can I help you? All I kept praying for was please say It's the police. Please come in here and see me like this. Then I heard a woman's voice. Are you this boy Victors parents? Brian said Stepfather. Why? What did that little idiot do now?

She told him, from what some of the other kids told her, they were playing hide and go seek up near the street, and I came up the hill mad about something and pushed her niece violently into the car, and that she's on her way to the hospital for stitches. She said that they should expect an ambulance and a hospital bill sometime in the near future. She asked why I was up there in the first place. Brian said he had no idea and I am already being punished for it. She said they were not going to press charges or tell the police it was on purpose because one of the little girls Laura had a completely different story from the other kids and they believe her more than the little punks that lived down here.

Brian thanked her and said he will take care of it. Send the bills if need be. Shut the door Janis. I heard him say to my mother we aren't paying that cunt anything. Fuck her and her niece. He came up behind me and put both his hands on my shoulders. He pushed down hard on them and asked me as I let out a holler. Did you go up there and do that on purpose? I cried no, I swear I didn't. I played with them for a few minutes and it was an accident. He pushed down harder for just a second than let go and said ok. If the little bitch is anything like her aunt she probably fucking deserved it. After he removed his hands from my shoulders he put them under my armpits and said get up, you're done. As soon as he let go of my armpits I reached down and tried to brush the rice off of my knees. A few fell off. A few stayed buried and had to be dug out.

I say a few and a few because as they were talking to the aunt at the door. I moved most of them from under my knees. I guess just praying I didn't get caught. And I am so happy I did. Him pushing down on my shoulders like that with the pile that was under there before would have been excruciatingly worse. At this place in time, I couldn't even imagine the pain if they were all still under there. A little later in time though, that pain would be all too real.

So I picked the rest of the rice out of my knee with a pair of tweezers and they made me sit down at the table. They told me to spit it out, everything. If I lied I would suffer way worse than I just did. I told them everything. I don't know if they felt bad or what, they kind of acted like they did for a moment. My mother told me to go take a bath, relax, and clean myself up and get ready for bed. Let me tell you something. I messed up pretty good in that bathroom. I put some Mr. Bubble in the tub before I got in thinking that it would help me to relax. You know the commercial if you are around my age. Calgon, take me away. Well nope. Big mistake. No relaxing. Terrible pain, Mr. Bubbles in all my cuts and scrapes was definitely not one of my brightness moments. I cleaned myself up and showered all the soap off and put my pajamas on and left the bathroom more stressed out than when I went in.

I guess they didn't feel as bad as I thought they might of. Brian looked at my mother as I was standing there and asked, do you think he learned his lesson on this one? You would think as a mother she would have said yes. She answered, how the fuck am I supposed to know? He looked at me and asked me, do you think you learned your lesson? I said yes. He asked why? I said because I don't want to have to kneel in rice ever again. He said wrong answer. The correct answer is because you want to be a good boy. So yeah, as you can probably guess. Another night. No dinner. And he took my fan too. So not much of any sleep that night either.

The next morning, early, very early, much before the sun came up, as I was sitting there, in the hot porch, on my hot bed, my pillow held up to the screen trying to get a breeze on it to cool it down, the door comes open. Brian walks through with his shotguns. He looked at me and laughed, what's the matter? Can't sleep in the heat? Go get your fan you little prick, it's in the kitchen, tell your mother when she wakes up I said it was ok. He walked outside and put the guns in the car, he came back in and grabbed his cooler and asked me where Zane's leash was. I said hanging up on the hook right behind you.

He grabbed the leash and called to Zane, Heel. Zane walked over, head down scared shitless and Brian hooked him up. I asked where he was taking him. He said he needed him to retrieve the ducks because he was going duck hunting. Brian said he needs his exercise and needs to get back to it so he doesn't forget how. I didn't think very much of it. It sounded plausible. He's done this before. They left and I plugged in my fan, threw that bitch on high and finally fell to sleep. My mother woke me up a few hours later. She asked me immediately. Where's Zane? I told her that Brian took him hunting to go fetch his ducks. She said come get breakfast and closed the door. She made me some apple cinnamon oatmeal and went into her room on the phone immediately. At this point I felt something was wrong. I was just hoping it was my imagination.

Brian came home a few hours later. I was in the living room with Joey playing Atari. I heard the front door open and expected to hear Zane's claws scrapping across the kitchen floor. Brian had the guns over his shoulder and the cooler in his hand. I walked past him and looked in the mud room towards Zane's food bowl and towards his bed. I looked out into the car through one of my windows.

Daddy Brian, where is my dog? Is he outside in the yard? He looks at me and says, first of all he was never your fucking dog, second of all he went to see a man about a horse. I said fine then. Where's your dog? Our dog? Where is he really? You brought him to a farm with horses? He snickered. Yeah, something like that. Don't worry about him. He can't come with us to our new house so I gave him to one of my cousins who has a horse farm. I said ok, why didn't you tell me? He said it was none of my business and there was nothing I could do to change it anyway.

Now I never got a straight answer about what ever happened to him. I never saw or ever heard anything about him again. I'm fairly sure I met all of his cousins in the years to come. And although one of them had a truly sweet log cabin out in the woods. I never saw or heard of a horse farm. I heard him and my mother talking about it through their door later that night. He denied killing him and said that they were hunting and he ran off into the woods and he never came back. One of those answers were obviously a lie. Ninety-nine-point eight percent sure they both were lies.

But this is how Brian operated. No one will ever know what actually happened to Zane. He always leaves just enough to think things one way or the other. Never a straight answer. He walks out with the dog and his guns to go duck hunting. He comes home with no ducks though. He's the great white hunter? How did that happen? He gave him to someone else because we couldn't keep him? No name though. He lost him in the woods? And just left without looking for him? I don't know what he did with this dog. I never will. Even if he did give him away to another family. Even if he did run away off into the woods. Us thinking he went out into the woods and shot him works way more to his advantage. He lived and disciplined by total fear. I wish I realized this a lot sooner.

The next three days were pack and move, pack and move, pack and move. With Brian running our things back and forth to Wallingford. Remember I said a few days ago I wanted to help. I guess I got my wish. He worked me like a slave. It was the first time in my life I ever knew what muscle aches were. I remember making even a bigger mistake than with the mister bubbles on the second day of moving. I rubbed Ben Gay on my thighs. Huge misjudgment. I rubbed it to high on my right thigh and got a very little on my testies. A little was all it took. I don't know much about anatomy apparently. Because it was completely baffling to me why it was such a difference between my thigh and my nuts. It burned uncontrollably for two or so hours. It is quite painful and I wouldn’t recommend it.

Our new apartment was the opposite of the one we just moved out of. Although it was a duplex. We were now the ones living on the second floor. While we were going back and forth to the truck for the three days I saw Freddy, the twin I didn't hurt and Miguel a couple of times, they were hanging out mostly at Freddy's house on the porch now. They only looked at me to flip me off.

I saw Laura and the other twin also, the one I hurt in up the hill. I was pretty sure that the one I hurt hated me too because she hardly ever looked over towards me. All I wanted to do deep down inside was tell her how sorry I was. So, on the last day of moving with the last load ready to go Brain told me to stay behind with my mother and Joey and help her finish cleaning.

After he left I went outside and sat on the steps to the porch to rest for a little bit. It was the first time that I was outside without Brian around for days. The three came over from across the street and the twin looked at me and said I hate you for what you did to my sister. And Freddy and Miguel started calling me names. I was just about to get up and go back inside feeling terrible when I heard the other twin yell over. Hey you guys leave him alone, and her and Laura came running over. The twin I hurt pushed Freddy and said get back across the street where you belong. He didn't hurt me on purpose and you know it.

The three of them left in a huff and that's when I knew which one that I hurt. Tabitha, five stitches on her forehead, she yelled at them you know he didn't do it on purpose, why are you acting like this? Go to hell Tabby her sister said, you can be friends with the loser that hurt you and the bible thumper. I have my friends. You have yours. And away they went. I was just about to apologize for the stitches in her head, when she apologized to me for everything else that happened to me after. Laura apologized too. She said they were all just jerks and deserved each other. We are good just the two of us. We wish you didn't have to leave.

My mother then came out with Joey. Come on Victor. Say goodbye. We have to go. I looked at the girls and we all started crying. They each gave me a hug and a kiss and said they would miss me. I told them I would miss them too and I wished I didn't have to leave this way with everyone mad at each other all because of me. I got into the car with my mother and Joey. We started to pull away when Joey blurted out. I'll miss both of you beauties. And off we went. I cried all the way to Wallingford and never heard from any of them again.

◆ ◆ ◆

PART SIX - THE GREAT WHITE HUNTER

Now I know you have to be thinking to yourself, or asking me, come on man, this shit can't get much worse? Can it? I don't know if I can say worse for this period in time. But I can say more of the same bullshit with different tactics. I have four different events from this time period stuck in my brain at this moment. I guess I'll call them episodes. I write from memory, not from any notes at all. I remember as I write. Or write as I remember. So, I can't say with complete certainly that any episode was worse than any one before or after. And there might be more than four by the time I'm done. This part takes place for almost two years. My little brother Bobby was born here a few months after we moved in. So, at this time I had just turned ten and Joey five. Enjoy.

When we first moved in on Allen avenue I remember walking onto the front porch. There were five steps to get up, and the porch was the length of the front of the house. Not enclosed so it wasn't my bedroom this time. There were two doors side by side. The door to the left was to the downstairs apartment and the right was to ours for the upstairs. The stairway up to our apartment was very narrow. At nine years old I could easily touch each wall on my way up with my elbows still quite bent.

As you got to the top of the stairs you could see a door a little to the left on the opposite wall. This was to the outside entrance and was located in the kitchen. To the right at the top of the front stairs was the living room. One doorway. You would walk up the stairs and turn right and after you walked through the doorway looking straight ahead was a wall about seven feet in. Turn to the right and it was the entire width of the house. Long narrow living room.

Back to the kitchen. Out of the living room walk straight past the stairs to the left used to get into the house. To the right past that was the back-entrance door and porch to the back yard. The back porch was about six by six feet with about a four-foot-high rail going around with stairs going down to the right. Back into the kitchen through that door, refrigerator to the exact right with a small wall and a doorway going to a hallway, down this hallway was the bathroom and the three bedrooms. Straight through the back-entrance door is the rest of the kitchen all the way to the front wall. Big kitchen too. Walk down the hallway next to fridge and you have the bathroom to the right, the door to my parents' room to the left, Joeys door to his room right past the bathroom to the right and my bedroom straight down the hallway at the end.

At first this was really a sweet setup. My room was at the complete opposite end of the house from where everyone else hung out in the living room. My grandfather bought me a small TV for my bedroom and I could play my Atari in there with Joey or by myself and not be to bothered. Colony lanes bowling alley was directly outside, out of the front door and across the street. They had an arcade and if I could get my hands on a couple of quarters here or there at first, I was gone. I would wait in line for an hour just to play asteroids. And Gramps started taking me with him every other week to go roller skating again. It was a great couple of first months.

Brian was seemingly happy too. He had a baby boy on the way and was working full time as a landscaper. My mother still worked as a waitress, and after I got home from school, I would pretty much be in charge of the house until one of them got home between five and seven o'clock. And you might be asking why don't you talk about school that much. And my answer to that is. Fuck school. I never liked it. I was bullied pretty badly, I guess I was an awkward kid. There will be some about it soon. But not much in these books. I could probably write an entire standalone book on the subject. We'll see what happens.

So like I said things were going pretty well. For a while. I don't know why it all went wrong when we were all so happy. My mother had my baby brother Bobby on January 21st 1982. All three of us born in January. Guess she was at her most fertile in April or some shit.

Alright, I know you're waiting for the bad stuff, fuck all this gushy getting along shit.
So here you go. The first event actually started fairly awesome. Brian took me to a shooting range with him and a buddy. I think his name was Jack. I'm not positive. I got to shoot all kinds of different guns. We were there for hours and it was truly the first time me and Brian went out and did anything just the two of us. I felt that maybe this is what he needed out of me, and if it would make him, my mother and my brothers happy. I would do my best to do my part. It also helped to think this was the way to not get myself beat up anymore.

A few days later he asked me if I wanted to go hunting with him. It was going to be my first hunting trip ever. I was a pretty excited. Though I can't say I wasn't a little, maybe just a tiny bit nervous about going to see a man about a horse, but the way we were all getting along and the fact he knew I told my grandfather about the hunting trip the night before on the phone I wasn't all that worried. Maybe more nervous about messing something up.

Brian said go to bed and set your alarm for three a.m. and get some sleep. We have to hit the road by three thirty. Brian was cleaning the guns and my mother was in the kitchen making us some sandwiches and getting drinks ready for us in thermoses when I went into my room. It took a while to fall asleep and before I knew it my alarm was going off. It was sometime in February, and back then we actually had snow in the winter. I put on a pair of thermal pants and jeans over that. A thermal shirt, a long sleeve shirt and a heavy flannel shirt. Two pairs of socks, winter boots, a hat and gloves.

I went out into the kitchen and Brian was already up having a cup of coffee. He said he already took care of icing the cooler and to take it downstairs and put it in the car. I brought that out while he was packing up the guns and the ammo. He said grab the thermoses and follow me. We went down the stairs and he put the guns in the trunk and I put the thermoses in the back seat next to where I placed the cooler. And off we went.

If you know Wallingford you know, or knew, I'm sorry. I don't know if it changed since then like everywhere else did. But down past the dog pound is the Wallingford dump. Near the dump is a large section of woods, and in those woods is a small river and a few streams. That's where we went. We got out of the car and gathered up the guns, ammo and the thermoses. He said to leave the cooler in the car and we'll come back to it in a few hours to eat lunch. He said we're only going about a mile in.

We walked for about a half hour. We stopped in a clearing that you could see has been used for target practice a lot. He said put everything you have near those logs. He handed me my gun. Twenty-gauge pump. He had a twelve-gauge pump. He showed me how to load it and he set up some duck targets. I remember I did really well. I liked it just as much as I enjoyed going to the range. We stayed in this spot for about forty-five minutes going through two boxes of shells each. He said we only have one box of each left so let's go to the river and shoot us some real birds.

We get to the river, it was about a fifteen-minute walk. We set up on a hill hiding in between and under some bushes looking down over the river. We were there for about three hours and I was starting to get very uncomfortable and impatient. When all of a sudden eight ducks come flying down over our heads. They landed right below where we were laying down. He whispered in my ear and pointed out which duck he wanted me to shoot. He said you shoot the tan one right below us and I'm going to shoot the black and green one farthest away. He whispered on my three.

One,,,,two,,,,three. Boom, Boom,,,,. Boom boom boom. I hit mine and he hit his. As soon as we shot the ones we were pointing at. The rest started to fly away and that's when he stood up and took the next three shots. I saw them scatter. I don't think he hit another one. He dropped his gun and grabbed me by my shirt and yanked me up to my feet.

Go, jump in the water and grab your duck. I jumped right in. His was way farther so he ran a bit before jumping in. I got to mine and as I looked down river he was just getting to his. He yanks his up and lets out a howl. He holds his up and yells. That's the way to do it son. Hold that thing up. Be proud of yourself. This is your first duck. I'm very proud of you son. That's our dinner tonight. Let's dry off and go eat lunch. Then maybe we'll go out and shoot for some squirrels. We have plenty of ammo left.

We dried off, grabbed our ducks, he stuffed them in his pouch, we grabbed our guns and thermoses and headed off towards the car. It took us about forty-five minutes to get there from the river. We put everything down on the trunk and he starts digging and looking through his pockets, and going through his pockets. And looking through his pockets, and again, looking through his pockets. FUCK. He yelled. The keys. I LOST THE FUCKING KEYS. They must have fell out in the brush where we were laying or in the river. He then took off his pouch with the ducks inside and laid it on the trunk with the rest of our stuff. He said you stay here. I'll be much quicker by myself. I'm going back for the keys. Or were walking home. I'll be back.

He goes running off into the woods. I was there by myself sitting on the hood of the car for about twenty minutes when I heard a noise coming from behind me near the trunk. Smack smack smack smack smack. At first, I thought it was Brian messing with me. But there is no way in hell he got back that fast. I got off of the hood and walked slowly around the car on the passenger side. Smack smack smack. I couldn't tell where it was coming from. Was it a woodpecker? Is it Brian? Is it Zane? Wolf? I am standing here all alone in the woods with weird noises coming from behind me. Ten years old. Scared shitless? Yeah, understatement. I got up on my tippy toes and looked through the back-passenger window to the back window and heard a smack and saw Brian's pouch fall off the other side of the trunk like someone pulled it off with a rope.

I dropped down to the ground next to the back-passenger side door near the back tire. I looked under the car to see what just pulled the pouch off of the trunk praying that whatever it is doesn't rip my face off. As soon as my ear touched the ground I saw it. The pouch was puffing up and down. Flapping. I stood up and walked around to the back. I look on the ground and now I know what it was. There is definitely one of those ducks still alive in that pouch.

I just left it there, I'm not Jeffery Dahlmer. I'm not pulling that thing out and killing it. I kind of felt bad shooting mine in the first place. As a matter of fact, I'm not even opening that thing because if I do and it's still very alive and it gets away I have to deal with Brian. No thank you. Everything is too good to mess anything up. Just wait. Brian will be back soon enough and he will take care of it. About twenty more minutes go by and here comes Brian running out of the woods. Huffing and puffing and sweating bullets. I found them in the bushes right where we were laying. Record time. He says give me that thermos. I'm parched. He throws me the keys and says get the cooler out of the car. Let's eat something. There's still time to get a couple squirrels or something if you want to afterwards. I saw a bunch running around when I ran through back and forth from the river.

I told him about the live duck and he walked over and picked up the pouch. He asked, why didn't you just kill it. I said I didn't want it to get away. He bought that excuse. I got it he said. Just get the cooler. I grab the cooler and he pulls my duck out. He says, oh shit, you're right, it is still alive. He took it in both hands and slammed its head on the trunk. Blood splatters all over the trunk, I say gross. That's where I was going to eat. He laughs and stuffs it back in the pouch.

I pulled the cooler out and placed it on the ground and opened it. I looked up at him. He says hand me a couple of sandwiches. What did she make? I didn't know what to say. I dig in under the ice. I knew it was a stupid question so I couldn't ask it. So, he did. You never put the fucking sandwiches in the cooler? Did you? I said I thought you did. You said you put the ice in already so I figured you put the sandwiches in too because you never told me to. You just said bring it to the car.

He just snared at me and said, you truly are a retard. I should just leave you out here in the fucking woods and make you find your own way home. You are so fucking useless. How the fuck would you not check the cooler before you bring it downstairs. He said his father would have tied him up and would have dragged him home from the bumper of the car. He said put everything away. We're done. Sit in the back seat because if you're up front with me you're probably going to get backhanded.

We drove home with him complaining the entire way. All I could think to myself is this actually wasn't my fault this time. He was up before me and told me to bring the cooler to the car.

Not to put the sandwiches in it and bring it to the car. I swear it was almost like he did it on purpose.

We finally got home after it felt like hours. It was actually only about twenty minutes away. I got out of the car and walked to the door with Brian still bitching behind me like I stole his lunch from him on purpose. Not that I simply just forgot it. I opened up the front door and my mother is standing at the top or the stairs looking down at me. She asks, how was your lunch fellas? She smiles and Brian walks up behind me and says shut the fuck up bitch, I'm glad you think that it's funny. I told your fucking retard good for nothing son to put them in the cooler and bring it to the car and he brought a cooler full of ice.

I didn't say anything. I was ready to go to my room absolutely knowing I'm to go to bed with no meal at all for the day. I didn't care, I was used to it. I walk into my room and started getting my clothes out of my dresser and I hear a bunch of paper crumpling around down the hall. I was on my way down the hall to take a shower. I ask, does anybody need to use the bathroom? I'd like to take a shower. I'm really sticky from the river.

Brian laughs at me. Put your clothes down and get the fuck over here. You're not showering yet, you have to finish your job. Job? What job? There was newspaper covering the entire kitchen table with the two dead ducks on top of it. His in front of him and mine in front of an empty chair in front of our aquarium at the end of the table. There was a boning knife sitting next to my duck.

You shot your duck and you're cleaning your duck. Sit the fuck down. Right there, right now. You have to learn this if you want to survive. I'll show you how to do it. Just watch me. I didn't want to do it. I guess you can say my Chef maturity didn't kick into any type of butchery yet. I then did something I've never done before. I asked my mother to tell him no. Please tell him no mom. I don't know how to explain it because I have no problem doing that kind of stuff now. I just knew there was no way I could gut an animal when I was ten years old. It simply wasn't in me. It just wasn't. It's Unexplainable.

My mother looks at him and of course he says don't you dare baby him on this one. Make him be a man. She tried sticking up for me. Kind of. I guess. Ok if you don't do it you go to bed without dinner tonight. I was already expecting that so I was good. Ok, no dinner. I took a step to go pick up my clothes. GET THE FUCK OVER HERE AND SIT THE FUCK DOWN. You're not going to coddle this little bastard anymore Janis. He is going to sit here until it's done. I don't care how long it takes. I reluctantly sat down and he plunges his knife into the ass end of his duck. Cuts upwards and sticks his hand in the duck's ass. He yelled pay attention to how I am doing this and just do it, DO IT NOW.

I had no problem putting the knife into the duck. I had a little problem slicing into it. But I did it. It was still warm and smelled really gross to me. I couldn't bring myself to stick my hand into a dead animal. It just didn't feel right to me. I wanted to make him happy and proud of me but something in my mind wouldn't let me go through with it. I tried, I really fucking tried. The guts were all squishy and felt like wet dead worms and snakes and between the texture, the blood and the smell I couldn't do it.

He rips the rest of the guts out of his duck and slams them on the newspaper in front of me. It splashed everywhere including on my face and a little got into my mouth. Absolutely nasty to me. I stood up and almost threw up in the fish tank that was behind me, but he grabbed me and put my head over the kitchen sink. I puked up liquid and foam for just a second and spit the taste out of my mouth. He yells and pulls me back. Sit back down. Stop being such a little girl. Stick your hand in there and pull the guts out. One minute, that's all it will take, get it over with then you can take a shower and eat dinner. He just would not stop badgering me. Four hours, no break from his yelling in my face to just do it, aggravatingly spitting in my face the entire time. I'm not going to sit here and write everything that happened for the next four hours. But that's how long he made me sit there.

He finally gave up, he was livid, and he threw my duck in the trash can and told me to go to bed. No shower and don't let me catch you in the kitchen eating sometime later tonight. If I catch you, I'm telling you now, if I catch you in this kitchen you are going to get the fucking beating I should give you right now. Get the fuck out of my face.
Looks like the good times are over again. I go hunting with him one more time. Deer, not duck. Wait until you hear how much fun this trip was. To be continued.

I'm going to give you what I believe to be the main analogy for my early life really quick. To me it is definitely like riding on a see saw. Ridiculous up's and downs. Always. I guess it really just mattered who was riding on the other side of it at the time. Some people in my life played it the right way. They knew how, new the right way from the wrong way. I can say with absolute certainty that less people knew the right way than the wrong.

Let's use some examples. Example one, Gramps. Gramps gave me a chance to sit down on an even seat and to push off with my legs and shoot up with me trusting 100% that he was going to help me down. Up and down in a fluid motion. Sharing, helping, caring, loving. He understood that the use of his leverage on the other side of me is what is going to either make it easier or harder for me to push off or have a safe landing. He used his leverage to keep me safe and to make sure I wasn't stuck at the top or I didn't come down to hard and crash.

Some people tried to play the right way. Trying to be fair. They just either didn't know how to play correctly or simply lost their concentration during the game. Example two, My mother. Put my mother on the other side now. I think she tried to play right. She would start off perfect, paying attention to me and to where we were going for a little bit, but then someone else would come into the picture. Walking up to her side, and then she would pay more attention to them rather than me on the other side. She would then keep her leverage towards them, forgetting about me and leaving me hanging in the air. No matter how much my legs would flail or I would ask for her help to get my feet back on the ground. She was just to overwhelmed with trying to concentrate on both of us. And I was just simply left in see saw purgatory.

And now some people that just play the game for themselves. Not caring about fairness. Just simply out to win. Even in a game that shouldn't have a winner or loser. Example three, Brian. His game. His rules. Go ahead, get on, I got you. This is going to be fun. So, I get on. Trying to believe in him just one more time. He'll pretend to play fair for a minute. Gaining my trust. Then knowing his leverage is much greater than mine he jumps on with all of his weight and as soon as I am far enough in the air for his purposes, he then jumps off at just the right moment and lets me slam right through the ground with no compassion whatsoever. His game is rigged and all about him.

Looking back on five years with this guy. I think it's safe to say he was just a split-up personalities kind of motherfucker. You would think he was an ok guy for a while and he would just turn on you in a heartbeat. His dimmer switch was definitely broken. It was either completely on or completely off.

Let's get on with the next event on wonderful Allen Avenue. I remember the news of the day on TV that it was a few weeks before the one-year anniversary of Ronald Reagan being shot in an assignation plot. It was all over the news. It was a strange night all in all. It was late and I was at the kitchen table with Joey eating dinner. We were there for at least two and a half hours already because my mother and Brian wouldn't let us leave the table before we finished everything on our plates. We couldn't eat it though. It was liver with mushrooms and onions and every bite I tried to take I would almost vomit. Joey couldn't eat it because in his words it was an all-day chewer. He couldn't chew it enough to swallow it. It was very tough and, in my experience, now, as a chef, I would probably say it was quite overcooked. And years later we would come to realize that I am allergic to mushrooms.

We heard knocking on the door downstairs while we were still at the kitchen table. Joey yells. Mommy, Daddy Brian, someone is knocking on the door downstairs. My mother comes out of the living room and goes downstairs to open the door. I hear someone talking to her. A man, crying. I hear her say come in. Come in and talk. It will all be alright. As they got to the top of the stairs I see him going to turn the corner into the living room. He was a big guy. White T shirt all ripped up with blood and dirty clear as day perfect handprints all over it. I ask the man if he was ok. He turns his head towards me. Greg?

Now keep in mind, and I can't explain it. I didn't think about or remember at this point what he did to me three or four years prior. It simply was not in my memory banks or in my conscious mind. And I never told my mother or anyone else for that matter what he had done to me. I don't think. When he turned towards me it was very clear that he was beaten up pretty badly. Both eyes swollen and his face was quite bloody. Oh my god Greg I asked, are you ok? What happened? He said nothing, you don't have to worry about it. I'm ok. I think you and Joey should go into your room though, I have to talk to your parents. And of course, they made us do exactly that. Not that either one of us complained due to the food.

We went into my room and closed the door, but not really. I put the Atari on for Joey and turned the volume all the way down. And I kept the door open a bit to hear what they were saying, because, well, I guess I was a nosey ass kid. No real other excuse. They all sat down now at the kitchen table and my mother was making a pot of coffee. I could smell it. I heard her say I'm throwing this shit out, they're obviously not going to eat it. Brian says fine. But I'm making them the same thing tomorrow and they are going to eat every bite of it. Whatever. Dick.

Greg was still crying so his words were louder than they probably were normally. What I heard is that Greg's father had done this to him in Wawa's parking lot. From their conversation in what I understood, his father found out something he had done to somebody else and that an argument started at their home and his father tore his room apart and found something to do with pictures that he shouldn't have had.

Greg left the house in the middle of the argument with his father still going through his dresser drawers in his room. He said he had to get out of there because he knew his father was going to find something else he shouldn't have had. Greg said when he left he went straight to Wawa's and ordered a sandwich and while he was waiting for it to be made his father burst through the door and dragged him out to the parking lot and beat the ever-living shit out of him. I this point I think they either noticed that I was trying to listen, or their coffee was just simply done and they got up and moved the rest of the conversation to the living room.

They were in the living room and I could still hear muffled voices. But couldn't understand the context of what was being said. I could hear that Brian was starting to get very vocally angry though. I didn't know if it was towards my mother, Greg, Greg's dad, or someone or something else. I soon found out, or at least I think I did. About fifteen minutes into the living room conversation Brian shouted get the fuck out, you expect us to help you out with this? You expect to be able to stay here? You get the fuck out of my house now. I was very confused. I know Brian and Greg met through my mother. So, they probably only knew each other for less than a few months. I don't know exactly when they met but from my knowledge they didn't know each other in any form beforehand.

As he was walking down the stairs I could hear Greg shouting and begging my mother to get Brian to help him or someone was going to kill him. Brian showed him out of the door. He slammed the door and he came back upstairs and the fireworks began. He called my name and told me to get out of my room and to sit down at the kitchen table right the fuck now. My mother kept telling me to stay in my room. Don't come out here. You stay right there. I had no idea who to listen to or what was going on.

The fight on them asking me to come out to the kitchen shifted to them fighting and shouting at each other about Greg. Your fucking friend did this and you want me to protect him? Fuck you, I refuse. This is his problem and your problem not mine. Brian then told me to stay in my room. And close your fucking door this time. The screaming and fighting made its way back into the living room. At this point I was absolutely scared that it was me now that had done something wrong but was no longer listening and trying to block it all out in hopes that it would all just stop and go away.

All of the sudden, my mother yells my name. Victor, get out here right now. I opened the door and heard her say he would never have done that and if he did I would have known. You have no right to make assumptions about something you know nothing about. I won't lie, I had no idea what assumption meant at that time. I thought at the time it meant some kind of threats.

I started walking down the hallway and made it to the kitchen doorway. I asked if I did something wrong, my mother said no, but we need to ask you something. Out of nowhere Brian comes flying out of the living room and grabs an iron off of the ironing board and grabs my mother by the throat. He reared back and I really thought and could actually picture in my head him beating her with the point of the iron and killing her right there and then.

He looked over at me now as I'm crying and screaming please don't hit my mom with that. You'll kill her if you hit her with that. He let out a blistering holler and slammed it on the counter. Once again, I was confused. What the hell did they want from me? This is crazy. What did Greg do? Who else besides his father wants to hurt him? Brian yells at me to go back to my room again and that they would call me back out in a few minutes if they needed me. I turned around again to go back and saw a surprising look on my brothers face as he was now standing outside of his room. He yelled out my name. VICTOR!!!

I panicked. Put my hands over my head and ducked. By the look in his eyes I thought that I was going to get hit with something from behind. As I hit my knees to the ground there was a terrifying smash. Loud and muffled and sounded like glass breaking. I get up and turned around as fast as I could. I could see water run under the fridge and much more hit the door to the outside porch and splash up. I looked towards them and they were both just staring at each other. I looked down upon the kitchen floor and saw a small crab running across the room and a grouper sliding across and flapping on the tile.

I looked where the iron was put down and it was gone. I took a squishy step off of the rug and onto the now flooded tile and looked to the right. There, with the iron on the bottom slightly buried in little rocks and its cord dangling over the side. There, on the beautiful brass tank stand was a now a smashed through seventy-five-gallon salt water aquarium. I looked around to glass and little rock pebbles everywhere, crabs running over the glass and about six or so fish flapping all over the tile floor. I heard Brian say, are you happy now? You stupid bitch.

Now, listen carefully. For years I blamed Brian for this mess. I thought it was him that threw the iron. I think because of all he had done to me and my mother over the years it just made more sense in my mind that he did it. So, whenever I told the story in passing over the last couple dozen years or while hanging out with friends drinking or whatever the situation was where the story came out. It was usually just a quick story with the ending of the mess that was created as the main point. Everything else in the story were just schematics. As I have been sitting here writing and having to dig through the details out of the depths of my mind. Shit. I have been wrong about the middle of this story for my entire adult life. Lost details that I just never brought to the surface. My memory now tells me this.

I remember Brian saying, well the fish are done. Victor grab all of the towels out of the bathroom closet and bring them over here, watch out for the glass. I handed him the towels and he told me to go get mine and my brothers' shoes on. I handed him the towels and ran into Joey's room and grabbed his slippers and ran from there into my room being pretty damn happy that the water never made it that far.

As I was putting on Joey's slippers I said, that guys an ass hole huh? He said, not this time big brother, the hole in the tank belongs to our mother's ass. I asked what? He said I saw her. It was her. She threw the clothes iron thing at Brian and missed. I don't know if I just didn't believe him or I didn't care over the years, but that wasn't in my story. It wasn't in Brian's or my mother's story later in that evening as a matter of fact either, wait until you hear this bullshit.

I get done putting my shoes on and heading down the hall when the front door starts to be beat on. Hey, open the door, hey hurry up. We need your help. I hear my mother say, oh shit, someone's banging on the door downstairs. Brian grabs a baseball bat that was just inside the living room door and we all run down the stairs. The couple that live down there are scrambling. What in the hell is happening up there? Did a pipe burst or something? I ran across the porch and looked through their apartment door to see a bowl like light fixture hanging in the exact middle of their living room.

It was very dim and looked like smoked glass. There were buckets all over their living room floor with water dripping from at least six or seven spots in the ceiling. I know how that feels now. Brian runs back upstairs with the bat almost immediately as we could hear sirens getting closer and closer. My mother looks in and says that actually doesn't look that bad. The girl that lived downstairs said, oh yeah, and climbed up on a stool and pushed the light fixture ever so slightly. You could see the water pouring from each side as it tilted back and forth. It was big enough as I remember that it could probably fit at least three gallons in it. In my mind I was like, aww shit. You guys are in big trouble this time.

Brian comes back down and whispers something in my mother's ear and she starts up the stairs behind him. You stay here Victor. Watch your brother. About two minutes later a fire truck is just starting to pull up as Brian runs back out of the front door straight at me. You listen to me right now. All you have to say is you're not hurt, you're fine. Go upstairs and bring Joey to his room and put him in his bed and you go to your room. When you come out you agree with whatever I say or when they leave you're fucking done. You got it. I said yeah, yes, I got it. I asked what are you going to say? Don't worry about it and get upstairs, I don't have time right now, put your brother in his bed and go play your game.

As I am bringing Joey to his room I look over to the fish tank. The iron is now gone, get this shit. The aquarium was closer to the kitchen table now than it was before, not too far from where it was earlier but closer. When Brian called my mother up they slid it over on its stand and leaned a chair up against it with the top knob of the chair leaning into the hole. I knew it pretty quickly, and amazingly so did Joey. He laughed and looked up at me and said. Sorry man. They're going to say you did it. I said I know. This was a complete and total frame job. And we both were right.

I could hear all the commotion downstairs and then all kinds of footsteps coming up the stairs. Baby Bobby is now awake in their room, crying, probably from all the sirens. Joeys in his bed probably laughing himself to sleep now. I can hear them saying. No, he's fine. It startled the hell out of him when it broke and the cold water hit him but he's fine. We checked to make sure there were no cuts on his body and dried him off and we sent him to bed so we can clean up.

My mother went to get Bobby from his crib and she saw me looking out of the crack in my door. She made a mean face and mouthed, go lay down in your bed right now. I left the door open and shut off my Atari and my TV and laid down in bed. I could still hear everything going on even over Bobby's fussing and the police radios.
One of the officers were very skeptical. He was questioning them extensively.

The couple downstairs claimed that there was a lot of commotion and yelling up here right before it happened. Brian said yes. We were yelling at Victor at the kitchen table to do his homework. We yelled at him that he couldn't go to bed until it was done. The officer asked, he was sitting in that chair? Brian said yes. The officer asked did you push him towards the fish tank in anger and that's how it broke? No. He said. We weren't even in the room when it happened. In fact, we only made it a few steps into the living room after yelling at him when we heard the smash. That's why the yelling was so close to the water going downstairs.

My mother then said. He must have leaned back in the chair being a smart ass as soon as we left the room and lost his balance. The cop then asked one more question. The chair is awfully dry if it went through the tank that close, are you sure that's what happened? Oh yeah. We didn't throw the chair through it if that's what you're getting at my mother said. Why would we do that? Victor was on it so he must have soaked up most of the water. The officer then says I need to see Victor and Joey to make sure everyone in the house is safe. I heard a couple of seconds of complete silence.

I'm serious the officer says. My mother than says ok. But let's go into their rooms. I don't want them anywhere near the glass. They go to Joeys' room first. Joey, Joey, Joey wake up. He says leave me alone, I don't know anything, I need my beauty sleep. Go away. I hear the cop say. Ok. I guess he's fine. My door opens. The officer asks, are you ok? No cuts? I say no. He asks what happened out there. I said, exactly what they said. He said, ok. Exactly what was that? I knew better than telling the truth. I leaned back in the chair because I didn't want to do my homework and I broke the tank. It was my fault. Are you sure? Yes.

The officer looks at my mother, and she says, see, we told you. He shrugs his shoulders and says ok. Have a good night's sleep pal. They walk down the hall and Brian asks if they're done and if they can leave now so him and my mother can clean up this mess. I hear the cop take one deep breath. I know he knew I didn't do it. Alright guys, let's go. They left the apartment and I can hear their very muffled voices outside for at least twenty minutes probably talking to the downstairs neighbors. I could hear Brian as they were cleaning complaining that they still hadn't left.

As it got quieter and the sound of talking and the sound of glass going into buckets slowed to a stop. My door comes open and they're both standing there looking at me. My mother says thank you and we're sorry you had to go through all that. Brian said yeah, thanks, even though you know if it went any other way it would have been your ass. We have a surprise for you in the next couple days for doing that so get a good night's sleep. Goodnight., That was that with that. I never even found out why or how this particular night was all started. I mean I think I know, but I don't know all the facts or any of the questions they had for me. Not another word ever again about it from any of them. And I never asked. I will give you my theory on it though after an event that happened a few years later.

I am going to take some time right now to break up the monotony of fear and beatings and assholes and being hungry and all that good shit. I'm going to talk about my first taste of real freedom I actually got to experience every once in a great while. There was a couple of kids in the area. Tony and Alex that lived in an apartment complex directly behind our building. There was Jeff and Gary who were brothers and the sons of one of Brian's distant cousins. Alex and Tony were both lifelong friends of each other. Also, Francis and his sister Melanie that lived next door.

Whenever I was outside these were the kids I hung out with and I played with. Me Alex and Tony were always working whenever I could get outside. We would have five-gallon buckets and walk the railroad tracks gathering up railroad spikes and selling them to a scrap yard that was right down the street.

There was a car wash directly across route five from the bowling alley where there were four trash cans near the car vacuums and one giant dumpster where we would go over and search for returnable cans and bottles that we could cash directly on the opposite side of the bowling alley from our apartment. We would rake yards in the summer and during the winter we would walk up and down the street to shovel driveways. I learned at a young age that if I really needed or wanted something I'd better work for it. I would get what I needed from work or Gramps. That's really all I had at the time.

We would make enough money to somehow, almost daily, be able to play video games at the bowling alley arcade. Ten, Twelve, sometimes Fifteen, maybe Twenty dollars or more a day for the three of us, usually depending on how early we got started. As gramps would say we had a pretty good racket going for ourselves. Their parents weren't exactly rich either, and they definitely knew my family situation was for shit. We would usually go to the bowling alley after we cashed in all our stuff for the money and we would go grab my little brother Joey from home and all go get a hot dog for $2.00 each, share an order of fries or two for $1.50 an order, and a drink to share for another $1.00 from the bowling alley concession stand and then used the remaining cash for the video games. We definitely shared it very well.

We would sometimes stay there for hours, my mother and Brian didn't really approve of me being there, especially bringing Joey there with me. But this was my escape and the only way to keep Joey near me and away from them. And I wasn't going to give that up for any amount of threats or beatings. You could say I started my rebelling a little sooner than most. But most hadn't been through what I have. At least not any that I knew of personally.

My grandfather had bought me a bicycle for the previous Christmas. It was not to long after we moved into this apartment if my memory is correct. Waiting for the summer to come was excruciatingly painful to wait for. This is what I usually did with Gary and Jeff. There is a hill going up from our house and we used to walk our bikes half way up and coast down and hit the curb at the edge of the bowling alley parking lot for a jump. This was always fun for me. We got away with doing this for many months even though all our parents dis approved. This bicycle freedom ended abruptly pretty quickly after our friend Alex went from the top of the hill and hit the curb and crashed himself into a coma. Within a week from this crash my bicycle suddenly and conveniently was stolen from our backyard.

We did have fun though when we could. I just tried to make the best of the situations. During the winter when we weren't shoveling we would make huge forts in the bowling alley parking lot with elaborate tunnels and rooms. We would spend days on it. We would hang out in there for hours at a time. And I have to admit we would often throw snowballs at cars traveling on route five and then hide inside the tunnels. This was actually Brian's thing. I think this is what he thought of as bonding time. It helped. It was really the only time we had fun together and the only time I wasn't afraid of him.

Myself and the kid Francis and his sister would play in their back yard mostly when I wasn't with the other kids. They're parents were very elderly so they did pretty much whatever they wanted to do outside. This is when the kid in me would be able to come out. We played actual kid games. Tag, hide and seek, they had an army tent in their back yard we would lay in it and play board games. We would build snowmen and igloos in their back yard during the winter. It was a good place to hide from everyone else. They pretty much kept to themselves so being in their yard was kind of a safe space for me.

Like I said earlier, the bad really did outweigh the good. The good is here and there and not quite as clear in my mind as the bad. It is all foggy to say the least. And to me It really sucks. I remember some of the fun stuff with my brothers and a few friends. But I honestly have to say that I feel my childhood was most definitely robbed from me. Stolen or killed like my bicycle and Zane.

I need to bring some clarity to what happened next, before you even hear it. It is not something you jump in and just say out loud. I need to make sure that everyone knows basically what happened before they read it. I am not making any excuses for my actions or behavior. What I did in this period was wrong. I know it was. What I will do is tell you what are my reasonings for having this type of behavior in the first place. Up until this moment in my life I thought this behavior to be acceptable. This is me at ten years old, seeing what I've seen for the last five years, and going through some of the things that have happened to me gave me the mindset that this behavior was OK.

Let's start with something I've only talked about a few times so far. The sexual conduct that was going on around me ever since the last day of living with my father. After my mother had Joey she was quite promiscuous to say the very least. She was a beautiful girl and received an awful lot of male attention. She absolutely flaunted everything that she had too. In front of a number of people. I hate to say it. But I personally saw way more of it than I should have. I can't reiterate it any more. Way too much of it. I obviously won't get into the exact details as this was my mother and it's very uncomfortable to speak of her in this way. The only way I can explain the magnitude of what I have seen without the actual details is like this. I either saw an adults naked body, I heard some type of sexual activity in another room, or actually saw the act of sex at least five or six times a month without any question by this time.

If you couple that with what happened with me at my grandfather's house and the daughter in the mud room in Meriden a little while before. This next episode should come as no surprise to anyone.

About a week or so after the great flood, was the actual surprise they promised me for taking the rap for the aquarium. It was obviously three or so months since my birthday but I really didn't get anything at all because my mother was very pregnant and didn't have the time to do anything. So, this was mine and Joeys belated birthday party and Bobby's birth party all wrapped into one. It started out great.

Now I am only comfortable telling what had happened next because I know the girl I did it to does remember it as well. She once told her stepsister who I was seeing in my middle school years what had transpired on this day. Carol was a single mother with two children, Stephanie and Paul. I had actually met them and played with them before this day a few times. Carol was good friends with my mother and Brian and lived right around the corner and up a catwalk from my grandfather's house.

I will make this fairly quick, because as I explained earlier this is not a porno. The parents were all out in the kitchen and the kids were all in my bedroom playing Atari. One of the parents yelled to come get cake and cookies. As all of us were going towards the door. The last two were me and the girl Stephanie. I grabbed her by the arm and asked her if she wanted to go into the closet to play. She said ok and we went inside. Let's just say that while inside the closet we got semi naked and I was kissing her and touching her very inappropriately. It was only about two minutes in. The closet door blasted open and all three of the parents were standing right there glaring into the closet. The beating I received didn't go quite as quick as the dirty part of the story just went.

We got out of the closet and Carol said it was time to go. Brian pushed me into his and my mother's bedroom and grabbed the bullwhip off of the wall. My mother was telling him no, that's too much. He stood there taunting me with it waiting for the sound of the front door to close and for them to leave. Put your fucking hands under your stomach immediately you little pervert fuck. Every time they come out I am going to hit you two more times. Don't fuck with me. You've had this coming for a long time.

The door shut. Whipap, holy fuck. He hit me perfectly in the area right above my butt crack. Cross ways. My Hands come flying out. Whipap. A little lower across the width of my butt but my hand blocked some of it. I fucking told you. Put them back. NOW. I looked at my right hand where he hit it and it was bleeding straight across my palm. I put them both back under my stomach and waited for the lash.

He reared back and I could hear the whip cut through the air. My eyes were closed waiting for the slash when I felt my mother run into my leg and foot. She had grabbed Brian's arm and yelled enough. I rolled towards them still laying with my legs hanging halfway off of the bed hoping not to get hit in the face. He said fine and rolled it up and hung it back on the wall. But I'm not done with him by any fucking means. He yanked his belt off from around his waist and grabbed my mother by the face and pushed her out of the door into the hallway and closed it and locked it.

He turned towards me and I went to get into position on my stomach. He yelled fuck no and just started whaling on me like he was trying to kill me with a leather belt. This went on for a solid minute, or more. Fore hand and back hand, over and over, and a shit load more overs. You name a part of my body, he hit me on it. He beat the fuck out of me. Literally. I even tried to pretend half way through that I passed out but he just didn't stop. I really thought he wanted me dead.

My mother finally broke the door open and got him to stop. But the damage was way more than done. He ripped me up off of the floor where I was now laying curled up in a ball by my hair while I was crying my eyes out. He dragged me back into my bedroom and stuffed me in my closet. You can fucking go to sleep in here for the rest of the night you little fucker. There was plenty of room for you to try and touch that little girl like a fucking little pervert scumbag kid, then there's plenty of room for you to sleep in here. You're a fucking embarrassment to your mother and your whole family. Don't you let me see you leave this fucking closet. If I see you at all I will beat your ass with that whip twice as bad as I did with that belt. I will beat you into a bloody fucking pulp. Don't you think for a second that I won't. If you come out of there at all, your mother, nor anybody else in this fucking world is going to stop me from fucking your entire shit up. He slammed the door.

I could hear him as he was walking away that if my mother or Joey tried to help me in any way he would stuff them in the closet too and we could all stay in there together. I just laid in there crying, and thinking about how they are always doing sexual stuff around us. I was trying to wrap my mind around why what I just did was so wrong? Why was it so bad that I deserved to be beaten the way I just was?

Brian was yelling from inside the kitchen that he had to go to Carols house and find a way to apologize for what I just did. My mother asked him if she could bring me a blanket and a pillow and he told her no. He can use the clothes that are in there. He gets nothing for the rest of tonight. He has to learn, and if you give him anything he will think he can do something like this again. To hell with that fucking kid. I am calling for him to go to military school on Monday. He's done. He's gone. He is not staying here with us any longer. As soon as he heals up you can say goodbye. He then stormed out of the door.

I could hear my mother open my bedroom door about a minute later, she walked in and opened up the closet door. I could never forget the look on her face when she saw me. She just said oh my god. Are you going to be ok? Does anything feel like it's broken? I said I don't think so but I do have a lot of cuts. I need to go to the hospital mom. Please. I saw Joey behind her and he was staring at me crying his eyes out. He asked if he could go get a washcloth to clean up my cuts. To my surprise she said no. If Brian finds out or notices he's been cleaned up he will lose his mind and hurt us too. Let's just give him time to calm down after he gets back. My mother told Joey to just go into the living room and watch TV. I told him thank you for trying to help and that he could bring my Atari into the living room and play it there if he wanted to. So, he did.

My mother left for a couple minutes to help Joey set up the game in the living room. She then went into the kitchen and made me a peanut butter and mayonnaise sandwich and a cup of fruit punch. She came into my room and said I had to try to eat something and we had to talk. Don't ask. Peanut butter and mayonnaise sandwiches were just one of her things. Maybe because she was pregnant all of the damn time. Who knows.

Hurry up and try to eat that before he gets home. She started talking to me. She explained to me that she realized I have seen a lot of things in my life that have never been explained to me and that I cannot act on some of those things I have seen and why. As she's explaining the do's and do nots, Joey being Joey pops his head around the corner. Hey mom? Don't you think daddy Brian or maybe Gramps should have told him all this stuff before? She says yeah, probably. He says, well I don't need them to tell me anything. I just learned it all from a girl. She smiles and says, go in the living room I'll be in there in a few minutes.

I explain to her that I was sorry and I really thought it was what you were supposed to do with girls and thanked her for telling me. You're a little late mommy, but thank you. She took some clothes and a sheet down from the closet shelf and made me a little bed in the closet, she said just pretend you are camping for the night. I know you are hurting and I am sorry you just had to go through that. Everything will be better tomorrow. I'll try to talk to him. Do I really have to go to military school? I don't want to leave you Joey or Bobby alone with this animal. He will kill one of you if I'm not here to take his anger out on. She started balling her eyes out. She said that I would probably be better off away for a while. We'll see what happens Monday.

I tried to eat and take a few sips of my juice but my lips were bloody and very swollen. I told her I couldn't eat it and I asked her straight up why she just doesn't leave him. She made the excuse that in his head he was brought up this way and he thinks it's the right thing to do when someone disobeys the rules. I looked at her and said. I just thought that what I was doing was right? I know it was wrong now. But look what happened to me. How is that fair and why does nobody punish him for being wrong? I said I'm sorry mom. But I don't think what he just did to me was right. I received no answer. She took the sandwich and the drink and that was all I heard from anyone else for the rest of that night.

I was in my room healing for more than a few weeks. My grandfather called up to come get me the very next weekend and they told him I had caught bronchitis from the kids being here the weekend before and that I couldn't go. I guess he bought it because he never saw me in that condition. I was a swollen beaten mess for quite a while. Sore all over my entire body. Here's the kicker. This was the first, I'll say, REAL BEATING of many that would come just like this one. I've gotten quite a few spankings before this but this was a different beast all together. But as long as my grandfather, uncle Bob or my aunt Debbie didn't see what was happening to me. Nobody else seemed to give a single solitary fuck.

I constantly asked myself. When the fuck are the cops going to come save me and put this violent alcoholic prick away? They really should have been called by someone by now, at some point, but they never were, way too many times to count. And I'm not saying that I didn't deserve something for what I did with that girl, but, once again these people made me like this and a beaten like that to a ten-year-old kid from a thirty year old grown ass man is completely fucking unacceptable. A spanking? Fine. Corner kneeling on rice? Fine. No dinner? Fine. A beating like the one I just took? Not fucking fine. Not one bit.

Here's the problem. The argument if you will. I hate to admit it because the beating did teach me never to do that again. I learned that day that no matter what I see around me. That behavior was obviously much worse than my brain at the time had computed it to be. Even more than the talk with my mother that clarified what I did was a NO-NO. To get a beaten like that taught me that what I did was not going to be tolerated in any way. And the fact that I was beat up like that made me think that if no one feels bad that I got messed up like this than I definitely did something I should never do again. And I never did. I didn't touch another girl in that way for many years and even with my first few girlfriends it was only kissing. I knew NO MEANS NO way before it was a thing.

OK. No more sexual stuff until I actually start getting some when I'm at a more appropriate age. I'm not going to tell you every time I saw a sexual act around me or someone naked or anything else in that category for now. And I'm not going to tell you when I started or how many times I whacked it in my life. That's another book altogether. Not that the sexual misconduct stopped happening in front me or around me. But now that I've learned what I've learned, the sexual stuff no longer had the impact that it had before this. The abuse did. So that's now my focus.

So back to some more of my wonderful amazing youth. About a month had passed since the closet incident. I know this because it was the very last snowfall at the very ending of that winter. And in between the closet and this next episode is pretty much a blank besides healing from the beating. Probably just doing all the stuff I laid out before. Cans, Igloos, arcade, hiding outside, etc. etc. I obviously never got dragged away to military school. Maybe he forgot because it took so long for me to heal and he couldn't send me there in the condition that he caused me to be in.

On this day I remember there was a big-time event that was an all of a sudden thing. Quite literally all of a sudden. There was no notice whatsoever. I was woken up out of a dead sleep in the middle of the night. I looked up and there was Brian. He said, get up, get dressed really warm and come with me. I honestly thought I was having a nightmare. I looked at the wall hoping I would just wake up for real and he would go away. He shook me again. Come on. I really need you to come with me. I got up and got dressed. I went out into the kitchen and remembered from the day before that Brian was all set to go on a hunting trip that morning. And I was all set to not have to deal with this guy around all day. I remember how stoked I was in bed thinking about it the night before that he wouldn't be around at all. It's so funny how quickly my plans always seemed to change in an instant.

Brian exclaimed. I need you to come hunting with me. I remember looking around for my mother. I thought to myself, FUCK NO. Does she even know about this? He said I really need you. Please. You will be doing me a huge favor. I won't try to make you gut anything or skin anything or anything like that. I just really need your help because the person that was supposed to come with me isn't answering their phone. I felt a mix of things. Obviously, first, he's going to kill me, and this is just the set up. That's what was in my mind on that. Next, if I do him this favor maybe he'll be nicer to me and it will make my mother and my little brothers happier.

Being me. I just went along. Ok, I said, let's go. Like I had a choice anyway. We drive out into the woods, basically the same area as the ducks. He pulls his tree stand out of the trunk of the car. He says get the guns. Follow me. I felt better knowing I had the guns in my hands and not in his. But at the same time, I was thinking he had me carry them to try to gain my trust and he will kill me later. We walked a couple of miles into the woods and he stops. He looks down and there were deer hoof prints in the dirt. He shows me what they look like and says this is the perfect spot. We'll set up right here.

He said you wait right there and just keep your eyes open and if you see anything don't yell. Just try to get my attention quietly. He climbed the tree like a monkey man and set up his tree stand. He sat up there for about twenty minutes just scanning through the woods. He comes down and loads up the guns and he handed me the twenty gauge, then he very quietly tells me like this.

I want you to go to the left a little and walk quietly till you hit a road. You will see the guard rails if you go the right way. When you hit the road, I want you to walk fifty feet to the right and zig zag back towards me. If you see the deer pull your gun up slowly and point it just like you did with the duck last time. Remember to breath out while taking the shot. You got this. If you don't see them that means you will be scaring the deer right in my direction and I will kill one from my tree stand. You got it? Yeah. I got it.

I take the gun and walk almost all the way to the road. I didn't walk all the way because I saw a few cars drive by and I didn't want anyone to see me by myself with a shotgun in the woods. I walked to the right about twenty-five steps. I figured in my head that every step was about two feet. I took a few steps back towards the street when I saw no cars around and started to zig zag my way back.

I thought I was doing exactly what he told me to do. I still do. I counted my steps twenty-five to the right twenty-five to the left. In between I walked forward ten steps. He didn't tell me how far to zig zag, he didn't tell me to walk on an angle, he told me to zig zag my way back to where he was.

I was walking back and forth for about ten minutes when I hear a bunch of rustling to my left and what sounded like in front of me a bit. I tried to go back towards the road just a little to try to get around the noise I heard because I thought if they were deer moving in this direction would push them closer to Brian or let me get a bead on them and shoot one myself. I returned to zig zagging towards where I thought Brian was and the tree stand was set up but I think I lost count of my steps when I got excited thinking I was close to the deer.

I walked slowly and quietly, everything around me was quiet. I was expecting to hear the gun shot any second now and the closer I thought I was getting the more nervous I got that this was something else. My mind started racing about Zane out in the woods and Brian killing him somewhere out here. I started thinking I was sure that the deer were forced towards him and he didn't shoot at them because the plan the entire time was to shoot and kill me. My mother didn't even know I was with him. She was still sleeping when we left.

I was feeling that I was really close now. This is the area that we were in when I left. I look up into the trees and I spot the deer stand, it's empty. I look around for a second pointing the gun towards the ground like I was always told to do, when all of the sudden Brian comes flying around the corner of this huge tree to my right, pointing the shotgun directly at my face, I close my eyes knowing he's going to shoot me before I even have a chance to bring my gun up. I'm burnt fucking toast, this is it, my mother, my brothers, Gramps, Zane, my friends, my life, everything zipped through my head with incredible speed just waiting for the sound of the shotgun and for it to all be over. When they say in the face of death your life flashes before your eyes they are not at all joking. It honestly does. It wasn't the first time this happened to me and it sure as fuck wasn't the last either. It is a very helpless hopeless feeling.

I opened my eyes just in time to see him take his last step towards me, I saw his boot dig into the ground and as I looked up he reared back with his shotgun and hit me square in the middle of my chest as hard as he could with the butt end of the gun. My gun fired into the ground and I felt every ounce of breath I had leave my lungs as I dropped it. I hit the ground on my back and scratched at my chest trying to get some air into them. Gasping and clawing thinking he burst open both my lungs and I would never be able to catch another breath ever again and die right there.

As soon as I hit the ground he was standing over me with the shotgun once again pointing the barrel directly into my face. Again, I thought he was going to pull the trigger. At that exact second, I really wished he did. The pain and the burning sensation I felt trying to breath was the worst thing I ever felt in my life up till then, I simply wanted that feeling to be over and to be able to breath. It was honestly worse than almost drowning to death. Worse than the whip and worse than the belt. The muffed sound of his voice screaming over me started to become clearer and clearer as I was gasping for any kind of air.

I should fucking kill you, you didn't listen to a word I fucking said. Come here. He threw his shotgun next to where mine laid. He then reached down and grabbed me by the front of my sweater and ripped me off the ground like I was a rag doll. I felt my back bend and crack in a way it definitely shouldn't have. He grabbed me by my hair and stood me upright. As soon as my feet hit the ground he let go of my sweater but kept the handful of my hair and started dragging me through the woods. The grasping of the hair was definitely one of his favorite moves but my mother would never allow me to cut it. Maybe she wanted a little girl. Who the fuck knows.

Still trying desperately to catch a full breath as he is pulling me behind him while my hands are now clenched onto his wrists trying to take the pressure off of my head. After a full few minutes of this he tosses me to the ground and grabs me with both hands by my head. He turns my face towards the ground and puts me on all fours and screams, LOOK, LOOK AT THOSE, WHAT DO YOU SEE? I force the words out of my lungs. They are hoof prints. He lifts me up with one hand grasping my hair again and points to the road. WHATS THAT? OVER THERE? I say, the road. He screams in my face. THEY WE'RE RIGHT FUCKING HERE THE WHOLE TIME BEFORE YOU FUCKED UP AND SCARED THEM THAT WAY.

I was waiting for the punch, or him hitting or kicking me to start, but it didn't. He turned my head again. I want you to look at that, do you see that? What is that? I didn't know what it was he wanted me to look at so I said what, I don't see what you mean, I'm sorry, I didn't mean to mess up. He yelled that, that right there. On the ground. Just as I noticed what he was talking about he angrily sighed, Ahhhhh, go fuck yourself kid. He dragged me about five feet with my head facing towards what he wanted me to see. I yelled out, I SEE IT, I SEE IT NOW. ITS POOP, ITS DEER POOP.

He dragged me down and put my face right above it and I was expecting him to shove my face in it but he reached down and grabbed a handful of shit and smushed it into my face. There you go you little prick, do you see it now? Do you? You fucking see it now? I cried out, yes, I see it. Please stop, I see it. He yells I'll stop when I'm good and fucking ready to stop. He pushes me with his foot to the side and starts to walk away towards where the tree stand was. It took me a minute or so to get up to my feet. By that time, I couldn't see him anymore. I walked towards where I thought the tree stand was for about fifteen minutes or so crying and wondering how in the fuck this has become my life.

I finally reached where he was and he was just standing there with the guns in his arms staring at me. He walked away and leaned my gun against a tree about ten feet away. He pointed to the base of the tree with the tree stand in it and ordered me to sit down behind it and then he climbed back up. Don't you move and don't you make a fucking sound. I sat there. I didn't make a sound. He was up there for hours, I can't say for sure how many but it was a long time. The entire time he was up there I just stared at the gun leaning against the tree wishing I had the guts to go for it and shoot him right out of that fucking tree. But I didn't. Obviously.

He finally yelled at me to move and started taking apart the tree stand. I should drop this fucking thing right on your head you little fucking piece of shit. He came down and said I should make you carry this fucking thing back to the car all by yourself. But your father and your stupid fucking mother raised a little pussy and I know you can't. He then told me to grab my gun. You point that thing towards the ground and you follow me. You walk quietly behind me and you keep your eyes on the back of my fucking head. If I turn my head and point somewhere you aim your gun there and look at what I am pointing at. If you see anything moving you shoot it. I have to carry this fucking stand and my gun so you have to do it. And if you miss something you shoot at it's your ass.

I didn't understand any of this logic at the moment. This guy just beat my ass and shoved deer shit in my face. Why in the world would he think I wouldn't shoot him in the back of his head. We continued to walk when all of a sudden something in my brain snapped and told me that this was my only chance, you have to shoot this cocksucker, but what if you miss? You can't miss from this close Victor. Shoot him. But you're so close you can't say it was a mistake. But this is the only way out, I can get away with this, I can't get away with this, can I? look at me, I'm all beat up, dirty, shit on my face, they will believe me, I have witnesses as to what he has done to me in the past. You can't shoot him in the back of the head though, he has to be facing you for self-defense. You're only ten. How long will you possibly have to go to juvie anyway? Until you're eighteen? He's going to try to send you to military school someday anyways. It's worth it to never have to see him again. But you'll go to hell and burn forever. Is that worth it? To hell with that. God will forgive me if he sees everything this scumbag has put me through. SHOOT HIM, SHOOT HIM, FUCK HIM, SHOOT HIM.

I'm still walking behind him staring at the back of his head, it's cold outside but I am sweating like its one hundred degrees out there, my stomach is turning, I feel like I need to throw up, my mind is racing uncontrollably, I feel sick, my legs are rubbery, the gun feels like it was a thousand pounds, my arms are rubber, can I even lift the shotgun up? is this a dream? It feels like I am in a dream. Everything around my entire body feels like it's in a cloud, my mother and my brothers will never have to go through anything like him again. I lift my shotgun up, shaking like I've never shaken before. Thinking he could actually hear the gun rattling because I was shaking so much. I was afraid that

I would miss. But. HEY BRIAN!!! He turns towards me with no expression at all. I aim perfectly and directly at his face. CLICK? He didn't even flinch. NO. I take two steps backwards and slide the pump, nothing comes out. CLICK? NO, NO, PLEASE GOD NO. PLEASE GOD HELP ME.

His expression didn't change one bit as he let his gun and the tree stand drop to the ground in super slow motion and started towards me. I fully expected to see his head split apart when I pulled that trigger. Well I guess this is not a dream. He snatched the gun from my hands and turned and threw it over near the rest of the stuff. He turned back around towards me and open handed hit me on my left ear so hard I thought my brains were going to squirt out of the right side of my head. I could barely hear him over the ringing in my ears and I saw my first stars ever in my life. Now I know what the cartoons were trying to show me.

I knew it, I fucking knew it he yelled in my face. I didn't think you had the balls but I knew you wanted me dead. I can't wait to tell your fucking mother you actually have a set of balls up in there somewhere. He then reached in his pocket and pulled out a handful of green shotgun shells. He started counting them out loud as he was chucking them at my head. I knew they were from my gun because his were red. He must have taken them out and hid them in his pocket when I was walking back from the deer shit incident. Two, Three. Go ahead. Pick them up. Go for your gun. I fucking dare you. Come on. Four, Five. Go for it punk, yeah, that's what I thought.

He had me carry that fucking gun on purpose to see if I would do it. He said there's no doubt in his mind that I'm going to kill someone in my life. You're too much of a pussy to take any sort of beating, discipline or authority. He was all types of giddy about it. Once again, he stated. I can't wait to tell your mother. We are going to have to call the police on you for this you know. You tried to kill me. What you just tried to do is attempted murder. He turned away laughing to himself, this little fucker actually tried to shoot me. He stopped at the tree stand and guns and turned around smiling from ear to ear. He said you'll have plenty of time to think about what you just did before you go to jail because your skinny ass is walking all the way home. And I wouldn't stop at a payphone if I were you and try to get a ride from someone because the cops will probably be looking for you.

He gathered up everything and he just simply walked away. I sat down and leaned myself up against a tree and stayed there for what seemed like hours. Probably because it was hours! I just don't know how many. My chest hurt really bad, my ear and the side of my face were throbbing like crazy, it was cold and only getting colder, I had dried up deer poop all over my face and I could still smell and taste it. And all I had ate or drank all day "Besides deer poop" was a hostess apple pie and a pint of chocolate milk like eight hours ago on the way there, so I was very hungry, at least I think I was. I remember that my stomach felt like it was completely empty. But I guess It could have just been a ten-year old's ulcer. Maybe, or hunger, who knows?

I stayed there processing all that had just happened. Not really focusing on the cold or being that hungry, I was more freaking out thinking that he was going to come back here and find me and kill me, or the police would have me surrounded at any second now and drag me off to jail. I stayed there until a little while after dark. I don't think I noticed the sun going down or that it started lightly snowing out of nowhere. I thought to myself if they were going to come get me they would have been here by now. I stood up and just headed in the direction that Brian went. I was lucky in the fact that the moon was almost full and there was a tiny bit of snow on the ground. It was really scary but I could see all around me just fine. It was like someone out there wanted to give me some extra light to guide me in the right direction.

I found my way out of the wooded area pretty quickly, and I knew my way home once I hit the dump and the dog pound. It was about three and a half miles from home I believe. I made it about a half a mile when I heard a car screaming behind me and headlights coming up fast and screeching to a halt. I could see in the car that it was my mother driving and I could see Joey peaking over from behind the front seat. My mother jumps out and screams WHERE THE FUCK HAVE YOU BEEN? I was extremely cold at this point, extremely tired and extremely pissed as I was standing there, so I guess you could say I had developed a little bit of an attitude in that moment. I WAS IN THE DAMN WOODS WAITING FOR THE POLICE, WHERE DID YOU THINK I WAS? WALKING IN CIRCLES AROUND THE DUMP LOOKING FOR FOOD?

Of course not she said, stop being a smart ass or that's exactly what you'll be doing, you're in big time trouble mister. Let's get in the car and get you home. I say where's Brian? He's home with Bobby, just get in the fucking car, NOW. He's not going to do anything else to you, don't worry, he thinks it's funny. FUNNY? Really? If there was a shell in that gun he would be dead, how is that funny? She says, but there wasn't so everything's ok. Did he call the cops on me? Am I going to jail? No, he's not going to call the cops. Don't worry, let's go. So, I get into the car. Joey looks at me from the back seat and asks, did you really try to shoot daddy Brian. I looked at my mother and asked why would guys talk about that stuff in front of him. Joey says, they didn't, they tried to talk quietly. Brian came home and told me to go to my room. I knew something was up so I pretended to go in there but snuck closer and I heard everything. Isn't that what you do?

Sooo, did you? Yeah but there were no shells in the gun. He would have deserved it I said. Joey leans forward and says, Wow, you’re fucking crazy dude. My mother back hands him back into the seat. He didn’t miss a beat. Did he really shove deer poo in your face and that's why you tried to do it? I said not just that, look at me. He beat the hell out of me in there. My mother says he never told me that. He said you walked past the deer and scared them away so he got mad and wanted to make sure you knew what it looked like and just got carried away a little. I explained to her what really happened, but, I begged her and Joey not to mention it to him. I didn't want him to go off the handle on anyone else. They both agreed and Joey said to me. I'm sorry there were no bullets in that gun, I think you're right. He would have deserved it. You just don't put animal poo on other people's faces. That's just groody dude. It was kind of funny the way he said it. I just couldn't laugh.

We got home and I went upstairs and he was sitting on a chair right past the doorway. Hey killer, what took you so long? Did you go and try to kill someone else? My mother told him to knock it off and I was waiting for the explosions. He looked at me and asked if I had eaten yet. I said no. Where was I going to eat? He looked at my mom and said make this kid something to eat. He'll never be able to kill anyone if he's that skinny. He thought this was funny, some kind of joke, I guess it was over. I washed myself up and ate dinner and I don't remember if we ever really spoke of it again. It's simply fucking amazing how that seemed to always happen that way. THE UNSPOKEN. Maybe that's what I'll name this first book.

Well, I would hope you could guess this but I never went hunting with Brian again. Fishing two or three times but never hunting. There were a few more episodes while we still lived here through the next year or so but nothing that hugely affected my life the way this next one did. There were a few more beatings and explosive days but nothing there in my mind that would help me really remember the reasons why. So, no real reason to talk about them

. This next and last episode from Allen avenue affected my little brothers lives a little more than mine I think. I was the one that started it and ended up getting hurt from it but it was all my fault anyway and had nothing to do with my mother or Brian except the fact that they left me at eleven years old watch over a six-year-old and a one year old.

Those ages are a little bit deceiving because it was around September. It only snowed once so far in this year so I figured it to be around that time. Give or take a month. Here's what I did, and it won't take too long. After the attempted murder fields, I was our substitute babysitter for most of the days. My mother and Brian would both leave after we left for school and Bobby had a babysitter during the day. When we got home Bobby's babysitter would pretty much just up and leave us alone to our own devices.

On this specific day, and don't ask me why. We were playing hide and go seek and tag for a while throughout the apartment. At some point I had this big Idea that I would make the game more interesting by handing Bobby a knife and smacking him around a little to piss him off and then having him chase us around with it. He surprisingly remembers this day very well. I dared him to try to stab me with it and taunted him that he couldn't catch me and cut me. At one point me and Joey were taking pillows and putting them in front of us and having Bobby throw the knives at us and we would block them with the pillows. The amazing thing about this is that even though it ended badly for me it wasn't the last time we did this.

This went on for a while on this day and at one point we put Bobby in my room with the biggest knife in the house laying in front of him on the floor. I stood him against the far wall and I stood by the bedroom door and said when I close this door you can grab the knife and come after us. I closed the door. Joey ran first and got out in front, I waited a second and waited until he opened the door. He opened the door and as he got a little closer he lunged at me. I going to get you this time asshole. The look on his face told me he might actually do it. I ran away from him as fast as I could hoping he wouldn't throw it at my back.

Now there used to be a screen door to the back porch, but it wasn't there anymore, Brian had ripped it off in a tantrum a few months earlier.

The regular door was wide open because we were all hot and sweating from running around the house like maniacs for a few hours. I saw Joey pop his head from the living room where he was now hiding, and I wanted to keep Bobby with me because if Joey got hurt it would be my ass. I looked once more behind me and Bobby was way closer than I thought he was. I took a sharp left and vaulted myself over the rail of the upstairs porch and down I went.

On my way over, at least in my mind, I was going to land on my feet and roll forward, you know, like in the movies, and everything would be just fine. I would get up brush off and walk away. How wrong was I? I did land on my feet, still facing straight just the way I pictured it. But instead of landing and rolling forward my knees slammed really hard into my chest and I crumbled like an aluminum can. Just like getting hit in the chest with the butt of Brian's gun, I couldn't breathe at all. On my side in the fetal position tears streaming from my eyes gasping for air. Again.

I finally got enough breath in me to roll a little more to my back and I looked up. Joey and Bobby were standing there laughing their asses off. Joey yelled down, did that hurt dude? I couldn't answer him at all. That looked like it really hurt dude. He says you probably should have let him catch you. Did you break anything? I tried to say my ribs but the words wouldn't come out. I heard Joey tell Bobby to put the knife away and that he'd be right back. Joey came down the stairs and stood there with me for a few minutes. Should I call an ambulance? No, no, no, I'll be ok. I just couldn't breathe for a few minutes.

I finally got to my feet. They hurt, bad. My ribs hurt, again, and my knees hurt. Joey looks at me and says see, the hell with daddy Brian always picking on you for being so skinny. If you were a fat guy that would have hurt a lot worse. You'd be in China right now. Let's clean up this mess before they get home and never speak of this ever again. Like I said, the kid was smart. I ate all of the pain never checking to see if anything was broken. It was sore and it hurt bad for a long time but Brian and my mother finding out would hurt way fucking worse. We cleaned everything up and Bobby and Joey kept the secret from them, for a few years anyways. Bobby told the story later, but by that time it was so long ago, no one cared and it was treated like a joke.

Life went on, we stayed there for only a few months after I jumped the rail. I don't remember any other real important events that happened there. It was time to go. Wharton brook drive, get ready baby, here we come.

◆ ◆ ◆

PART SEVEN – MEET YOUR NEW FRIENEMIES

I'm going to try to paint a picture for you. Before I can explain to you the story of living in this neighborhood I want to try to give you the layout. It was a very self-contained neighborhood and we mostly stuck to our own with a few outsiders coming and going. It was known to everyone in town as The Wallingford Projects. Let me make something very clear. There have been many debates and arguments that they weren't considered a "Project" by some because it was primarily white people. To all of you people that argued against this fact. Fuck off. You always argued from outside of the neighborhood, you would never say that shit on the inside. And if you did you usually left with some stitches.

Most of us there were poor as dirt, not a pot to piss in for a lot of us. And even though we really didn't have shit there. We had each other. There were fights there almost daily with some of the toughest people I ever met in my life. Plenty of stabbings, all of the drugs you could possibly want, and alcoholism rampant from top to bottom. But all of this didn't mean we had to destroy our neighborhood just to be certified a project. Sorry if we kept our neighborhood nice and clean and didn't shoot at each other for a dime bag of weed. It did happen at times. But we were mostly civilized. Mostly.

We fucked plenty of shit up in our time there. But what we had there was pride in what little we did have in that neighborhood, and we were all in this mess together instead of stealing and robbing from each other. Not many from the outside came in and fucked with us I will tell you that. And when they did they were usually the ones being carted out in an ambulance It will always be the projects to me and mine. A lot of us were a huge part of each other's family's and lives. Sorry if we didn't meet some of the other fools' criteria for a ghetto project because we were mostly white boy's in Wallingford CT.

Just driving down this street for the first time was very exciting. There were kids of all ages all the way down the road. As you drive around the first corner up a driveway on the hill to the right there is Fairview dairy, you can pull up into one side of the driveway and down and out of the other. Behind the dairy there is a path to Pat wall field. Driving past the Dairy to the right is an elder community. Across the street on your way by and then on both sides for about an eighth of a mile there were multiple unit apartment buildings.

You then pass over a small bridge overlooking the brook. Three more multiple unit buildings to the left and one more to the right and a wraparound street also on the right called Louis Circle that horseshoes and spits out of the other side still on Wharton Brook.

Past the three last multiple units on the left, and the entrance of Louis circle and the one multiple unit on the right, still on Wharton brook drive, there were the duplexes, three duplexes down on the left hand side and four on the right side . On the left-hand side was our new home with a catwalk directly next to it that went up and around behind our apartment into a more upscale neighborhood.

Right past the brook, behind all the buildings all the way up to the catwalk on the right side of the street were "The Canyons" About a two square mile patch of woods that separated all the other neighborhoods around from ours. You will hear a lot more about this area throughout my story.

Across the street from our building were the three duplexes going to the exit of Louis circle. In the very middle of the Louis circle horseshoe was The Steps. It was a set of stairs that went down to a path that lead to Lyman Hall High School. On the right of the path was the high school football field. And to the left was a patch of woods that went from the steps to the school. A little larger than the football field itself.

At the end of the path straight ahead and a little to the right was the school. Huge. One floor. All the way to the right around the school was the front of the school. And To the left of the path is a huge parking lot in the back. Going around the high school either way are more paths going to Dag Hammerschold middle school and E.C Stephens elementary school.

Coming out of the exit of Louis circle, to the right was still Wharton brook and driving straight ahead was Tremper drive. It went up and wrapped around to the right and past the other end of Wharton brook drive. Tremper drive kept going for about another mile and ended at long hill road. Now back to passing Wharton Brook on Tremper. If you take a right onto Wharton Brook from Tremper towards Louis circle you will pass the high school to the left and on the right were a line of houses and a few more duplexes to the corner of Wharton Brook, Louis circle and Tremper drive.

I'm sorry about all that and I tried to make it as un confusing as possible. If it gets too much and you want a better picture. Or if it becomes important to you to get a clearer picture. You should google earth that shit. Keep in mind that housing developments destroyed our canyons. So, when looking down at the multiple unit buildings on the left past the brook. Behind that was the canyons. I almost cried when I found out they bulldozed it for more construction. We all had so many memories there. Let's get on with them.

When we first moved in it was total chaos, these were Brian's stomping grounds. He knew almost everyone in the neighborhood. His sister Denise, Aunt Dee, lived two duplexes down towards where the brook is on the same side of the street. She was married to Bob, uncle Bob two, he had his own nicknames for me, Weictor Agee. Or Hector Agee. Don't ask. They had four girls. Kimberly, Heidi, Jill and Melissa. In the same duplex but separate apartment was Brian's brother Ronnie, uncle Ron, his wife was Beverly, aunt Bev. They had three girls. Lynn, Vicky and Samantha. They were a huge part of my entire time living here.

In between our duplexes were the Cases, Michelle was the biggest factor in my life for a while so we'll stick with just her from that family for now. The Sepulveda's. Julie was my babysitter so we'll concentrate on just her for now. In our duplex, in the right door, were the Sabatucci's. I'm sure I'll get to them.
These were the people that were around us the most when we first moved in, and helped us to get settled in even though the process of settling in was very unsettling. It was a madhouse to say the least.

So like I just said, madhouse, madness, complete and udder chaos. I'm not going to get into the whole moving in process. It was too much to take in then and way too much to sort through now. What I can start with is this. What I considered to be the best part of the move. Even though there was a lot going on, and this atmosphere was where I thought Brian would probably get stressed out and snap. He didn't. We went a few months without any aggressive alcoholic or violent episodes.

In the beginning living here for the first few months were awesome. Brian quit drinking for a while and was working landscaping every day, when he wasn't working he was in the yard making the outside of our apartment look amazing. My mother worked for a nice upscale restaurant and things were going very smoothly. We actually had food all the time in this period. Me and my brothers had three pretty much full-time babysitters that would watch us sometimes two at a time from almost as soon as we moved in. Julie S. And Annie Case from next door and Christine Meager from one house up across the street. They were all awesome.

Looking back, I credit Brian's new-found attitude to now being around his friends and family, and with a new son, and he was trying desperately to prove to everyone around him that he had changed for the better. No one knew what was going on for the last two years and I was told straight from the get go that when we got there to keep my mouth shut. I listened. No reason to say anything, things are going great and there was no reason to cause any static.

A quick apartment layout. And when I talk about being in anyone else apartment in the neighborhood, it's exactly the same in each and every one. With one exception. They are perfectly flipped from the left apartment to the right. Looking at the building from the street there is a walkway straight up the middle to the steps There is a patch of grass on each side for our front lawns about thirty feet by thirty feet squared. On each side of our lawns were our driveways. Enough room for at least two cars each.

Going up the walkway to four steps going up to a porch about eight feet in width with two doors in the middle. Ours was on the left. You walk into the front door into a mud room. Only about three foot by three foot with a door to the left. You open that door into the living room. As soon as you walk through the front door, if you turn to the right there is a cubby to the immediate right with enough room for a regular size oval or rectangle kitchen table. Walking straight ahead past the cubby to the right and the living room to the left is the doorway to the kitchen.

Immediately through the kitchen doorway to the left is the basement. Full size, same as the apartment. Walking through the kitchen straight ahead is the door to the back yard. It was a big back and side yard. We'll get back to that. Returning to the front door. Standing with your back to the cubby next to that door straight ahead is the living room. Also, good size. Walk through it and take a right there is a bedroom just off of a stairway going to the upstairs. This downstairs bedroom was mine.

Walking out of my bedroom door and taking an immediate left was upstairs. At the top of the stairs is a small hallway, to the right is my parents' bedroom, straight ahead at the top of the stairs was a small closet, to the left a few steps straight ahead was the bathroom and standing outside of that doorway to the left was Bobby and Joey's bedroom. Once again, I hope it wasn't too complicated. I'm positive this information will come in handy through this entire chapter.

Living here at first like I said was an extreme one hundred and eighty degree turn. My mother was happy, Brian was being on his best behavior, my brothers seemed to be loving all the extra space, especially in the yards, and even more now with all the kids around. All kinds of kids, all ages. If you couldn't find at least a dozen friends in the confines of this neighborhood around your age within a few weeks? You probably had cooties.

I started with basically hanging out with my new-found cousins. I had only met a handful of them in the past at birthday parties or what not. All it would take is walking through one-yard front or back and we could all play together. Within a week or two I met Jesse and Corey Thompson. They had two younger brothers Jimbo and Benny. Me and Joey and the Thompson brothers became friends almost automatically. And right up until now. They introduced me to Pete Dunebietta. Alex, Efrain and Robert Vasquez, Dave Zocco, Daryl, Michael and Eddie Nielander. Rick Warner. A bunch more that will be mentioned later I'm sure. And I knew a kid living here already from a few years ago named Mike Lazzarro because his sister Stephanie used to babysit me at my Gramps's house.

The big thing in this neighborhood was bikes, BMX bikes. Now the Vasquez's lived on Louis circle and Mike lived across the street from the Thompson's. Directly behind their apartment complex was the canyons. And the canyons were the shit. There was a path cut out next to their complex that went into the mouth of the woods. The first time walking in I heard, and then saw my first live dirt bike in action. The kid riding it sped by waving, then put his hand on the throttle and hit a jump and just flew through the air like a bird. Jesse looked at me and said, that's Mike Nielander. He the best on any bike of anyone around here. I was in love with this place immediately. It really sucked that my bike was stolen.

We walked into the mouth and as far as you could see were Giant boulders, trees and trails cut in between it all. Bike trails zigging and zagging in between massive trees and smaller trees alike. Trails, hills and jumps everywhere. They told me that they have been working on them for many years. This was my new home. This is what I have been waiting for my entire life. Friends everywhere and a place to hang out and have a little extra freedom from the monotony of being at home.

I can't say I made friends with all the kids here right off the bat, I was a bit stranger than most kids, you could definitely say I was a bit awkward from what I have been through. So, I can't lie, I got picked on by some of them quite a bit. The friends I did make were mostly from the poorer, single mother / alcoholic or druggie absent father type families who didn't have much growing up. And I would never put anyone down for that. The one thing I can say is that most of the parents there did all they could do to keep their kids safe and happy. They worked with what they had. Most were on welfare and received food stamps so at the very least there was always food around. At least in the beginning for my family anyways.

It started out as very fun, even with the few douchebags that didn't like me. I had the canyons, my step cousins, my new friends. It was like heaven. We would all play outside in front of the buildings or in the canyons from the time we got home from school till it got dark out. We always had food in the apartment, Brian wasn't drinking and was being nice to me, my mother and him were both working, I had some new clothes, Joey was funnier than ever and made new friends everywhere he went. Joey Hollywood.

There was even a point where Brian took me aside and apologized for everything he had done to me in the past few years, he told me he was just stressed out by having a family so quickly, and wasn't ready for all the responsibility, and that now he was, and everything was going to change for the better. He explained how he was going to be a better father to me and he would never hit me or my mother again. It was the most relaxed I had ever been. Even more than Gramp's house. This was it. No more abuse, no more being nervous, I have a bigger family with all the new cousins, Me, Joey and the Thompson's were like brothers. It didn't get any better than that. No Really. It didn't get any better. Ever.

We were there for a few months, everything was awesome, Brian and his friend Dennis Culver were building me a sweet bed that looked like it was recessed into the wall of my bedroom, it was a twin sized bed that you would have to crawl into through an octagon shaped entrance with two drawers underneath and a large cubby hole above. They worked on it every night after they got out of work. I wasn't allowed into the room until it was finished and I slept in Joey and Bobby's room with them. I slept in Bobby's bed because he was still kind of young to be trusted not wandering around and he slept mostly in his playpen.

I remember coming home from school one day and they told me to close my eyes and brought me in. I was super excited and when I opened my eyes I was amazed with what I saw. It actually looked like a bed in a wall. Painted to blend in perfectly. I jumped on the bed and thanked them vigorously. They said your welcome and Dennis said to Brian let's celebrate bro. I'll run to the store and grab some beer. Brian said yeah, your right, I deserve it, but I'm just having a couple. I made a lot of promises I and don't want to break them.

I laid in that bed for like three hours just listening to Deep Purple and looking around the inside of it. It had a curtain and a little light hanging from the inside and I was very proud to have it. It was the best Gift I had ever received. And coming from Brian it gave me some hope that things really have changed for the better. I remember the side of the cassette stopping and me wanting to go thank them again. They were upstairs in Joey and Bobby's room looking around drinking and saying what they were going to do special in their room. The feeling surrounding everyone there was the most positive vibe I could imagine. I couldn't stop smiling. But that would come to a drastic end in the next few hours.

Dennis had a blonde girl with a white dress on with him and my mother was also in the room now. They were passing around a joint as I walked in, Brian had a measuring tape in one hand and a forty oz of beer in the other. I was laughing watching him try to juggle both at the same time. My mother said something to the affect that Victor shouldn't be in here with all the smoke and Dennis said don't you worry about that Jan, he's almost a man now, he'll even be doing this soon in his new bed. He dropped onto his knees in front of the blond girl and lifted up her dress and buried his face in her crotch and started shaking his head back and forth like a maniac. The girl was laughing hysterically while looking straight at me. I knew exactly what was happening.

My mother told him to stop and he popped his head out and made some sort of remark to her and I saw Brian's entire posture change as I looked towards him. Brian told me to go outside and play. I had no idea what to think. I went outside and went over to my cousin's house with Joey. Bobby was sleeping in his playpen in the living room. We were playing on the swing set on the side of their yard for only about five minutes. Me and Joey were now playing with Kimberly and Jill. They were on the see saw swing in their yard and me and Joey were pushing them.

We were doing this for a few minutes when Joey fell down and the corner of the swing caught him on the side of the fore head. He immediately started bleeding and the first thing I thought is Brian's drinking right now and here comes the first beating in the new neighborhood. As we are all yelling for help I look over and here comes Dennis running over towards us with Brian trucking close behind him.

I thought for a second that they were running over to help us. Dennis took a sharp right about twenty feet before us and started running towards the woods in between the Cases and my cousins building and Brian took the same right turn. Dennis stopped right before he entered into the woods at a recessed cement-built water stream that ran the length of the neighborhood from behind our apartment to the brook.

Now Dennis is only about 5'9" at the most and now looked even smaller standing in the stream. He stood there and Brian went in for a tackle. I thought for a split second that they were playing around but Dennis hooked Brian's arm and slammed him down and the fight began. It lasted for about four minutes and was one of the best, brutally violent fights I've seen live even to this day. Swinging for the fences. I thought for sure when I realized they weren't playing that Brian would just take him out fast but Dennis held his own like a champ. They looked like they were literally trying to kill each other. They both walked away after it was over bloodied and battered.

I had forgotten all about my brother bleeding from his forehead because I was so enthralled with what was going on with the fight. I was still kneeling down with my hand over his cut with blood running down my arm but it was completely drowned out by all the excitement. My aunt Dee ran outside and pulled my hand off of his head and grabbed Joey and brought him into their house. I followed Brian back towards home. I don't know if it was to see if he was ok or to see what he looks like semi defeated. As I walked behind him I saw my mother on the front porch and heard her ask. Hey big guy, Did Dennis do that to you? What happened to baddest motherfucker in the valley? Oh, what the shit mom. Why? Here we go.

She laughed as she turned around and walked inside, he stood there for about three seconds, I heard him take a deep breath and knew it was on. He walked up on the porch and threw the screen door open smashing the neighbors screen door and burst into the house. I walked in right behind him for some reason and stood in the mud room looking into the living room. Bobby was still sleeping in his playpen in the middle of the living room and my mother was standing on the far side of it. Brian roars you want to see the baddest motherfucker in the valley you entitled little cunt? Bobby started crying immediately grabbing up towards the padded rail of the playpen. She asks, what? Are you going to beat me in front of your own kid now? He replied. Yeah. You're fucking right I'm gonna beat you.

He let out another roar and grabbed the playpen from both sides with Bobby still in it and threw it over her head as she ducked and it slammed against the far wall. It landed on its side and Bobby looked like he was knocked out laying on the netting of it on the floor. Brian ran over and grabbed her with both hands around her throat and I could see the shock on her face. He squeezed like he was trying to take her life from her.

I could see her face turning purple and her eyes immediately going blood shot as her tongue was protruding out of her mouth. He was screaming in her face that no one fucks with him and after he's done with her he's going to go find Dennis and kill him. He thinks he's a tough motherfucker, I'll show him who he's dealing with. I'm standing there thinking that she is going to die any second and he's then going to turn on me and my brother Bobby before he goes to kill Dennis.

I don't know what I was thinking but I didn't want him to kill my mother. I was shaking uncontrollably and thought this was it. I had to do something or she was going to die. I picked up a baseball that was in the hallway and threw it at Brian's head with all of my might. It hit him on the side of his head perfectly on his left ear. He let go of my mother's neck and I knew I was about to get hurt badly. But it was ok. My mother was free.

He looked over at me as he put his hand over his ear and then looked at his hand to see if it cut him. He already had blood everywhere from the battle outside but I think he thought at that moment it was me that did that to him. The look on his face made pure horror flow through my entire body. He looked at me and asked you want to fuck with me too? After what I just did for you. You're nothing but an ungrateful little fuck. He took one step towards me and I froze in fear. Knowing for sure that the beating I was about to endure, was going to take the last fifteen minutes worth of pure frustration he had balled up and was all going to be taken out entirely on me. I closed my eyes and covered up my face and my head, and the next thing I know is the door bursts open and I get slammed up against the wall and fall on my ass.

Three cops rush in and towards Brian and get him down fairly quickly but with a huge struggle and get him cuffed. It took a solid minute. My mother ran over and grabbed Bobby to get him to safety before they rolled over on him. She ran him upstairs.

I don't know if he was up or still unconscious. They finally get Brian up to his feet and he's still screaming that he's going to kill everyone. They tell me to move and drag him out of the front door. He looks at me and says I should have never built that bed for you you little piece of shit, are you the one that called the cops on me? All I Said was no. I was standing right here the whole time.

They took him away in the cop car and I went to check on my mother and brother Bobby. He was awake and seemed fine. I don't think he even knew what had just happened to him. I walked back downstairs and Aunt Dee and the girls came in with Joey who now has a band aid bigger than his head on. I look at Joey and tell him I'm sorry for not paying attention to him while the fight was happening. The kid looks at me and says. I don't care. I was watching it too; did you see that little guy go? Dude takes a licking and keeps on ticking. I laughed and asked how his head was. He says Aunt Dee said it needs stitches, but I hope Brian needs more, in his butt, from jail. I just saw them stuff him in the car and I hope they stuff something bigger than that car in his butt. My mom just asks where do you get this shit from? He said you guys. She had nothing else to say. I couldn't help but laugh. Like I said earlier. This kid was nonstop clownery no matter what the situation was. He really should have been a comedian.

Bobby, like I said, incredibly, didn't get hurt at all from what anyone could see, my mother had broken blood vessels all through her neck, her eyes were bright red and bloodshot and could hardly talk. And Joey needed stitches. No one else was ever told about Bobby hitting the wall. My mother asked me to watch him until a babysitter could get there and her and Joey went to the hospital in an ambulance a few minutes later. I think the cops called it for my mother.

I don't remember which babysitter it was that came over. Probably because they weren't there for very long. While my mother and Joey were in the hospital Brian ended up coming home. What? Are you fucking kidding me? It wasn't even three hours. Promise to appear. A Wallingford police joke that always seemed to happen no matter what this guy did wrong. Just wait. It gets incredible with later episodes this guy put us through.

He walked into the door and asked how Bobby was. I couldn't even look him in his face as he asked. I said he's fine. He picked him up and sat in a chair and put Bobby on his lap. He asked where my mother and Joey were? I said at the hospital. He said come on. I didn't choke her that hard. I replied yes you did. I told him about the blood vessels and that Joey got hurt and needed stitches also. He asked how did that happen? I didn't even see Joey. I told him what happened, he asked when? I told him one minute before you started chasing Dennis. I said you ran right past us. He said he didn't remember most of it. He asked if I threw a ball at him. I said yes. I thought you were going to kill her. He said good job. You should try to protect your mother. Even from me.

He told the babysitter she could leave and that my mother would pay her later. I looked into his face with both eyes swollen from the earlier battle with Dennis. He looked at Bobby and put his head down looking horribly deflated. I have to say I kind of felt sorry for him for a split second but at the same time I was happy he finally got someone that stood up to him and showed him that he wasn't as invincible as he thought he was.

He told me to go to my room, so I did. I heard the phone ring a short time later and Brian answer. I heard him say yes, I'm home. What do you mean? I got a promise to appear and I have court in three weeks. He said ok I'm on my way and hung up. I heard him call his sister Dee and ask her if she could drive him to the hospital to pick up my mother and Joey. He brought Bobby to me and laid him down in my bed and said I'll be back with your mother and Joey. I'm sorry for today. I shouldn't have drank that much. It won't happen again. I'll make it up to you all. Very soon.

I promise. This was his entire M.O.
Beat us up then promise to make it up to us.

About an hour later I had Bobby in his high chair and was feeding him dinner when I heard the car pull up. I saw Dee hand my mother the keys and give her a hug. Joey was sleeping and Brian scooped him out of the back seat. They walked into the house without a word. Brian carried Joey up the stairs and my mother sat down next to me and just pouted. Also looking defeated. Brian came back downstairs and asked me to go to my room again. So, I did again. Being me, I left my door open a little and heard them talking.

For the most part what I heard was him apologize and promise to make it up to her and I heard her arguing that it can't happen again and he has to make it up to us too. He agreed and said he'll have a surprise for us in the next few days. I wasn't holding my breath and didn't believe a word of it. The last thing I heard was him promise her he wouldn't drink again and everything would be ok again. I laid down and didn't hear a sound for the rest of the night.

A few days later everything seemed back to normal. Well as back to normal as normal could be I suppose. What the fuck is normal anyway? Ok, it was quiet again. That's better. I had slept over the Thompson's on one of these days that were quieter. I had a little more freedom probably because Brian felt he owed it to me. I loved staying there especially during the summer. I had no air conditioning in my room and could never sleep like that in the heat. Beautiful bed or not. They had two industrial fans that when on high it was even cooler than an air conditioner on the hottest of days once they got rolling. Colder than cold and we all loved it.

We would hang out in Jesse and Jimbo's room and play Tecmo bowl on Nintendo when we weren't outside. I remember I was sitting on the edge of the bottom bunk sitting next to Jimbo and it was our turn to play. I had long hair like I always did and still do to this day and I heard giggling coming from the top bunk. Now I don't know which one did it but either Dave, Corey, Petey or Jesse flicked a lighter on my hair, and mind you this was the eighties and I was a hair band rock and roll kid so there was Aqua net involved. Poof. I saw the flame shoot out of the top and corner of my eyes. My whole head went up into flames.

I even laughed at this, just for a second though, then panic set in, I ran to the bathroom mirror, you could smell burnt hair everywhere. I was fucked if my mother sees this. She loved my hair, sometimes I thought it was the only thing she loved about me. As I'm freaking out Jesse and Dave come up with the Idea to buzz cut my head. They grab the clippers from the hall closet and take turns buzzing me down. Connie "Their mother" comes home with her friend Debbie. All I can hear from downstairs as soon as the door opened was Debbie, What the fuck is that smell? Then Connie, what the fuck is that noise? Then yelling, What the fuck are you damn kids up to up there?

They run upstairs and there we are all in the hallway with Jimbo with the clippers just a smiling. Hey mom. OMG. Why are you letting them cut your hair Victor? Jesse says, well mother, we kind of, sort of lit it on fire a little bit. You can see the fire in her eyes now, do you know how long it's going to take to get that smell out of here. Damn kids always messing shit up. Hurry up and finish. Don't let him go home looking like an idiot, his mother is going to kill him already.

We finish up with my head and Connie's house phone rings. It's my mother telling me to come home right away and that it's an emergency. I still have hair all over me and I don't know what to do. I ask them to come with me and they all say no. Jesse finally agrees because he said they might not kick my ass if he's there. We run out the front door hair blowing everywhere off of my back and shoulders. We get to my driveway and my mother, Brian and Joey are all standing there with the most baffled looks on their faces.

My mom yells what did you do to your beautiful hair? Jesse looks at me and says I'm done, and turns around and runs back home. Brian comes over and rubs my head and says it looks good like this, my brother Joey is just laughing his ass off, you actually let those clowns talk you into this, idiot, it's because the girls dig your hair more than theirs. Dummy. My mom yells I loved your hair. You better let it grow back out.

Now I'm standing there baffled. I said Hello? What's the emergency? Joey says your head dude. Knock it off already kid I said. Really, what's wrong? Where's Bobby? Brian says follow us. We walk inside and all I hear is Bobby giggling, I look in his playpen and there jumping all over him are two St. Bernard puppy's. The girl was brown and white the boy was brown, black and white. They were so fucking cute.

My mother looks at me and says, I shouldn't do this after what you just did to your head, but their yours. I freaked out. Brian picked up the boy and says you have to name him. He handed him to me and without hesitation I yelled out Heineken. My mom asked what? Heineken? I say yeah, remember the picture in Gramp's back yard when I was like two years old, I was holding a Heineken in my hand. And in Harry's beer can collection Heinekin was always my favorite. You guys always told me about how you all got me drunk that day in Gramp's back yard and I got all kinds of sick. Remember? Yeah. It's Heineken.

Brian picks up the girl and I stood there staring at her for a minute. I don't know why? I don't even know where I ever heard the name before. But I blurted out Keisha. Heineken and Keisha. They said ok. Then they walked me out into the back yard where they had a new doghouse for them. It was out in the way back of the apartment near the catwalk that went up into the other neighborhood.

Brian walked over and attached two chains to the doghouse and said this is where I want you to have them in the morning before you go to school. Make sure they have food and water. That's your job. If they are in the house and they poop anywhere that's on you too. The puppies would sleep in my room with me at night. Well. Stay in my room at night. They played with each other a lot and barked way too much. Not a whole lot of sleep going on.

When I got home from school and went out to play with my friends I usually put them up in Joey and Bobby's room for Bobby to play with. They shit all over that room. I don't know why. But when they pooped anywhere else in the house I would clean it up immediately. When they pooped in there I just ignored it. Seemed like everyone else did too. I remember having a couple of friends over and we opened up the door once and Mike Lazzaro looked inside and screamed. DOODY MINES. LOOK AT ALL THE DOODY MINES. We all died laughing. But I still ignored it for that day.

It was about a week into having them and I remember Brian coming into my room and making me go upstairs to clean up the mines. Most of them were rock hard. It took a while and it sucked. I brought the puppies into my room and It was a couple of hours before bedtime. Brian came in and said not tonight. They are going to have to sleep outside tonight. I was mortified. There are crazy rabid raccoons out there. You can't let them stay out there by themselves. His answer. If you don't want them by themselves you can sleep out there with them. No way I was going to do that. I was terrified of raccoons because they were always right outside my window going through the trash. I would bang on the window for them to go away but they didn't give a shit about me. I'm pretty sure they wanted me to step out so they could fuck me up and take me out. Little bandit looking jerks. I have a funny story about them later.

We took the puppies outside, I chained up Keisha and he chained up Heinekin. He handed me their bowls and said make sure they are filled and bring them back out. So, I did. I went back inside afterwards and they were barking up a storm as I was staring at them through my bedroom window. I remember them jumping on each other and playing while I kept my eyes out for the raccoons. I planned on watching them all night long but I got very tired and laid in my bed. I figured I would just lay down and listen and if I heard a ruckus I would just yell for Brian. I ended up falling asleep though.

The next morning I awoke to pure silence. I ran to the window and saw Brian on the lawn walking towards them. I couldn't see them at all but saw that their chains were in a weird position going on an upwards angle towards the catwalk fence. I left my room and ran out of the back door as fast as I could and saw Brian up against the fence pulling up one of the chains from over it. I noticed the colors on the puppy and I yelled stop you're going to hurt him. He looked over at me and said it's too late. They're both dead.

I looked at Heineken and his head looked like it was blown up to twice the size of his body. Brian set him on the ground and I ran over as he was pulling Keisha up and I tried to get Heinekens collar off of him but it was too tight. He pulled Keisha over and she looked exactly the same. I started crying hysterically. My mother came outside and asked what was going on. Brian held Keisha up by the chain and said they must have seen something they wanted to chase on the other side of the fence and killed themselves.

I have to say right at that very moment I didn't believe a word of what he was saying. I thought with all my heart that Brian waited until I went to bed and went outside to stop all of the barking and just simply threw them over the fence to hang them to death. Brian looked at me and told me he was sorry. These kinds of things happen. We will get you a new dog soon. An older dog that will know better. I should have let you keep them in your room.

My mother walked back into the house and I stayed outside sitting on the back porch crying. I heard her ask him straight up. Did you do this? He said no. She said there was no way those puppies could have both climbed that fence. She said that she noticed that the doghouse was moved way closer to the fence than it was yesterday. He said well they could have pulled it there together. She said no way. They weren't in any way strong enough. You know that. He went into defense mode and said well maybe it was Dennis trying to get back at me or someone else who didn't want to hear them barking anymore. She said maybe. I better never find out you did this.

To this day I never got the answer of what really happened to my puppies and I know I definitely never will. I was devastated for weeks over this. It could have been any of those scenarios. Or even something else. Who knows. All I know is it took a long time to get over seeing them both dead like that. So much so that I actually named a daughter after one of them ten years later. It could have been Brian? It could have been something else? But to me it will always be more than likely Brian. This isn't the first pet I thought he has killed on me. And it wouldn't be the last one. And with the last pet there are no questions or debates because he killed him right in front of us.

The feeling in the apartment was clear now. Very mistrusting. Myself and Joey were hanging out more and more away from the house. If we weren't outside playing we were at the Greenlaws, or the Thompson's place. Mostly the Thompson's. Winter was coming and after school you wouldn't see us at home almost ever. We even ate somewhere else most of the time. Connie and aunt Dee always asked if we were hungry and fed us. I don't think my mother or Brian even cared that we weren't home most of the time. The only rule I had was don't let Joey out of my site.

At the Thompson's their mother was working most of the time and we had almost complete run of the place. Jesse and Corey were about my age, Jimbo a few years younger and Benny and Joey were the same age. Joey and Benny would become best friends and there was another that was there all the time with them. Pete Dunebietta. Over the years we would all become the best of friends. With a few more that will all be a part of this story as the years go by. Right now, they are just friends and acquaintances. As they become more involved in the upbringing of my life and my teenage years, the more you will hear about them.

At home like I explained, when we were there, everything was very weird. Everyone was very quiet. We would just pass by each other. Something happened with Brian's job and was just home bumming around for a while. He wasn't drinking but was very down. He had gone to court and gotten two years of probation for the fight and what happened with my mother in the apartment. If he wasn't bumming around he was down in the basement for hours building something. None of us were allowed down there with a threat of death. I'm just not allowed in basements I guess. Kind of Ironic as you will later see.

◆ ◆ ◆

PART EIGHT - THE VIOLIN, THE GUITAR AND TWO BROKEN LEGS

My mother was now working only part time nights and we were heavily depending on state welfare. Government cheese, powdered milk and the whole deal. I won't complain about the government cheese though. I would cut that shit about a quarter of an inch thick and make grilled cheeses for myself Joey and Bobby like a pro. When we had it. The powered milk on the other hand. You can keep that shit.

One other way we would eat besides Connie and aunt Dee was almost like on Allen avenue. I would go out and shovel driveways or rake leaves for money to go to the dairy. Back in the day when we were young it was owned by an old couple named the Tremper's. I don't know if they have anything to do with the street. I would usually get cold cuts and bread so there was enough for the three of us. They also made the best hot dogs I have ever had to this day. I don't know what kind they were, but they buttered and grilled the buns, deep fried the dogs in peanut oil and topped them with mustard, relish and a mound of chopped onions.

I would always try to make enough money in most days to also get Joey one and get a bag of fries. They would fill a double lunch size paper bag and salted and peppered them in the bag itself. We could share the fries with Bobby and cut off a piece of each dog for him and there would be plenty. If I had a very good day we could also get a milkshake. Chocolate malted. My favorite. I busted my ass usually a few days a week at eleven years old to feed myself and my brothers if someone else didn't feed us. When the food stamps came in and shopping was done for the house Brian would mostly get only the things he liked and rip through that shit in days. Liver, clams, spam, cream of mushroom soup. Stuff we didn't like at all. Yeah, I know. It was on purpose so we wouldn't touch his shit.

School wasn't going any better than at home at this point in my life either. I was being picked on badly because I was almost always wearing the same clothes daily, sometimes even very visibly dirty clothes. I had a nemesis in school. Every morning while waiting in line to go into the building myself and another kid Billy would fight for the other kids. Every single morning. The other kids would egg us on and we would just do it. I was called to the office often and they would call my mother and Brian. My mother would get mad and Brian would just say well if you gotta fight you gotta fight.

I was in fifth grade at this time and I had one teacher by the name of Mrs. Bruce. I could always see that she felt very badly for me. She even had a star system for me where if I would behave she would take me out for lunch on Saturdays. My Grandfather wasn't coming around as much at this point as he had met a woman and they were getting closer. I remember having three different lunches with her and I always felt safe with her around. I believe part of the whole thing was to be able to pick me up and drop me off so she could see what was going on with me at home. But of course, that's when you saw Brian and my mother do their Mr. and Mrs. Cleaver routine. Sorry. It really wasn't fooling anyone.

This all came to a crashing halt with my teacher on one stupid day. Well, the next day after a stupid night. Me and another friend from the neighborhood Seth Pastore. Whose single mother was as dirt poor as my family. They lived in an apartment building right next to the steps on Louis circle. Their apartment was on the corner closest to the steps. We wanted to go to the high school one night because we were both interested in playing an instrument. They were having a music program workshop where they had all the instruments on display. We both knew it was a pipe dream that neither of our parents could afford but we wanted to go anyway to see what it was like.

We walked in and I was immediately drawn to a beautiful saxophone. I stood in front of that thing for five minutes just staring. The price tag on it was $1,200.00. I knew I would never be able to get it. Seth came over to me and said come check out the violins. We walked over to where they were which was right next to the exit. He said look at the price tag on this thing. The tag said $865.00.

I looked at Seth and just said if I take it we can share it. He said go ahead, I dare you. I didn't skip a beat or hesitate in any way. I shut the case and snapped the latches closed. And instead of just walking out of the door I walked it back over to the saxophone with Seth following me. I looked at him and said grab that thing. He said no fucking way. I called him a wimp and turned towards the door. Standing right in front of us was a teacher or someone. He looked down at us and asked what are you doing with that? Is that yours? I looked him dead in the face and said yeah. My grandfather just bought it for me. I'll go get him for you.

I walked forward towards the exit knowing this guy was still staring at me. I didn't care a bit. I opened the door and just walked out. It was about fifty feet to the woods and we just booked it straight in. We got about half way in. Just about the very middle in between where the school is and Seth's apartment. We stopped at an old underground fort and sat down on a couple of rocks to hear if anyone else had followed us into the woods. They didn't.

We sat there for a few minutes and discussed what we were going to do with it. We both wanted to take it home with us but he said we should bury it for now in the fort. I said I didn't want any of the other kids to find it because a lot of kids would stop right there to smoke before school. That's what I said. The real reason is I knew he would go back for it as soon as I went home. We decided that the only fair way to do it seeing how I did tell him I would share it with him was to take turns. I'll take the violin and bow tonight. You take the case and we will switch tomorrow.

We both went home. I walked through the front door with it and my mother and Brian were sitting on the couch watching TV. They looked at me and asked where the hell did you get that. It looks brand new. I said it was Seth's and he was letting me borrow it so I can practice and learn how to play. Brian looked at me and said bullshit. Did you just steal that thing from the music show? I said yes. He said you didn't take the case? I said yeah, Seth has it. We're switching back and forth. He laughed and said if you get caught I don't know shit. My mother only said, nice Brian, and I took it in my room.

Now what I thought next while in my room staring at my new toy was extremely stupid. I knew for a fact that the next day in our class was a show and tell day. I was very excited because I never got to show off anything in class because I never had anything worth showing. I was most definitely the poor kid. I was the one who never had anything. Kenny McCormick didn't have shit on me. That was all going to change tomorrow. I'm going to have the coolest thing to show and when I am done I'm going to try to sign up for music class.

I wake up the next morning and look through my clothes for the best that I had. Which wasn't much. But I was proud none the less. I was going to show everybody. I made sure neither my mother or Brian saw me leave with it. I walked outside and waited for the bus. Oh shit. Yeah. A few things. Sorry again. I took the short bus to a school across town. I was expelled for fighting at Stephens school. So, I was in Pond Hill school I.E.P. Class. As soon as I got on the bus I could see that no one believed that it was mine but I wasn't budging. The driver and the aid both drilled me the entire way there but I stood strong. My grandfather bought it for me.

I got off of the bus and stood in line. I looked at Billy and said not today pal. I'm going to have a good day with no trouble. Even with all the other kids egging it on he said ok. I was so happy with myself. We walked inside and Billy looked at me and said good luck with your day. I said thank you and went to class. I ran up to Mrs. Bruce and said look at what my grandfather got me. She looked at me like she was going to cry. She looked up towards the door and there was a man standing there with a police officer standing right behind him. He said Victor. You have to come with us. I'm John Bruce. The Wallingford youth officer. Where is the case to that?

Now to get it strait. Bruce and Bruce? No relation. Just coincidence. Mrs. Bruce looked at me with shear disappointment. Why did you take that Victor? I replied because I never have anything and I turned around in shame. John Bruce took the violin and the bow and the officer told me to put my hands behind my back. John Bruce said cuffing him in the front is fine and the officer cuffed me in front of Mrs. Bruce and the whole class. Everyone had a look of bewilderment on their faces but not Mrs. Bruce. She had no emotion in her face. Just tears flowing down it. She put her head down and they lead me away.

We walked into the principal's office and they explained to the principle that they had to take me away to jail. John Bruce asked if he wanted to give the violin back to Mr. Tuttle. The principal called into another room. Mr. Tuttle can you come over here for a second. I looked towards the door where he just called into and wouldn't you fucking know it? The same damned guy who spotted me with the violin the night before. I never saw the music teacher there before but I now guessed this was him. Dammit. Jigs definitely up.

He took the violin in his hand and looked at it all over. He handed it back to John Bruce and said there seems to be no damage, but without the case I'm not taking it back. His parents are going to have to pay for it. If the case comes back in perfect condition I will not make them pay and I will not press full charges. He looks at me and asked where's the case son? I just stood there staring at the ground. John Bruce then spoke up and said that there were officers collecting Seth from Stephens School right now and there were officers at his house right now obtaining the case from his mother.

I looked around confused out of my mind. How in the world did they know everything already? Mr. Tuttle looked at me and said you better hope nothing happened to that case. I have to tell you. I knew from the very moment I saw you that you were stealing it because it was from our music class. I let you go to see if you would actually try to walk out with it. I thought you were going to put it back down on its stand and leave. I was caught off guard when you exited the building or I would have caught up to you. Which way did you go when you left? I told him we ran for the woods to the left. He replied. Well maybe track and field for you then. Music most likely isn't in your immediate future.

John Bruce and the officer then lead me out to the police car and put me in the cage. They told me to scoot over and put the violin and bow on the seat next to me. I looked at the school and at least fifty students and teachers were staring at me through the windows. There were mixed emotions. Some probably think

I'm a bad ass kid. Some might already know what I did and just think I'm stupid. I wondered what they were all saying. John Bruce said you look at that violin very carefully on the ride to the police station and think about if it was worth what you have done. Silence from there the whole twenty-minute ride.

As we pulled into the police station the officer asked John Bruce if he wanted to go through the front or into the cell area. He said the front door would be fine. As we walked through the front door I had noticed my mother's Audi sitting in the parking lot. I was freaking out. We walked into the front door and my mother and Brian were sitting on a bench. Brian said I told you. Why the hell would you bring that thing to school if you stole it? You are not the brightest bulb in the package are you kid? Not to smart buddy. Buddy? Ok. John Bruce then asked where's the other one. The desk sergeant said they should be right behind you.

The door opens and there's Seth walking in front of an officer. He just looked at me and asked why did you bring that thing to school with you? All I said is I don't know but an awful lot of people keep asking me that so I'm guessing it wasn't too smart. He said no duh. They took us each in the back in separate rooms and I was in mine for about twenty minutes alone which felt like hours. I knew Seth was just going to tell the truth because it was me that took it. John Bruce walked in and sat down. He said I just talked to Seth and I know exactly what happened. Are you going to tell me a different story and keep me in here forever or do you want to go home?

I said I wanted to go home and just told the whole truth. He said another officer just walked into the station with the case and it looked like there was no damage done to it. I am going to give you a break for telling the truth and not trying to lie your way out of it. But I will have to write up a report on you and keep in our files. So, if you even think about doing anything like this again, we will know it was you and next time it's probably going to be juvenile hall and there will be nothing I can do to help you next time. He had an officer come in and take off my cuffs and told me I was free to go.

He walked me out to the lobby where my mother and Brian were still sitting. They stood up and I asked where Seth was. They said his mother came and got him already. She asked us to keep you away from him and she told him that you two can no longer be friends or hang out with each other. And we agree. All the way home all I could think about was that I couldn't talk to Seth right now and everybody was going to think I ratted him out to the police. But I didn't. My mother and Brian did.

We got home and I went straight into my bedroom and fell asleep. I woke up a few hours later and Bobby was in his playpen and Benny and Joey were already out of school and sitting on the living room floor playing Atari. I looked down at them and Benny was drinking a glass of juice or something. I asked Joey if he heard what happened. He said yeah. What do you think you're Beethoven or something? Benny shot juice out of his nose and his mouth all over the TV. Bobby even laughed at me. I can't believe I never beat Joey's ass for some of this shit. I asked where Brian and mom were. They said over talking to Seth's mother. I didn't know what to think.

They came back not that long afterwards. They told me to sit down at the kitchen table. They sat down and said we just came back from Seth's house and from having a conversation with his mother. We explained that it was you that took the violin and that you have been having a tough time since your puppies died. We explained to Seth that you never said anything to the police and it was us that told them. He said ok and that he understood and his mother said that if you promise never to do anything like that again she has no problem with the two of you still being friends.

It was really the first time they ever asked me to sit down to talk like that. Like a real person. I kind of even felt like Brian treated me like I was truly growing up. Benny and Joey were still sitting on the floor snickering and Bobby was looking over his playpen staring at them laughing at nothing. My mom intervened and told them to knock it off. He made a stupid mistake. You'll make plenty of them, don't you worry. It's also the first time my mother ever stuck up for me over Joey. I calmed down after the talk and was much more relaxed.

I thanked them for talking to Seth and his mother and for not punishing me. They said the police already scared me enough and John Bruce wasn't someone to take lightly. Brian said he knew him his whole life and if he says something he means it. Just stay out of trouble and you'll be fine. You're turning twelve soon and you have to start growing up. I agreed with them. But I'll admit it now. That wasn't mine and Seth's last hoorah. And it was far from my last dealings with Mr. John Bruce. They were right though. I was growing up. But I was growing up the way they taught me how to grow up.

They were right about one more thing. My birthday was coming up pretty quick. Gramps somehow found out what happened with the violin. Brian had found a new job doing something or other and wasn't home on the day Gramps came over. He came inside and gave me a little love tap on my face and said I heard what you did. You can't be doing those things. I'm very disappointed in you. I'm sorry I haven't been around much but I have been very busy working and I have found a new love interest. Her name is Mary. I am going to be here with her to pick you up on Saturday. We are going to take you roller skating so you can get to know each other. Are you ok with that? I said hell yeah. He said watch your mouth.

He got down on one knee and gave me a kiss on my cheek. I told him my roller skates didn't fit me anymore. He said not to worry about it. I'll have you a new pair. What do you want for your birthday and Christmas. I said I can't ask you for what I want. It's too much. He said nothing is too much right now. I would rather get you what you want than have you out stealing it. I told him I would like a new bicycle because someone stole mine from Allen Ave and a Nintendo game system. I said Joey needs a bike too please. And Bobby needs a big wheel. He said I'll see what I can do. This was my Gramps. I knew it was all going to come.

He asked me to go outside and play or to go into my room for a little bit. I have to talk to your mother for a little while. I'll come get you before I have to go and am going to pick you up Saturday no matter what. Please just give us some privacy. I said ok I'm going to go listen to my music in my room. None of my friends are outside right now. That was a lie. I didn't know who was outside and when? I just wanted to hear what he had to talk to my mother about.

I saw Gramps sit down and I walked towards my room and closed my door until it clicked then opened it a crack so I could hear them. As soon as door clicked I could hear him. Janis? What the fuck are you doing with this guy? He's no good for you or your kids. Don't you see what's happening with these kids? You need to move on. What is wrong with you? You are my daughter, I love you, you are better than this and your kids deserve better. This guy is no fucking good. I told you that as soon as I met him. Does he hit these fucking kids Janis? It's the first time I ever heard my grandfather swear like that.

She said no. He disciplines them but he never hits them. What about you honey? Doug told me he was arrested for choking you or something like that. Is he lying to me? She said yes. Of course, he's lying to you. Doug has always been in love with me and would say anything to get rid of Brian or anyone I'm with. He got into a fight with someone that insulted me and that's why he was arrested that day. And he hasn't drank in months. He's on probation now and behaving himself and trying to be a father to kids that aren't even his. Give him a break. He's changing for me and these kids.

I wanted to burst out of my door and wave my finger at her and call her a fucking liar. He then asked ok what happened to the puppies that you told me you got for Victor. I heard their both dead? Why does this type of shit seem to be happening around this fucking alcoholic bum constantly.

You know I'm not stupid Janis? Am I stupid Janis? She said no Pops. I don't think your stupid. But your wrong this time. He's really getting better. He said yeah, I'm wrong? Whatever Janis. You have to start doing better for your children, and stop messing around with these bums you always seem to find. I will get Victor and Joey both new bikes and Bobby a new big wheel for their birthdays. You get them the game system they want. Don't you let me find out you didn't? I'll take Victor and Joey out for some new clothes next Sunday. I heard Victor is getting picked on in school for having no clothes. She asked where did you hear that? Doug too? He said don't worry about it. I know people. Don't you dare disappoint them on this. It will be the last time I do anything to help you if you keep letting them down.

I heard him say here. Don't you let this guy drink or drug this up. Use it for what you told me you needed it for. It better be done. My mother said you know what he did with Victors bed and what he's trying to do for them right now. Gramps said I don't care Janis. He's good with his fucking hands, big deal. I better not hear about this guy putting them on you or hurting my grandsons, ever. I will have him killed Janis. I don't give a fuck if you think you love him or not. Now give me a kiss and say goodbye. Do the right thing for once.

Victor. Come out here. What is your shoe size? I said 7-1/2. He said I'll have your new skates Saturday and we'll go skating and you can meet Mary. And I'm going to take you and Joey on Sunday to get some new clothes. I said I know. He looked at me with a sideways eye. I said that's the only part I heard. I swear. I was going to come out to look for batteries but you were still talking so I went back in. He looked at my mother as she sat at the kitchen table crying. Wow, Just like you. I'll see you Saturday kid. And he left.

My mother looked at me and asked how much did you really hear. I Felt so bad for her at that moment so I just told the truth. I said I heard every word mom. I said you know he would let us move right back in if we needed to. Why don't you just listen to him? You know he's right. Brian isn't a good person. At all. He actually acts like a wild caged up animal sometimes. She told me that I wouldn't understand until I get older. And I have no idea what he's sacrificing for me and Joey and we'll both see soon enough what kind of man he is. He built you that bed, didn't he? I said yes. And I love it. But. She said no buts. He did that for you. Respect him as your father because your real father doesn't do anything for you like he does. You'll see. I was confused again. See what? What the hell was all this doing something for us all about?

And no. She gurgled through her tears. We can't go live with my father again. So, stop talking about it. He has a new girlfriend now and they wouldn't want us there anyways. I told her you really don't believe that. Do You? He loves you and you know it. She told me to shut the fuck up and to mind my own business. You're going to get every fucking thing you want for your birthday and Christmas. And more. Yeah, he'll do everything you fucking kids want but what the fuck do I get besides fucking headaches. From you, from him, and everybody fucking else. Get the fuck out of my face. She was saying all of this to me as she scraped a pile of cash off of the table that I'm positive my grandfather just put down there for her. A couple grand I'm sure. Feeling sorry for her changed in that second. I walked outside and went to the Thompson's to wait for dark to throw snowballs at cars.

We went outside and we all hid on the side of a girl named Tamar's house. This was the last apartment before the brook with a huge bush we could hide behind with a clear path down a hill to the canyons to run if any cars stopped or the cops showed up. Most of us hardly ever got caught. Sometimes. But hardly ever. So, we're all there. Myself, Jesse, Corey, Jimbo, all the little ones, Joey, Benny, Pete. And a bunch of other kids.

As we are hiding behind the bush piling up snowballs waiting for cars we don't know to go by. Brian shows up. He says I heard your grandfather showed up today. I said yep. What did he say? I answered he just asked me what I wanted for Christmas and my birthday and told me not to try stealing things. Did he give your mother any money? I don't know. I didn't see any. He said well she's really mad at you for something. You want to go piss her off a little more. I was still upset with her so. Sure. How?

Let's go kids. Everyone can go over in the yard next to our apartment. For what? To nail the cars from there. A couple of us said but it's harder to get away from there. He said don't worry about it. I got it covered. We all walked over to the side of our building and got ready. There wasn't much cover to hide behind from there, but we were all game. We see a car coming down the street we didn't know and Brian says this is the one. Pelt this motherfucker.

I swear there were fifteen snowballs flying through the air. This poor car got at least half of them. Bam Bam Bam Bam Bam. The car slams on the brakes and slides to a stop. Two guys get out of the car and start to walk towards us. What the fuck are you little assholes doing? A few of us ran away. A few of us stayed. I stayed. What the fuck is wrong with you little fuckers one of them yelled towards us. Brian grabs a 2 x 4 leaning against the side of the house and walks right towards them holding it like a baseball bat ready to swing. Get the fuck back in the car or I'll crush your fucking skulls. They turned around and walked back to their car Immediately. Walking away you could hear them yelling. You're a sick fuck. Nice parenting Douchebag. We're calling the cops.

My mother comes outside in a tiff and asks what's going on out here. Are you throwing snowballs at cars with these kids? Yeah. We're bonding. That's what you always say you wanted. Right Jan? Give them and me a fucking break. He says anytime you kids want to throw snowballs from over here it's no problem. If you can't get away run into our house. See that Janis? Bonding with the kids. I have to say. We definitely took him up on that offer. A lot. Especially when they weren't home. The cops did show up that night. Verbal warning blah blah blah. Typical Wallyworld police.

A few days later just like he promised my grandfather showed up to bring me roller skating. He had a woman in the car with him and introduced her to me as Mary. She was very smiley and had very curly brunette hair. I have never seen my Gramps so happy before. He was definitely giddy. We went roller skating and she treated me like I was also her grandson. We skated for hours and it's the most fun I had there ever. I asked if we could start doing this again every week. She immediately said of course. He didn't buy you brand new skates for just one day.

On the way home, we stopped for dinner. They brought me to Tony and Lucille's on Wooster street in New Haven. It was the first time I ever had fried mozzarella. Holy shit. That was the best thing I ever tasted besides modern pepperoni pizza up till then. I was so happy. I asked if we could take Joey next week. He needs to try this. Gramps said no, we can't do that. Saturday's are only for my number one grandson. But, we can bring the number two grandson tomorrow after clothes shopping. Yes.

As they dropped me off I was very happy for my Gramps and for Mary. She was truly one of the nicest people I have ever met in my life even up till now. I went into the apartment and my mother asked me how my day was? I asked her if she had met Mary yet. She said yes of course. She is perfect for him. Don't be asking him for too much. Let him live his life. He doesn't need us ruining this for him. I said he's bringing me and Joey clothes shopping tomorrow and out for fried mozzarella. I had fried mozzarella today. It was the best thing ever. All that she said was, that figures. I don't know why he's always spoiling you kids like this. Like she was jealous. I just rolled my eyes at her and walked away into my bedroom and waited for the morning.

The next day went exactly as planned. They picked us up around noon. Joey met Mary. We shopped for clothes for like three hours. Joey loved her as much as I did. We had so much fun and got enough cloths to last a couple of months. Three pairs of pants each, a few shirts, under ware, socks and each got a new pair of shoes. It was the most clothes I ever had gotten at one time and we got to pick all of them out ourselves. No more getting made fun of for wearing the same shit every day. At least for a couple months.

We went and ate dinner, but this time it was Consiglio's, also on Wooster street. Gramps went all out. Fried mozzarella again. Plus, garlic bread, fried calamari, meatballs, the works. One big buffet in the middle of our table. I remember looking at Joey and he had more sauce on his face than on the plates. He just looked up at me and said through his still full chewing mouth. Good. Dude. This is so good. All I could do was laugh. We had the best day ever. Gramps was the funniest dude to be with out in public. He just didn't care. Like I told you earlier. Dressed like a gangster and played the part all the way through. There's no smoking here. Fuck you. Smoke hanging out of his mouth. Whistling everywhere and just plain fun. And Mary was just as crazy. Going through a grocery store opening up chocolate milk and letting me drink it while we were shopping and just placing the empty container on a shelf when I was finished. They were a match made in heaven. I was so happy for the both of them. They were the first really in love couple that I have ever seen.

A few weeks later was Xmas. Waking up in the morning and leaning up against the wall near the Christmas tree were two

Huffy BMX bikes and a big wheel. There were a couple of other boxes but I knew exactly what box I wanted. I opened that thing up as fast as I could. It was the Nintendo. Super Mario and duck hunt with the gun. Everything I Wanted was there. And one more thing. Hidden behind the tree. FROM GRAMPS. There it was. All wrapped up. Acoustic guitar. It had a note attached to it. If you wanted an instrument all you had to do was ask me. Live and learn. Love Gramps. It was the best Xmas since the headphones and the tent that I could remember. And better than any Xmas that ever came after until I had my own children.

Brian said to take a good look at the bikes. I have to bring them downstairs into the basement to get them out of the way. It's winter so you don't need them yet. I don't want any of you down there because I have your birthday present down there. If I see any of you down there it all goes away. Don't you dare. I didn't really care. I had my Nintendo. No problem. I promise I won't go down there. I was hooked. I played that thing until my fingers wouldn't work anymore. I got to where you jump on the turtles on Mario brothers for all the free guys in about a week. I worked on getting those free guys for about four days straight after I got there. None of us could do it.

We were all in the living room one day. Me Joey Jesse Jimbo Corey Benny. We all took turns trying to get all those free guys. Connie called the apartment and said that the boys had to come home for dinner. After they left I tried like three more times. Finally. Bloop. Bloop, Bloop Bloop. Over and over. I finally got it. I run to pick up the phone. I dial 265-9494. Yeah guys. I still remember your number. Jesse answers the phone. I got it, I got it. 44-45-46. I can't believe I got it. Jesse says congrats bro. 49-50-51. Joey comes running around the corner from the kitchen. Dude, nice, you got - CRASH. Crash? He came around the corner so fast and while he was staring at the TV he tripped over the games power cord and unplugged the system. I don't got it dude. Forget it. Goodnight. I'll talk to you tomorrow. I was so mad. But would never hit Joey. Not yet anyways.

For a while it was ok. Brian and my mother were hardly ever around. If they weren't working Brian was in the basement doing god knows what always banging and slamming and my mother was always locked in her room. The only time I ever really saw her was if I wanted to or had to do something and had to give Bobby to her. Him and Joey were mostly my responsibility now. My life at this point was either shoveling driveways when it snowed, Saturday's with Gramps and Mary, hanging out at the cousins or the Thompson's, playing with my guitar or we would be in our living room playing the video games. The kids pretty much had control of the house at this point.

My twelfth birthday came. I woke up to Brian and my mother already waiting in the living room which seemed very strange. Go wake Joey up and go down into the basement. Ok. I woke him up and we went downstairs. And this is what I mean by split personalities. I don't think we were ready for this in any way at all. As we got to the bottom of the stairs we looked to the right and there it was. What Brian was doing down in the basement all of this time. He has built us a railroad station with a race track. Covered in Astro Turf. All electric. It looked like a professionally built town the someone at the pentagon would build preparing for war. It was pretty awesome I have to say. About twice the size of a ping pong table. He had a knack for this kind of shit and probably could have made an awesome living doing it. But we all have our demons we have to fight off I suppose.

There was a whole town in the middle of the tracks and little plastic houses and people everywhere. Trees and bushes. The whole nine. He started up the train and handed me and Joey each a controller for the cars. I gave him a big hug and thanked him. I think it was my first besides the puppies. We started playing with it and it was fun. For a couple of hours anyway. I hate to say it but, in that day, and at that age with the video games, it just wasn't as exciting as it looked after playing with it for a little bit. We finished up and Brian told us that he still didn't want us down there without him. He didn't want us breaking it. I was fine with that. I looked over at the bikes and couldn't wait for summer to come.

Soon after was the announcement. Gramps and Mary are getting married. It was a small gathering but beautiful at the same time. I don't remember much about the ceremony but I do remember my gramps telling me afterwards that he and Mary would be gone for a few weeks for their honeymoon and he would come and see me after they get back and everything would get back to normal.

It was only a few days after the wedding. I was at school and got caught doing something stupid again. I was sitting on the floor playing with some other kid and we had a bunch of little green army men. There was a substitute teacher that day and I thought I would be able to get away with taking some of them home for the little town in the basement. I mean come on. They would have made a nice inclusion.

I am pretty sure the other kid I was playing with saw me stuff like four of them in my back pocket. About three minutes after I did it the teacher asked me to empty out my pockets. I turned my front pockets inside out and she looked baffled. She looked at the other kid I was playing with and shrugged her shoulders. I thought my shirt was long enough to cover them in back of me but I was dead wrong once again. As soon as I turned around she grabbed me by the arm and dragged me to the principal's office. She reached into my back pocket and slammed them on the front desk.

I looked up at her and said Mrs. Bruce would have just talked to me and not done this. She just said well I'm not Mrs. Bruce and walked away. I was brought into the principle's actual office with his desk. He picked up the phone and called my house and no one answered. I had to sit in there for the entire day. I went home at the end of the day and no one said anything. I thought I was in the clear. No suspension. No phone calls. I'm good.

The next day I went to school like usual. The bus came and I had a regular day. No one said anything all day about the army men. Did I totally get away with it? Maybe they won't say anything. I got home and went straight for my room. As I was walking across the living room I heard my guitar strumming. I thought it was Brian. WTF? I opened up my door and there was Joey. Beating on the strings. I grabbed the guitar. What are you doing home? He said I stayed home sick today. Brian told me to stay in your room. I think he's upstairs playing with his pee pee again.

My mother's car wasn't in the driveway and I didn't see anyone else around. I thought Brian was upstairs so I thought I was in the clear and got mad at Joey. I looked at him and said in a low whisper if I ever see you playing with my guitar like that again I'm going to kick your ass. Boom. Come on. Really? The door flies open. Brian snatches the guitar out of my hand. Joey runs out of my door. YOUR GONNA KICK WHO'S ASS. ANSWER ME. YOUR GONNA KICK WHOS ASS YOU LITTLE MOTHERFUCKER? He rears back with the guitar and hit me as hard as I had ever been hit before. Right in the head and face from eyebrow to ear with the side of it. It felt like my neck broke. I hit the ground behind the door really hard and threw my hands over my face.

I could hear that the guitar definitely broke a little when it hit me and it hurt like hell. I could feel blood run down my face over my hands immediately. I felt a wooden sliver stuck in my eyebrow and pulled it out. I looked up at Brian and I thought that was going to be all there was especially after him watching me pull the sliver out. YOU'RE GONNA KICK HIS ASS HUH? How about this you little bastard? I was laying down behind the door trapped in the corner and knew it was coming again so I just covered my head and face and he just let loose.

He beat me with that thing until there was nothing left of it that looked even similar to any guitar. It lasted about three solid minutes and I even pretended to pass out at one point again hoping he would stop. But no chance. I think he knew that trick. Just like the last severe beating. And I know what you did at school yesterday you little fucker he yelled. I stayed home with your sick brother so I got the phone call we missed yesterday. You're suspended from school and grounded for a week. Don't even think about leaving this room.

I was bleeding from everywhere. Scratches all over my body and all bruised up. He slammed my door and I heard him tell Joey if he ever touches you just let me know. He'll get that every time. He can't threaten you like that. Who the fuck does he think he is. A few hours I was in my room picking up the pieces of the guitar and I heard my mother come home. Your fucking son did it again Janis. He tried to steal toys from school. Then he threatened to kick Joeys ass for playing his guitar. I took care of it. No need to even talk to him. He's suspended from school for a week and grounded until he goes back.

She asked him what about dinner tonight? He's not getting anything tonight he said unless Joey wants to share his with him. I wouldn't give that little bastard anything. I laid in bed crying wishing there was a place to escape to. I needed Gramps but he was gone. I needed to use the bathroom so I opened my door and asked if I could go. Brian said no way. You can just stand there and piss in your pants. My mother said to knock it off. Go ahead Victor. Just hurry up and get back in your room. I'm very disappointed in you right now. Brian got up off of his chair and looked like he was trying to block my mother’s line of site to me. It didn't work.

My mother said come over here Victor. Oh my god Brian. What the fuck did you do to him? He sat back down and said he fucking deserved every bit of it. He deserved that she asked? Are you fucking kidding me Brian? Are you alright honey. Is anything broken? Do you need stitches? Brian said it doesn't matter if he does. He's not going anywhere. I said yes mom I'm fine. I looked over at him and said I think I'm getting used to it. He stood up again and reared back with his hand, my mother jumped up and screamed don't you fucking dare hurt him anymore than he already is. I swear to god Brian. I will call the police if you touch him right now while he's already hurt like this. Don't forget you're on probation and you will go away.

He said it would be better than having to live here with you fucking pieces of shit and just sat back down. All I said was my arm and my head hurt really bad. But I'll be ok I think? She looked at Brian and asked how the fuck are you going to hide this one? You are one stupid asshole. He said your fathers on his honeymoon, he's suspended from school and he's not leaving that fucking room for a week. No sweat. Clean him up and do your magic. Put some super glue on him. I've heard that works wonders. And if you call me a stupid asshole again you're going to need a gallon of it for yourself. He just chuckled an evil laugh and cracked open his beer.

You worry too much Janis. He's young. He'll heal fast. He healed fast the last time after molesting that little girl didn't he. He needs to learn some respect and he can't be bullying his brother like that. If you don't like the way I discipline your kid you can go back and live with your father. And that's exactly how it was. Only ones who ever knew about this beating were me Joey Mom and Brian Kimberly and Michelle. They only knew because they came to my window every once in a while, to check in on me. But I made them promise never to tell anyone what happened. I never said anything to anybody else. I was a prisoner in my room for a week and a half until the cuts on my face healed.

I was threatened by Brian that if I ever told anyone about that beating that he would take me downstairs and kill me and use my finger bones for light posts for the little town. He said he would cut the rest of me into little pieces with his table saw and bag me up and throw me in the brook and the current would take me so far no one would ever find me. If anyone asks you tell them you tried to ride your bike in the snow and you fell off. And that was that for that. That was the story and I stuck to it.

That was also that for me in that apartment for the most part. I absolutely hated being there and I absolutely hated him. Saturday's were still Gramps and Mary roller skating after I healed up again. But the other days I stayed outside more than as much as possible. Spring was coming. Almost bike time. My cousin Kimberly I guess you could say hooked me up with Michelle from next door now and I was with her a lot. Yeah. Boyfriend and girlfriend. I had a secret thing for redheads and she was a straight red-haired freckled ginger. I got made fun of a lot for that for some reason but I didn't really care. I liked her and that was all that mattered to me. All she ever wanted to do was kiss. Wherever, whenever. And I didn't complain not one bit. If I wasn't with her I would just roam the streets with the rest of the kids.

It was just before spring and I finally got to take my bike out. There was one certain day that I couldn't find any clean shirts to wear at all. My mother must have been working a lot during this time because the entire floor on the left side of the basement was filled with dirty clothes. Brian wouldn't do them and I wasn't allowed. I don't think there is a way to explain in writing how many dirty clothes were piled down there. Anyone that went down there was always in complete awe.

I got made fun of a lot by my friends when we snuck down there because of this and always having no food in the house. Someone once said to me that you could have hid a family of five comfortably under all the clothes. Let's say ten foot by ten foot three feet high. And the basement leaked. So, the entire bottom of the pile was always moldy. It was absolutely nuts. Mike Lazzarro one day opened up the fridge and said pew fucking wee man. You eat food out of this thing? I wouldn't drink a closed soda out of there. This was my life.

So anyway, no clean clothes for me to wear. I ran up into my mother and Brian's room and found a white t shirt in his drawer. The only one. I said fuck it. I put it on and put a semi clean sweater on over it. I went outside and grabbed my bike. I went into the canyons and rode around for a while. I loved it in there if I haven't mentioned it before. I was supposed to meet up with Michelle so I came back out. I noticed a bunch of the kids on their bikes ready to go in. The Thompson's, a few other kids and Dave Zocco.

I was hot from riding around in the canyons so I took my sweater off. As I was lifting it over my head I heard Zocco say, look at this fucking guy. Look at the yellow pit stains under his fucking arms. I looked at my under arms and there were yellow stains from Brian wearing it. I said this isn't even my shirt. I took it out of Brian's drawer. Zocco says yeah right. This Fucking Stink Guy. That's your new name. Stink guy. I really wish I at least tried to stand up to him up for that. He did have me by four years and at least fifty pounds but I still should have tried. Because that fucking name stuck with me for five fucking years. At this point in my mind it was definitely fuck all these pricks.

Fuck these assholes for picking on me, fuck my mother for not protecting me, fuck the police and my school for not doing anything at all to stand up for me, fuck everyone and everything. I started hanging out more and more with Seth again. The kids around the neighborhood picked on him too. We came up with our own little scam to keep away from the neighborhood as much as we could. We had a old coffee can and wrapped it in paper and wrote UNISETH on the can. We hung out in front of Wawa's with it. I'm pretty sure it didn't fool anybody but we somehow made bank with that thing.

In just a few hours a day we would bring in between twenty and forty bucks and ride our bikes over to colony lanes and eat and play video games without anybody bothering us.. We wanted nothing to do with anyone in that fucking neighborhood for a while. Nobody in my family gave a fuck where I was. We got away with this for most of the spring. Venturing as far as stop and shop which was about three miles away with the can. It all ended abruptly though. We were confronted by the cops one day and they took our can and told us if we ever get caught again we're going to juvie. What we were doing was fraud. They brought us home, took the money, told our parents and we had to stop. It really sucked. Stuck back at home again.

I was waiting on the front porch one Saturday for Gramps and Mary. But they never showed up. I called his house multiple times but no answer. The next day he came by alone. He asked all of us to sit down at the table. He placed his head in his hands and told us that Mary was diagnosed with terminal cancer on Friday and only had a few months to live at the most. I had never felt so sad for anyone in my life and never even came close to seeing my grandfather cry before. This was going to change everything. Again. And I knew there was no way anything was going to change for the better.

My grandfather left and I only got to see Mary once in the hospital before she passed. They had just gotten married. How could something like this happen? Life is so unfair. A little time passed. And then so did she. My Gramps was in a deep state of depression. I didn't see or hear from him for a long while. At least six or so months. Everyone was way off for a while after this tragedy. No one took it well. All I wanted to do was comfort him but he just wanted to be left alone.

Brian was out of work. Again. Gramps never came around anymore. Mom was at work all the time. It was a free for all. Again. Brian started selling weed out of the apartment. And pretty much just sat in the living room when my mother was at work and made all of us stay outside so he could watch porn and jerk off in the living room. You could see the porn on the TV from right outside the front window all of the time. We caught him dozens of times and he just didn't give a flying fuck. As soon as you would open the front door you would hear GET THE FUCK OUT. This guy was a complete scumbag way more than he wasn't.

There were different people in and out all the time now. That is when he wasn't beating himself off. It was all a madhouse again. One night a truck pulled up in the driveway. I was outside on the porch with Michelle, kissing, like always. The door opened and it was Greg walking towards us. Are your parents' home. I said yeah. Just Brian though. I asked him to hang on for a second and gave Michelle a kiss goodnight she went home and I brought him inside.

He looked at Brian and said they needed to talk. My mother wasn't home so it was a little weird to me that he would stay especially with what happened last time I saw him. Like you know I only saw him and Brian together once the night of the fish tank incident. I hoped everything was ok. He looked at me and asked if I wanted to sit in his truck and listen to some music. I said hell yeah. He said I have two new cassette tapes and they sound awesome in there. I went out and sat down in the driver's side. He turned on the truck and popped in a cassette. He said have fun. If you want to switch them just press eject and just pop in the other one in. Turn it up as loud as you want to but please don't touch the treble or bass levels. No sweat.

He shut the door and it hit me like a brick. Loud as hell. Dun dunnnnn. Dun dunnnn. Dun. Da nan na na na nan nan Def Leppard. Rock Rock till you drop. Holy shit this is the best thing I have ever heard. I listened to that tape full through twice. I was in complete awe. This is definitely my shit. No one ever even came out to check on me. I ejected the tape and popped in the other. Quiet Riot. WTF is this? Come on feel the noise. Are you kidding me. It was rocking. I was enthralled. I made it through about half way when my mother pulled in. She came up and asked whose truck is this! I said its Greg's, he's inside talking to Brian. I was just about to ask her if there was any way in the world she could buy me one of the tapes and she was gone. Straight into the house.

Greg came out almost immediately after she went in. Maybe three- or four-minutes tops. Like one song. She followed him outside and they talked for less than a minute and gave each other a hug and my mother walked back inside. He walked over to the truck and asked me what I thought. I said this is absolutely awesome. I love it. Can I listen to the rest of this one side please? He said he would let me and he's sorry but he had to go.

I got out and he sat down. He stared at me for a solid thirty seconds without saying a word and then he patted me on the top of my head. He said I'm sorry for everything kid. I didn't know at the time what he was talking about. I asked sorry for what? He just stared at me again with a blank look on his face. He said forget it buddy. Try not to grow up to fast. I saw you with the little red-haired girl. It's better to be young. Take care of your mother and your brothers. They need you. He popped the quiet riot tape out and handed it to me. He said this is yours. I can always get another one. He put his truck in reverse and I never, ever saw or heard from him again.

It was the middle of the summer. Still staying away from the apartment as much as possible but grounded to the neighborhood for the UNISETH scam. Mostly with Michelle or in the canyons riding my bike with my friends. Still dealing with the Stink Guy shit though. Whatever. I know I'm poor. Still no Gramps. Growing like a weed and running out of clothes again. No underwear at all. Brain still selling weed and jerking off in the living room and my mother never home and always working. All the rest of the kids in the neighborhood were getting ready for youth football coming up. Wallingford Vikings Football. I begged my mother and Brian to be able to play but they said there was no way they could afford my equipment.

I remember going down to pat wall field with Jesse and Corey who both played the year before. Even Jimbo and Benny were playing on the pee wee squad this year. I met with their coach and he let me borrow some pads and we played around for a little bit. He told me that tryouts were in a few weeks and if I could somehow pay for the equipment that I would more than likely be on the team with no apparent issues. Just get that equipment he said. I did everything I could. Borrowing lawn mowers and mowing lawns, raking leaves, collecting cans and bottles. Even broke out a new UNISETH can and snuck out of the neighborhood. That seemed to work way better when there were two of us though. I sincerely did everything I could at twelve years old to come up with the money.

There was a slight problem with the saving what I made though. And I'm not going to sugar coat this shit for anyone. Probably because the was never any sugar to coat it with. There was powdered milk I guess. There was never any fucking food in that apartment. If Connie or Uncle Bob and Aunt Dee didn't feed me I wouldn't have eaten that much at all. My mother would usually bring home food from work and by the time I noticed her car in the driveway and got home there weren't even scraps left. Brian would say if want to play outside and not be home in time it looks like you missed out, at the same time the dirty scumbag is wiping crumbs off of his filthy fucking face smiling at me.

I had to spend a good portion of my money on food for myself and sometimes my brothers because I felt so bad for them. This was no way for kids to have to live. Bobby is 2-1/2 and he is stuck in his playpen more than he isn't in this place. He had more freedom a year ago on Allen avenue. I hated my life. I hated their lives. I hated everyone. Except for Michelle and a small handful of cousins and friends. I could make out any time I wanted with Michelle and it kept my mind off of everything thing else when she was around. I should get used to hanging around with her because there was no possible way I was playing football.

And just then. On the last possible night for a miracle. Michelle went home and I went inside and went into my room. I was in a deep lost hopeless depression. I was counting what little money I had saved up cursing the world. While I was sitting there feeling sorry for myself someone knocked on the front door. I thought it was probably Corey and Jesse seeing if I could make it to the field in the morning. I was prepared to be embarrassed again because I knew I had to say no.

I walked out of my room and I opened up the front door. And standing on the porch was Gramps with a huge box in his arms. I heard my number one grandson needed something he said. Come outside with me. He placed the box on the porch and opened up the top. I could see right away. Shoulder pads, elbow pads, knee pads, jock strap, cup, cleats, couple pairs of pants and shirts, everything I needed for tomorrow. I jumped up on him and gave him the biggest hug. Oh my god Gramps thank you so much. I love you so much.

He cried and said he was sorry he hasn't been around. He said he knows it has got to be tough for me and my brothers having to live here with that animal. Your mother told me you were working really hard to try to get these things and you couldn't do it on your own. I told Gramps I would give him what little money that I had left and he said no. You keep that. I know you're going to need it for something. You need to eat more, you're too damn skinny. We both chuckled.

He exclaimed, I am so proud of you for trying to do this the right way. I love the thought of you working so hard for something you want. I'm happy you didn't try to steal what you thought you needed. Good boy. And I want you to pretend all of this is from Mary. I know she would want you to be happy and doing something you like to do.

She would have made me get this for you if she was still with us anyway. And she would be very proud of you too. All he said after that is I really miss her. And I love you Victor. Please have fun tomorrow. I'll come back and see you soon. Behave yourself, believe in yourself and do your best. He turned around and got into his car and drove away.

That night I sat in my bed and just stared at the equipment I had spread out on the floor in the shape of me wearing it. I stayed up way past 3AM. Adrenaline running through me. More excited than I ever was in my life. I am about to become a part of something. I am going to be part of a team. I have my friends there. I can learn everything about football. I am going to work as hard as I can and prove to everyone that I am not just another poor loser from the Wallingford projects. I am going to be a Wallingford Viking.

I tried to go to sleep for a long time. It was so hard. It was hot that night. I laid in bed staring at the equipment on the floor. I laid there with my eyes closed thinking about plays on Tecmo Bowl and thinking in my head about the NFL and making money playing football and never having to be poor again. I had my alarm set and nothing was going to stop me from making this team. I got over the biggest hurdle. Let's go. I finally fell asleep. My alarm went off what felt like immediately. Like it usually did for me. I hit snooze instead of jumping out of bed like I should have. But I didn't hit snooze. I turned it off. Next thing I hear is Brian. I thought you had somewhere to be today? Get the fuck up and go. You're going to be late. I hear him as he's walking away, fucking kid could fuck up a wet dream.

I jumped out of bed and grabbed all of my equipment. I was already late. I have to hurry. I looked out of the back window and Bobby and Joey were in the back yard playing which was weird in and of itself. They usually played in the front yard. I'm talking like ninety five percent of the time. I grabbed a string out of the box and tied up all of my equipment together. I run into the living room. Hey Brian, where is mom? He said she's not here. I sent her to the store. It's right down the street. Walk there, stop being a lazy fuck.

He sat down in his whack off chair and started looking out of the window. I said ok. Guess I'm running. Gotta go. I started for the door. He turns towards me and says stop. Listen. If you see anyone outside looking for me you tell them I'm not hear. I don't have any pot to sell anybody so I don't want to be bothered. I said ok and thought to myself nothing strange about that. Douche probably wants to jerk off and that's why the kids are in the back yard. I went outside and sat on the porch and started putting on my cleats as fast as I could.

Beep Beep. Beep Beep. A black Chevy nova pulls up into the front yard right in the corner of the drive way and stops. I've never seen this car before. It was beautiful. Beep Beep. Beep Beep. Victor. Hey Victor. Come over here. Hurry up. I stand up and place my equipment down on the porch. I walk over to the car and look into the passenger side window. Harry? What are you doing here? He says I'm looking for your father. I leaned my elbows on the window ledge of the door and I said he's not here. He'll probably be back later. Nice car dude. Seeing how he's not here and my mother's at the store I could use a ride down the street. Can you? Please?

He said yeah, sure, where are you going? I said pat wall field. Right down the street. Let me grab my equipment. I turned my head towards the porch and as soon as I started to raise my elbows up I heard the car hit reverse and the tires start screaming. I turned my head back towards the car and before I knew it the side of the door close to the front passenger side fender slammed into my hip as I tried to push myself away from the car with my right hand. I knew I was getting hurt somehow.

As I was falling to the ground the passenger side front tire ran over both of my shins on an away angle. Front of the tires pointing towards the street. I started rolling around uncontrollably from the grass to the driveway. Screaming in agonizing pain. I heard the car change gears and the tires squealing again over my screams. This time forward. I was mostly looking down at my legs while I was rolling around and screaming in total shock of what just happened. I could see that my legs were clearly broken. But I also saw the car with the tires now pointing towards me and the into driveway. It came to an abrupt stop as doors everywhere in the neighborhood flew open and everyone started screaming and running towards me. All the doors except for our door.

With every roll I took I could see that every time the toes of my cleats and my knees would face towards the ground so did the middle of my shins like they were made of rubber bands. I couldn't stop rolling or screaming. The pain was intense to say the least. I was no longer in any type of control. I couldn't stop from rolling around no matter how bad it hurt. It was my body reacting to the trauma. I heard Harry's car door slam and he ran right past me. He ran across the lawn and slammed on my door and I could hear him yell. I just ran over your son, he's hurt but he's still alive, it was an accident I swear. I don't know what happened.

They both run over to me and Brian reaches down and stops my rolling. He looks down and grabs under my right knee and lifts up. It was rubber. I shrieked in excruciating pain. He looked up at Harry and said, you ran over both of his legs you fucking idiot. They're shattered. Harry seemed to go into full panic mode. Pacing crazily around his car. He wouldn't look at me at all.

I was in a fog but I definitely was aware of all that was around me. There were about fifteen to twenty people standing around me within one minute. Harry ran to his car and jumped in the driver's side. Brian stood up in front of it and pointed through the windshield and said if you leave here right now I will hunt you down and fucking kill you. Shut that fucking car off right now and get out here. It was an accident. You won't get in trouble. I saw the whole thing.

As aware as I was I simply didn't think about it at the time. Maybe he didn't come outside immediately because he was the one that called 911. I didn't know. All I knew is that I was fucked and this shit hurt. I had Aunt Dee out there holding one of my hands and Christine Meager holding the other. I was kind of in love with her back then as a kid so that was just fine with me. Actually, why lie, I was in love with eighty percent of the girls in that neighborhood. We had some fucking hotties back then. Anyone who claims different is lying through their teeth. Anyway. They were talking to me telling me I was going to be ok. I was much calmer as I heard the ambulance getting closer. Two fire trucks, three cop cars. News people. Wow. All this is for me?

As the medics got out of the ambulance the first thing they did was take a pair of scissors to my brand-new pants. Everyone there told me not to look at my legs but I did. You could see the right leg looked like a pancake and the left had a bone sticking out of the middle with blood rolling over the sides of my shin. I was in complete and udder shock because they were just pretty much throbbing now and the pain wasn't that intense anymore. One of the medics looked at his partner and said we cannot move him at all without a morphine shot and stabilizing both of his legs. Don't move. Please don't move an inch.

There were now thirty or more people around me. As they stuck the needle in my arm I looked down at them putting it in and I saw in the background, purple jerseys with yellow writing. Wallingford Vikings Football. I thought I was seeing quadruple as the warmest feeling I ever had flowed throughout my entire body. What the hell is that I asked? Morphine. You like it? Is that better? Hell yeah, it's better. Do what you got to do my man. I feel like I can stand up on them and do a little dance right now. The medic chuckled.

Vic? Dude? Are you alright? Jesse, Corey and Jimbo were now

standing over me with Benny following close behind. We were all waiting for you at the field. What the hell happened Jimbo asked. I said you see that idiot talking to the cops with Brian over there? He said yeah. I said he ran over my legs with this sweet Nova. Corey or Jesse looked at me and said Damn man. It would have been way more fun if we got to break your legs playing football. I just laughed. I was feeling no pain at all in those moments.

It took them about a half hour to stabilize both my legs to move me. The crowd was now uncountable from where I was laying. Everyone was wishing me luck and talking amongst themselves. Brian and Harry were now done talking to the police. The officers went around the crowd asking everyone if they knew of anyone that saw what happened? Supposedly Brian was the only one.

The medics and a few firemen rolled me to my right side and slid an orange plastic board under my back. My legs were each sandwiched between two stabilizing boards with tight straps around them. They rolled me onto it and strapped my body down to the board. Everyone was saying goodbye when Harry came over as they were lifting me up onto the actual gurney. I looked straight up and there he was. He looked down at me and said I'm so sorry kid. I didn't mean to hurt you like this. You know it was an accident, right? I said I don't care if it was an accident or not. You take care of that car for me. I'm pretty sure that fucking thing is going to be mine soon. The look on his face was one of pure confusion.

As they were beginning to load me up I heard Victor. Can you look over here for a moment? I looked over at some girl and she said her name was Rachel and she was from the Record Journal. She then asked me if I minded her photographer taking my picture. I said no not at all. I'm going to be in the paper? She said most surely. The photographer stepped in front of her and asked are you ready? I said yes and threw up double peace signs with the biggest smile on my face. Click. The girl then said you just got both of your legs broken by a car. We can't put a picture of you smiling or they won't let it in. I said I'm sorry. I can't stop smiling. I said you can always change the headline from boy gets run over by a car, to boy waits for his legs to heal so he can drive his new sweet car. Needless to say. The picture never made it into the paper.

I remember the ambulance ride. They gave me another shot of morphine and asked how I was holding up. The driver yelled to the back of the ambulance, man I have to tell you, you're one tough kid. I said whatever that medicine is right there is definitely helping. All I can feel is the blood trickling down the side of my leg. No pain at all right now. Only numbness. He said just hang on a few minutes and we will be at the hospital. They are going to give you something to put you to sleep and they are going to fix your legs. You won't feel a thing.

We arrived at the hospital and they rolled me into a room. They hooked up a bunch of monitors and the surgeon asked me how I was doing? I said I'm fine. Did you hear I was getting a sweet new Chevy Nova? He said yeah, I heard something about that. And I hope you get it. You deserve it. They told me how well you handled yourself through the whole ordeal. Your parents should be proud.

Now I am going to put this mask on you and you are going count backwards from a hundred as far as you can and you will slowly drift off to sleep and you will wake up with full casts on your legs. Are you ready? I said I don't know. How bad will it hurt when I wake up? He said they are going to be uncomfortable for a very long time after but you will have pain medication for as long as you need it. I asked if it was the same warm feeling stuff. He said no. But close. It will keep you relaxed and keep the pain numbed. Now we have to do this. No more talking. I said good luck putting me out buddy. I can't fall asleep on my back.

He placed the mask over my face and turned the knob. I said out loud. 100-99-98. Why the fuck am I in the brook? How did I get here? Why is there a huge grey whale chasing me through the tunnel? How am I running right now? My legs are broken. I took three steps running away, turned my head towards the tunnel as the whale opened its giant mouth with its huge white teeth and its tongue hanging over the bottom teeth and VICTOR? Are you with us? Victor? How are you feeling?

Holy fuck to the fuckity of fucks. The pain was a hundred times more intense. All I kept screaming was to please put me back to sleep. I would rather let the whale eat me. Please please please. It hurts so bad. The doctor went next to my bed and pushed a button. Within a second, I felt the warm fuzzy feeling again. But I have to tell you. This time. It numbed the pain but most definitely didn't take it away. It was a streaming radiating type of pain. It kept running up and down. It felt like someone was breaking them over and over again. I asked the doctor why does it hurt so much more now than it did before? Something isn't right. Someone did something wrong. This hurts way too much. He told me I have a morphine drip in my arm and anytime I need it just push the button. It will numb the pain but won't take it completely away for at least a week.

He explained that the setting of my legs was what caused me all of my pain now compared to when it first happened. He said that plus the shock of it all. He said that my right leg was completely crushed and my left was a compound fracture. It is going to be very painful for a few weeks and very uncomfortable for a few months after. All you have to do is just to lay around and let your family take care of you any way you need. Do not try under any circumstances to stand up on your casts until we put boots on the bottom of them. That will be at least four months. Your legs will never heal if you put any pressure on them at all.

I asked how long do I have until I have to go home. He said about a week to ten days. I asked if I get to take the medicine button with me. He chuckled and said no. That would probably be nice for you though. You will have medication in pill form at home that your mother will have to go get for you. And the other reason you have to stay here for a while is because your family will have to set up your home for your return. You are going to need a hospital bed and a wheelchair and probably a wheelchair ramp. They have a lot of work to do. Speak of the devil. Here's your mother now. I'll give you a couple minutes with him then he should probably rest. He has been through quite a trauma.

Hi mom. WHAT THE FUCK HAPPENED? I was standing next to Harry's car and he backed up and ran me over. How does that happen? Next to his car? Did his fucking car drive sideways? Somethings not right here. Someone's is lying to me. What really happened Victor? You can tell me. Did he do this to you on purpose? I said no. I don't think so? Why would he do that? Speaking of which. How is my car? Have you seen it? It's really sweet. Enough with the stupid fucking car she said. Tell me what you remember. I told her how I just told all of you. It really is just what it is. Or is it?

Looking back a couple of things don't fit even my side of things. Harry said he was trying to avoid the trash that was on the corner of the lawn and the driveway and he thought that I had already backed away from the car. He said he thought that the garbage was to close near the door for me to open it and the only reason he hit the gas so hard is that he was simply showing off. He clipped me with the fender and I went down and he ran my legs over. Brian's recollection was he just happened to look out of the window as the tires went over my legs and he ran right outside immediately afterwards.

I'm calling bullshit on that for sure. Looking back now, I know way more than I knew then. Obviously about the molestation. You remember. But at the time of the accident or even for a few years after it was nowhere in my memories. I can't prove anything was on purpose. Not to anyone else. Not even to myself. It was a very confusing event from start to finish.

These are just my questions and opinions. I'm not straight up accusing anybody but they are valid questions to ask after everything I've learned. Was this really just an accident? Wrong place at the wrong time? What was that meeting between Greg and Brian a few weeks earlier? What was the meeting with them a year earlier that caused a night of total chaos with the fish tank? Why was Harry looking for Brian in the first place on that day at that time? For weed? I never found out why he was there that's for sure.

Why was Brian peering out of the window and telling me to tell anyone that asks that he wasn't home at that time? Did he call 911? Did someone else? Why was my mother not home and the kids playing outside in the back yard where they hardly ever played? Did Brian send her off on purpose? Did he tell the kids to play in the back yard? How much did he really see? Why did he say he ran outside immediately after my legs were crushed when I clearly know for a fact that he didn't? Why did Harry seem in no way surprised when Brian opened up the door when he wasn't supposed to be home at that time? Did he know anyone was there? My mother's car surly wasn't there.

Was this just an innocent stupid accident that broke my legs? Or was this car supposed to knock me down and crush over my chest or side? If I didn't push away when I did were the tires turned enough to actually do something like that? I honestly think they were. I really do. With every bit of my heart. If I had fell straight down I would be deader than dead right now. We're there people around me that wanted me or needed me gone that badly? Guess what? I have the answer to all of this. And you're not going to like it. We will never know the answer. That's the fucking answer.

I remember laying in the hospital talking to my mother when

my gramps walked in. First thing he asked was what the fuck was Harry doing over there in the first place? Where the fuck were you Janis? Why weren't you at football Victor? What the fuck is going on around here? This was quickly followed by my uncle Bob and aunt Debbie walking in asking the same exact things. Did any of them know something about what him and his brother did to me six years earlier? It just seemed extremely weird to me that the why was Harry over there question seemed way more important than what actually happened. Why was he there? There was definitely some importance to that question to everybody else at that time except for me.

I stayed in the hospital for a little over a week I believe. I received a ton of guests while I was there. They loaded me onto a wheelchair and into a van on my last day. I don't know what it was but I really felt uncomfortable and helpless with the wheelchair locked into the van floor on the way home. I believe I had my first anxiety attack on the ride home. I kept thinking that the van was going to crash and I would be stuck in there forever. When I got home it passed. But I will never forget the feeling.

As the driver pulled into the neighborhood he said alright, we're almost there. Are you ready to get home? I said no, not really. Then I saw the dairy. And all I could think of is I won't be able to go there by myself for a very long time and I'm probably going to starve to death. We were half way down the street when I heard the driver say HOLY SHIT KID. What? Holy shit what? He laughed and said I have never seen anything like this before dropping someone off. He said this will probably change your mind on not wanting to go home.

He said I am going to drive by and turn around so you can see before we pull in. I can see looking out of the back window driving past my cousin's apartment that there were more and more people starting to come into view as we passed. He drove past our apartment and I could see in the driveway that half of the neighborhood was waiting there for me to come home. I'm sorry. I don't have room to name you all. You know who you are and who else was there.

We drove past and he turned around at the corner, we pulled in and the back door opened to almost everyone I knew standing right there. I started crying immediately. I had no idea that many people cared about me. They unlocked my wheelchair and wheeled me off of the van. As soon as I got off I was bombarded with questions as to how I felt. There were a bunch of people kind of making a wall in front of the house and through them my mother and Brian broke through.

My mother came up to me and gave me a giant hug and said look. Look at what Brian and a couple of his friends did for you. The people move out of the way and there in the front of the house up to the door was a beautiful wheelchair ramp. It was pretty bad ass. It looked like it was professionally done. I stayed outside for about an hour with everyone while I tried to learn how to use the ramp without flipping the wheel chair over.

We finally said goodbye to everyone because my legs were starting to throb and I wanted to lay down. They rolled me up the ramp and through the living room. Everything in the room looked way different. All the furniture was now placed against the walls to give me enough room to get through when I needed to. We rolled into my room and as soon as the door opened I could see my room was also changed. There was a huge hospital bed up against the far wall.

With the bed that Brian built for me basically at the foot of the hospital bed. Brian rolled me in and scooped me up with my mother holding my casts to get me into the bed. It definitely didn't look easy. Once they got me in my bed they brought in my medicine. Everything up till now in the hospital was done through IV and relief was immediate after they gave me my pain medication there. Here though they were in pill form. Percocet. Brian said here Victor. Take two of these. My mom says no. Just give him one. He gave me two.

I was hurting bad from all the movement for the last few hours. It took about a half hour to hit me but I could feel the pain slowly start to dissipate. I closed my eyes and that was it. Meditation. Full on and beautiful meditating. I could think of anything I wanted and control it like a perfect dream. I could pretend I was flying through the air or swimming through an ocean without the fear of falling or drowning. I fell in love with these pills. I still couldn't fall asleep easily stuck on my back with the casts on, but the meditation felt even better than sleep anyway.

I was home for about an hour when my parents called out to me to open my eyes. It was Michelle and Kimberly standing over me. We talked for about fifteen minutes about how they were both jealous that I didn't have to go into middle school right away and that they were both nervous about going. All of the sudden Kimberly said she had to go. As soon as she walked out Michelle closed the door.

She came over to me and told me how much she missed kissing me. She bent down and we kissed for a good ten minutes. It was her thing. Always. Brian opens the door. What the hell? When did this start? She said to him months ago. Why didn't you tell me? I thought you were a gay wad all this time. Janis, did you know your son liked girls? Knock it off Brian. He just got home. You know he does. Fucking jerk. Let me make him some dinner. Michelle you have to leave now. You can see him tomorrow. I wasn't even home for a few hours before this guy started messing with me. Michelle gave me a kiss, said goodnight said she would see me tomorrow and off she went.

That first night sucked very bad I have to say. One of the worst scariest nights of my entire life. My mother brought me in dinner a little while after Michelle left and told me to eat and then try to sleep. I ate and she came in a little while later to take the dirty plate and my water jug, and said she was going to empty out my urinal and told me she would be back with my medication for the night and fresh water for me. I was exhausted and somehow fell asleep before she came back. I usually woke up within an hour or so if I slept on my back in the hospital to try and roll over to my side. This time was different. I think they put something in my food or drink to make me sleep without telling me because I fucking slept like a rock starting at around six thirty.

I opened up my eyes and looked around the room. It was dark, pitch black. Except for the red lights on my alarm clock. It said 3:11 A.M. I looked on my table next to my bed for my water because my mouth and my throat were extremely dry. I looked for my meds because my legs were pounding. I looked for my urinal because I had to pee really bad. Nothing. None of them were there.

I tried to yell for my mother, or Brian, or Joey. I couldn't get any words out of my throat. I tried again. Mom. It was so low. My throat scratched every time I tried like there was sawdust stuck in my mouth and throat and sandpaper on my tongue. Ten minutes in I couldn't hold my pee any longer and I had no choice but to pee on the floor over the side of my bed. Well, Kind of. Most of it was on my bed because I couldn't roll all the way to my side due to the casts and the rails on the bed. I tried to yell for about an hour after that. It got worse every time I tried. I thought I was going to die. Seriously. I did.

I got so desperate I tried to reach for my wheelchair that was on the other side of the room. I tied my pillowcase to my sheet and tried to throw it at the chair to hook it and drag it over to me. I didn't know how I was going to get in it if I did get it over to me but I had to try because no one was coming to help me. No one can even hear me. I got it hooked through the wheel but I couldn't drag it over. The wheels were locked and couldn't get it to slide over the floor.

After about an hour and a half all together. At a little past 4:30 I really thought this was it. I couldn't breathe. I felt like I could barely move. I took one last shot and lifted my right cast up with all that I felt I had left, I sat up as much as I could and with both hands I started to slam it on the metal rail of my hospital bed. If nobody hears this I'm done. I did this about five times through excruciating pain and almost not being able to breath at all. I honestly thought on the last time that I did it that I re broke my right leg. I laid my head down and let out all of a scream that I could. It was nothing. No one heard that at all I thought. I am going to die tonight.

I started crying, actually trying to lick at my tears for some kind of liquid in my mouth but my tongue wouldn't come out. I took my finger and swiped one of the tears from my face and put it on my tongue. That didn't help. I looked over at my wheelchair one more time asking myself if I have the strength to try again and standing behind it was Joey rubbing his eyes and yawning. Are you crying dude? What's all the ruckus down here? I tried to say water but nothing came out, I mouthed please water. He said I don't know what you're saying. I pointed at my mouth and towards the living room and got a course sounding wa-wa out of my mouth and throat. He finally understood and walked out of my room towards the kitchen.

It took so long I honestly thought he forgot. I started to hit my rails with my hands now. Not caring if I broke them or not. I needed water right now. I never felt like I was so close to death my entire life. My throat was literally closing up. I couldn't breath and my body pretty much just took over. Joey finally came back in. He handed me my jug of water and said this was on the kitchen table next to your potty jug. Dude. Did you pee on the floor? I drank the water so fast that it hurt. I was in so much pain at this point too. I could finally speak a little. Please get me more water and get mommy quick. Ah geez. Fine. Will you be quiet after so I can go back to sleep? Yes. I will. I promise. Hurry please.

So he brings me the jug back full of water and hands my urinal. He said don't go peeing all that water you just drank all over the floor. People have to walk around here. I'll go get mommy. Just hang on to your wee wee. A minute later my mother comes into my room and notices the sheet and pillowcase stuck in the wheel of the chair and the pee on the floor. Why the hell did you -- OH MY GOD, Victor, I'm so sorry honey. I forgot your water, I went to bed and forgot your stuff. I'm so sorry. Do you need more, do you need anything? I'll get your jugs. Do you need your medicine? Yes please. Ok, ok, I'll give you two pills. I'm so sorry honey. I'm so sorry. She got me two Percocet, the rest of my stuff, and I laid there for hours by myself wide awake while everyone slept half the day away.

This wasn't the only time I was stuck in there with nothing for the next month or so, I had to build my upper body strength up to be able to squirm around for myself. I started walking on my full casts way before I should have because I had no other choice. My Mom, Brian or Joey helped me "sometimes" but like usual I was mostly on my own. I got through it obviously or I wouldn't be here writing this to you today. It wasn't easy. In any sense of that word. I remember the constant struggle of every single day. But like I said, I found a way and I managed my own way through them.

I am sorry to leave you all hanging like this in the middle of a disastrous chapter of my life, but hey? Isn't that how the TV shows do it? The story from here is to be continued at a later date. I need a break and I need to get this out and make some money to survive before I start exposing the next chapters. Don't worry. You won't be disappointed. And it won't be too long. A few months at the most. I promise. Unless a publisher makes me wait for maximum revenue.

I have a lot more to tell including three more years with some wonderful abuse from the baddest motherfucker in the valley. Plenty of alcohol and drug use not only from the adults in my life but also from myself. Two more apparent attempts on my life. Another beautiful husband that my mother somehow dug up from the bowels of who the fuck knows where. My first real jobs. My first arrests. My first major accidents. More broken bones and stitches. Etc etc etc.

I should be able to get at least twelve to fifteen more years out of the next book. Who knows. There is still a lot in my mind and I can't wait to get it out to all of you. I pray every day that I write these books that it is the way to change what would be the outcome for the ending of my life. And to finally help me to change the final paths my family and my children might have to take without this. Hopefully it all changes for a better future. Take care of yourselves and the ones you love. Be kind to each other and protect the young and the weak. Remember my story and don't let anyone go through my life if you can do anything at all to redirect it.

I will see you all very soon. Goodbye for now.
And thank you all for your support.
Sincerely. The Newly Published Loser.

P.S. Some names have been changed to protect the innocent as well as the guilty. I don't feel like being sued. You know who you are.
And if I forgot anybody in volume one I am sorry. I'm more than positive you'll make the cut in volume two.

Made in the USA
Middletown, DE
11 July 2019